THE KRAYS - THE FINAL COUNTDOWN

THE KRAYS
THE FINAL COUNTDOWN

THE ULTIMATE BIOGRAPHY OF
RON, REG & CHARLIE KRAY

COLIN FRY

MAINSTREAM
PUBLISHING

EDINBURGH AND LONDON

First published in Great Britain in 2001 by
MAINSTREAM PUBLISHING COMPANY (EDINBURGH) LTD
7 Albany Street
Edinburgh EH1 3UG

Reprinted 2006

ISBN 1 84018 448 5

A catalogue record for this book
is available from the British Library

Typeset in Apollo and Espionage
Printed and bound in Great Britain by
William Clowes Ltd, Beccles, Suffolk

Contents

Dedication   7

Acknowledgements   9

Introduction   11

1 – October 1933 : Twin Terror – The Birth of the Kray Twins   15
2 – Summer 1939-49 : Running Away from Trouble   19
3 – December 1951: Fighting the Good Fight   25
4 – March 1952: Privates on Parade   31
5 – Summer 1954: Doing the Business   36
6 – April 1955: Organised Crime   41
7 – November 1956: Prison   43
8 – Spring/Summer 1958: Taking over the Asylum   47
9 – October 1960: Clubbing   53
10 – July 1964: The Case of the Brighton Peer   58
11 – Summer of 1964: Safari   65
12 – April 1965: Getting Hitched   71
13 – Summer/Autumn 1965: Bonds   76
14 – March 1966: Button Man   85
15 – Spring 1966: The George Raft Story   91
16 – Autumn 1966: Sinatra   97
17 – December 1966: The 'Mad Axeman'   103
18 – June 1967: Suicide   108
19 – Summer 1967: Stars   113
20 – October 1967: 'Jack the Hat'   119
21 – 1967–68: The Killing Fields   124
22 – April 1968: NYC   127
23 – April 1968: The Net   133
24 – May 1968: Gotcha!   140

25 – January 1969: The Trial 149

26 – March 1969: The Sentence 153

27 – 1969-81: Life 155

28 – August 1982: The Last Farewell 159

29 – December 1985: Another Way of Life 164

30 – 1988-94: Double Exposure 167

31 – March 1995: Death of the Don 170

32 – June 1997: The Dope 175

33 – July 1997: Married to the Mob 193

34 – April 2000: Death of a Clown 197

35 – August–October 2000: Freed – to Die ! 207

Epilogue 218

Dedication

The Krays loved their Mum – so it would appear fitting to dedicate this book to my mother who, like Violet Kray, had the great satisfaction and undoubted immense irritation of raising twins.

Being a twin is a great privilege, but it is also a responsibility. I was often blamed for my brother's misdemeanours – as he was for mine. In the end, though, it worked out even – although I am sure that my brother Rod would dispute that vehemently over a drink or two.

Violet took great pride in her twins, and her eldest son too – but Charlie Kray didn't get many of the advantages, only the responsibilities. And could Charlie or his mum tell the twins apart?

Who is who – and who did what? Was it you, or you – or both of you? I can hear Violet calling to her twins, 'Come here Ronnie/Reggie!' I am sure all twins in the world can identify with that. And I am equally sure that all mothers of twins, no matter where they may be, understand the importance of being a twin.

So my mother is special, just as Violet called her twins 'special'. In fact the whole twin relationship is something that needs further explanation and analysis and I have already attempted this in my book *The Kray Files*, also published by Mainstream Publishing. This biography, however, has not been designed to explain, but to present the facts and only the facts.

This one's for you, Mum!

Dedicated to Mrs Rosetta Ellen Fry.

Acknowledgements

To everyone who has helped me to become a writer, especially Bill Campbell of Mainstream Publishing who doesn't mind paying for the privilege of publishing a book about the notorious Kray brothers.

For those of you who think that a writer should not be paid for writing stories about people such as the Krays, I acknowledge a debt of gratitude. After all, I am a writer and writing is what I do. Without the constant hassle and all the dubious arguments that I have had to face through the years, I would most likely not have been able to thoroughly enjoy writing about gangsters. It is now, however, something that I consider to be a part of my life – and therefore worthy of the writing. I ask simply 'Why not?' and I have never had a satisfactory reply. But all that bickering has helped to focus my mind on the process of organising and administrating the writing process – and the result is *The Krays – The Final Countdown*.

I have been privileged to work with many people throughout the years – some of them major, some minor. But life itself is a learning curve and when embarking on a career we never really know where it may lead. I started out writing songs and acting in movies, then I worked in the oil business and the record business – and now I write books and film scripts. My mentor through recent years has been an American, Charles Rosenblatt, a man of many talents. Thanks to him I undertook a university degree at the age of 50 and his encouragement has helped me with my projects – both films and books – time and time again. Without Charles as my guide during the writing experience I seriously doubt whether I would have made it. My thanks also go to his lovely wife, Denise.

And I would like to extend a personal and public thank you to the Krays – without whom, obviously, this book would not exist. Ron and

Reg Kray were helpful, as always, by staying in the news even up to their deaths, and I will always fondly remember hearing Ron tell his outrageous stories when I visited him in Broadmoor. But the sad way in which Charlie Kray died will stay with me forever. He was not a bad man, but he had a couple of brothers who terrorised the East End of London and who killed for a living.

Call it selective or false memory if you will — but I will always remember Charlie Kray as a great womaniser, a fun person to be with, as the true 'Del-boy' of real life.

Introduction

The East End of London has seen some bloody times – from the chaos caused by that caped crusader Jack the Ripper, to the havoc wreaked throughout Bethnal Green and the Mile End Road by those kings of crime, the Krays. Their doings and killings were only matched back then by the blitzkrieg of the Second World War, but these murderers of London did their dirty deeds in peace time, where ordinary people were trying to make a living, trying to stay out of trouble, trying to get ahead in life. Death, though, has always stalked the shady streets of the East End.

I first met Charlie Kray in 1985 in a pub just off the Mile End Road. He was a charmer, a real diamond geezer and didn't the ladies know it. Always the centre of attention, Charlie Kray was constantly on the look-out for a 'nice little earner', as he would call it. He liked to 'put people together'. (Ultimately he would put a couple of low-life drug-dealers together with an undercover cop – and there went the neighbourhood!)

He was introduced to me as a man with connections within the music industry. And since my business was to buy and sell records and CDs, we had a chat. During the conversation he mentioned that he had a couple of brothers who were twins, but when I asked about them his whole manner and tone changed.

'They're in jail – but they should be out soon,' he told me straight. His demeanour had changed totally – he looked embarrassed as he tried to mingle with the other guests. A friend took me aside and explained the situation.

'His brothers are the notorious Kray twins – Ron and Reg Kray' he told me in a whisper. But it didn't mean anything to me – I had lived abroad for some 20 years and the name Kray hadn't been on the top of any editor's 'most wanted' list in Denmark.

Again I approached Charlie and we began to talk.

'So your brothers are in jail?' I said casually.

He gave me a quick look-over and decided that I was no threat; neither cop nor crook. Gradually he opened up and began to talk – all about the old days and how they had run something called the Firm. This was all very interesting, since I had never met a gangster before. Sure, I had met some dodgy dealers in my time, crooks who called themselves businessmen. But gangsters – that was something completely different. Over the years to come I would be proud to call Charlie Kray my friend.

By the time he died, Charlie had tried it all – from selling knick-knacks in an East End market, to trying to put together a consortium to clean up the sands of Kuwait after the Gulf War. He even tried to import fruit and veg. from Nigeria – but even that scheme went rotten. His only way out was to deal in drugs. But Charlie was never interested in supplying cocaine – he only wanted the money. Still, he did the deal, and in the end he died in jail.

It was Charlie who introduced me to his brothers – the Kray Twins. I was naturally keen to meet them, since I too am a twin – and twins who terrorised London were a must on my 'must-see' list. Ron and Reg Kray were not a disappointment.

I first met Ron Kray one sunny summer's day in 1988. I had arranged to meet him in the meeting-hall at Broadmoor Hospital, where he had resided for many years. When I got there a guard opened the huge doors and ushered me in to the open yard, which separated the gatehouse from the main living-quarters. The first thing that struck me was the string of keys on his belt – more keys than it would take to open Fort Knox. I was beginning to wonder where we were going, when he opened yet another locked door – and showed me into a large, dark, damp hall. This was it then – now or never.

We shook hands warmly and he gave me that famous stare. I had been warned about it and I was ready.

'Nice to meet you,' he said simply. I was surprised. He looked so well, so smart, so normal – but this was Broadmoor.

'I'm a twin too,' I said, squeezing the words through gritted teeth. That was it, the ice melted. 'I knew it when I saw you' he told me with a glint in his eye. 'Sit down – what do you want to know?'

He introduced me to his wife, Kate, and we all sat down and got on with the chat. I couldn't understand why Ron Kray, an open homosexual, could get married – to a woman. But on seeing the chirpy, delightful Kate, I immediately understood.

I saw him on many occasions in Broadmoor and he introduced me to many a friend. They were colourful characters – all murderers and villains, but colourful nonetheless. The only one, it appeared, he didn't get on with at the hospital was another infamous inmate – Peter Sutcliffe, the 'Yorkshire Ripper'. But generally he smiled at them all and everyone smiled back. After all, this was Ron Kray, once the 'Godfather' of London and the man who had met the Mafia in New York.

Ron was a great talker. He would tell the stories and relive the moments of his gangland past. And he loved every minute of it. Driving the long way to Broadmoor was no problem for me – in fact, it became a pleasure.

Meeting Reg Kray for the first time, however, was no fun at all. Initially it was simple enough – a few viscous handshakes and some complimentary words, followed by tea and biscuits. But all that would change dramatically – because Reg Kray was slowly, but surely, getting drunk.

I visited Reg in Nottingham Jail to discuss the matter of a new film. They had made pretty good money on the last one and the Kray brothers wanted more of the same. However, what started out as a request for £500,000 quickly became a demand for at least £2 million. What made it worse was the drunken Reg Kray breathing all over me and saying, 'If I ever find out who did that *EastEnders* t-shirt deal, I'll skin 'em alive!'

The booze had been smuggled into the prison by visitors at the adjoining table, who had a baby with them. The baby bottle was the perfect way to bring illicit vodka into jail – after all, who could object to bringing in a drink for a child? The baby stared hard at Reg when he reached over for his booze. He just couldn't understand why that funny old man kept drinking his juice.

The talk of t-shirts brought home a few truths to me. I was the one who set up the deal for the so-called *EastEnders* t-shirts – with full permission of elder brother Charlie. But somehow Charlie had failed to tell his brothers about the deal – and he had pocketed all the money for himself. This, I was to learn, was typical of the Kray brothers. I can even remember being told that Ron's favourite trick was to run protection rackets on their own establishments. It was just his way of saying 'I'm the boss – and don't forget it!'

But all this secrecy was new to me. I had been told so many stories of these twins; they would do anything for each other – and I mean anything. This was a very rude awakening to what it really meant to be a part of the Kray family. It was something that I just had to get used to (or get out of, knees intact) if I could.

I decided to stay with it, but I have regretted that decision many times through the years. Did I really need all those phone calls saying, 'I'll sort you out, even if I have to spend the rest of my life in jail'? I don't think so. All I did was to help – nothing wrong or illegal, all above-board and squeaky-clean. But the Krays just didn't like being helped. They hated the idea of control being in the hands of someone else, so threats were a constant thing – to keep everyone in check. Well, it had worked well enough in the past, so why not in the future? Ultimately, they just couldn't change the habits of a lifetime – their past, their present, their future. This was the way the Krays did business.

When discussing the format of this book with my publisher, a pattern clearly developed. It would be impossible to recount every single Kray story and do them justice in one volume, so I have selected a number of topics that I personally feel require further attention. These I have listed chronologically, as the reader can see.

Some of these chapters are lengthy, others only a single page or two. But all are significant in the lives of the Krays and therefore deserve a mention. Other biographers would naturally choose other topics, but I have chosen those events that I feel best explain what it was to be a Kray.

During my time as a 'Kray writer', I have had to endure both the slings and the arrows – and I never quite got used to them!

1.

October 1933: Twin Terror – The Birth of the Kray Twins

When Violet Kray was told to expect twins, she couldn't be sure. Seven years earlier she had been told the same thing when she was pregnant with her eldest son Charles David, but they had been wrong then, so she didn't know what to expect this time. But this time they were right. Ron and Reg Kray were born on 24 October 1933.

The first to be born was the one soon to be known as Reginald, followed almost an hour later by his twin brother, Ronald. It changed everything for Violet and father Charlie Kray. Charlie had to work even harder to feed his growing family, and Violet had three children to take care of, instead of just one. Having to take care of toddlers was not easy in 1933, especially if you lived in the poorest community in the country.

Charlie had met the young Violet some eight years earlier. They had run away and got married, much to the annoyance of Violet's father, who wouldn't talk to them for many years – not, in fact, until the twins came along.

Violet Kray was from the Lee family, and lived in Bethnal Green along with her mum, dad, two sisters and one brother. Her father, John Lee, was known as 'the Southpaw Cannonball Lee' – a born fighter and showman. Of Irish and Jewish extraction, he would appear in the music halls licking a red hot poker or walking along a line of bottles, all stood on their necks, facing downwards. He would do his tricks anywhere, even appearing in the local parks. At one time he even owned a string of horses – some 22 in all.

Cannonball was a teetotaller, a keep-fit fanatic who rode the 42 miles to Southend on a bicycle when he was well into his 70s. He was well known in and around Bethnal Green, having also worked in the local market there. It was a sad day when his young daughter, still only 17, ran off with Charlie, the smart little man from Hoxton.

Charlie Kray came from fighting stock too. After all, there were only two ways of making a living in the East End in those days: either as a boxer or as a crook. Charlie's dad, 'Mad Jimmy', was a fighter and a drinker. He was a real character and everyone in Hoxton knew him. He was a flash dresser and was keen on the ladies, but he was no 'Dapper Dan' and never gave up in a fight – that's the way he was, that's the way the Krays were.

Violet's husband, however, didn't take so much after his father. Sure, he was a fighter in his younger days, but he was more of a talker than an out-and-out brawler. It was his chat that got him into buying and selling, going from door to door trying to buy good clothes and gold and silver especially. He would cajole, he would persist, he would pester his way to something of value. The little man was very clever with his mouth.

Being of gypsy and Jewish stock, Charlie found it easy to leave his family. Forever a wanderer, he would stay away for weeks at a time, scouring the country for something sellable. At first they lived in Gorsuch Street, just off Hackney Road, but later, in 1932, they moved. Charlie Kray should have been on a trip around the country, 'on the knocker', but on that day of 24 October 1933, he had to stay home at the new address in Stene Street, near Kingland Street.

Hoxton was the home of pickpockets and pubs. People who came from Bethnal Green looked down on the inhabitants of Hoxton. It may have been only a half mile down the road, but to Cannonball Lee it was no-man's-land, never to be mentioned. He didn't even want to see Violet back home in the house in Bethnal Green.

All of Violet's family lived near the old house. Her brother, John, had a café over the road, which he ran with his wife Maude – and her grandparents lived nearby too. Violet was very unhappy about being separated from her family, but she made a good home for her husband and her children – and when the twins were born her father came to call and pronounced her 'forgiven'.

Violet would take her twins out in the pram. Everyone would stop and look at the lovely youngsters, since twins were by no means a regular sight around the streets of London. The young, blonde woman with her two dark-haired sons were a delight to behold and soon sisters Rose and May would be around asking if they could take the little darlings for a walk. Being the centre of attention had its own attractions for the young ladies, who were trying to charm young men.

Violet protected the twins. She provided a warm home, sheltered from the noise and brash daily life of the East End. And she tried to treat the twins equally. Since having twins made Violet feel special, it made her twins special in her eyes. For the young Charlie, however, it made things only just tolerable. He was the oldest and he had to do everything – run errands, help with the house chores, even help tidy the toys. He turned his attention to sport to get him out of the house that would soon become ruled by the twins, especially Ron.

Reg was the talker of the two; always keen to please, light hearted and amusing. Ron, however, was the shy one, always wanting his way at any cost. He would shout the house down for attention, especially if anyone had been nice to his twin brother. Both twins always wanted to win, but it was normally Ron who triumphed, with his outlandish behaviour and his tricks.

The twins would always stand up for each other all right; always protect each other. Ron in particular soon spotted this and he would constantly get his twin brother drawn into fights. He did what he wanted to do, all the time and without a thought for others. He never asked his brother if it was all right with him, he never questioned his actions – he just did it and took the consequences later. He soon began to dominate.

By the time the twins were three years old, they had never been unwell. But things changed when Reg was taken ill with fever. Soon Ron was ill. And when the doctor came to tell their parents that it was diphtheria, the dreaded day arrived – the twins were split up. Ronnie was taken to the isolation ward of the General Hospital, Hoxton. But twin brother Reggie was taken all the way to St Anne's Hospital in Tottenham. This was the first time that the twins had been separated, and Violet journeyed from one hospital to the other to see her boys.

Reggie improved almost immediately and after some three months he was back home playing with the kids in the street. But Ron was still not well. He couldn't breathe and was continually gasping for air. Violet took the bus to the General Hospital and collected her son.

'He's fretting,' she told them. 'He's missing his brother,' And she rushed him straight home to Stene Street.

Just before the war, in 1939, the Kray family moved to 178 Vallance Road, just across the street from Violet's brother John, and just around the corner from her mum and dad. Her sister May lived only two houses along the road.

Their new home was by no means luxury. There was no bathroom and the toilet was in the yard, where Charlie Kray kept chickens. The house had a large, oak door and a giant, oversized knocker. It was home – and Violet now had the support of her family, especially her sisters. The small, terraced cottages that made up Vallance Road were typical of the village-type properties of the East End and soon everyone called it 'Lee Street'. Soon, during the war, it would become known as 'Deserters' Corner'.

They had a short spell in the Suffolk countryside during the war, but Violet never liked it. She was too far from the family, too far from home. The blitz didn't seem that bad compared to the solitude of the country. Those little things, so readily available in the East End, were not to be found in Suffolk. The luxuries of life were missing and those who could provide them were a long way off.

The twins, however, loved the countryside. The family stayed at a place called Hadleigh, near Tring, where there were huge, open fields for the youngsters to run around in. They admired the big houses there and hoped one day to settle down in the Suffolk countryside. Later they would often talk of retiring to the peace and quiet they found in their youth.

The Krays were soon back at 178 Vallance Road and the twins were soon out in the bombed-out buildings of the East End, learning to fight and learning to win. This was their training ground, where they played by their own rules. Winning was the name of the game – and they never forgot it!

2.

Summer 1939-49:

Running Away from Trouble

The war changed everything for the Kray family. Like many East Enders, old man Charlie Kray didn't like the idea of fighting for his country. Just why so many ran to fight in the killing fields of Europe was inexplicable to the Krays; why fight for your country when you had to fight for your own survival?

But Charlie Kray senior was more intent on having a good time 'on the knocker' than being at home helping Violet take care of the twins. He didn't seem to have much to worry about. Vi's sister Rose lived just around the corner – and there was the young Charlie to give a hand with the housework.

So Charlie Kray, deserter and hence wanted man, travelled the south of the country – even going as far as Wales to make a living. Being on the move made it difficult if not impossible for the authorities to trace him – and it kept him out of harm's way. But he was away from his family at a very important time. And when he did see them they had to hide him from the police, who were, even at this early stage, keeping a watchful eye on 178 Vallance Road, Bethnal Green.

This was where the twins, Ron and Reg Kray, developed their hatred of authority of any kind. It became a constant concern and it occupied their minds. The game had begun – the Krays versus 'the old bill'.

Other up-and-coming villains from the East End had different ways of staying out of the army. 'Mad Frankie' Fraser earned his nickname when he was before the draft board. He flung himself across the table and grabbed the throat of the officer interviewing him. 'He must be mad,' said the red-faced officer, as he lay choking on the floor. The name stuck.

Many crooks from the East End used similar dodges – and many continued during the war to ply their trade up and down the Mile End Road. They did well. Goods were in demand, since the regular supply lines were severed on a daily basis. Anyone who had anything good for sale was welcomed into many an East End house – and so it was at Vallance Road. This buying from the back of a truck soon became the usual practice in the East End, where money was in short supply and goods were scarce.

With old man Charlie on the run it was the younger Charlie who took over many of the responsibilities normally undertaken by the father. Aunt Rose was a great influence and the twins adored her, but it was Charlie who did the housework, did the jobs to bring in some urgently needed extra money – and who tried to keep the twins in check.

It wasn't easy for the youngster. As soon as the twins were born his life changed – things were never to be the same again. Some seven years older than his brothers, he showed caring and maturity far beyond his years. But somehow, in the back of his mind, he knew that his brothers would not only change his own life – but would change the lives of people all over the country.

Violet devoted herself to her twins. They were special – and this made the Kray family special. But Charlie didn't like being singled out as the older brother of the twins; he didn't like missing out on the normal childhood his friends were lucky enough to have and he didn't appreciate being forgotten by his own father. The start of the war was the end of normal life for the Krays.

Whether or not their father, old man Charlie, would have made any difference to their lives at this time is debatable, but there are good psychological grounds for saying that families without a prominent father figure have more problems with their male offspring than those with a so-called 'normal' two-parent family.

Ron and Reg would even join in when their parents argued – always taking their mother's side in any row. They didn't know their father very well, even after the war, since he was still a wanted deserter. So with all his years of buying and selling all over the South of England and Wales before the war and trying to escape the police after the war, old man Charlie Kray really didn't know his sons.

But Violet encouraged the twins to respect their father. He was, after all, the breadwinner and he deserved their love and devotion. The twins agreed to her wishes, not because of any strong feelings towards their father, but because of the promise they made to their mum, who they idolised and worshipped. They would protect their father, all right – but not if it caused their mum any harm.

Playing games with the police, who often came to the house in search of their father, soon became a cherished pastime for the twins. On one occasion they hid their dad under a table. Ron saw the policeman trying to peer under the tablecloth and threw him off by quickly saying, 'You don't expect to find him there, do you?' Another time they hid him in a cupboard and used the same trick to great effect.

The idea of beating the law made them feel better and more powerful than the law. They now began to make up their own rules of conduct. If anyone broke those rules then they would be punished. The Kray twins would soon become the judges, the jury and the executioners.

Ron and Reg Kray settled into school, where they didn't do very well academically, but where they excelled at after school 'activities' – such as gang fights in the bomb craters of the East End. Ron, the younger of the twins, dominated here too. Reg would let Ron take the lead – wherever Ron went, Reg was sure to follow. At only eight years of age Ron and Reg Kray became known as the 'terrible' twins.

The twins learned how to handle any situation, thinking on their feet. Sometimes, when the police came to call, they would tell them that their parents were divorced. 'Dad don't live here any more,' was something the old bill got used to. They would go from house to house over the back fences and through the yards of the neighbouring houses, many of which were inhabited by members of the Lee family. Aunt May's husband was also on the run, away from 'Deserter's Corner', so they had many a willing helper nearby when it came to finding a suitable hiding place for old man Charlie.

But in other ways too, things were different when their dad was home. He wouldn't tell them the usual pleasant night-time stories, as favoured by their mum and Aunt Rose. He would tell them tales of pickpockets and thieves he knew; of people who worked in the fairgrounds and in the streets; of low-life villains who used violence and conflict as a way of life. Soon the twins relished the idea of having a father who was a 'wanted man', someone who had escaped the clutches of the law and who had survived to tell the tale.

Shortly after the war, the fairgrounds opened up again and the twins were able to meet their dad's pals and the folk of his adventurous tales face-to-face. It was Grandfather Lee who took them to their first fair at Victoria Park, with their father, old man Charlie, scowling in the background trying to evade the eyes of the ever-watchful police.

The twins especially liked the boxing booths, where professional fighters would take on anyone. Ron and Reg loved the blood, the sweat – and the tears. And they loved the sight of the pain and anguish – fear even, on the fighters' faces. This was where the local lads got to perform and where they could earn a name – as hard men, tough guys and men who were not afraid of confrontation. This was where they could build a reputation by sending a man crashing to the floor.

This first occasion here after the war was to teach the twins an invaluable lesson. They were watching the fights and enjoying every minute when the ringmaster called for men from the audience to enter the ring and to take on the champ. No one volunteered.

'Who'll be next?' shouted the ringmaster once more. Again silence. 'There's a fiver in it for you!' he said. The lure of the money did the trick. 'I'll do it,' shouted Ron Kray as he made a dash for the ring. At only 11 years of age, Ron Kray was no match for the heavyweight standing in the ring. As the audience began to laugh, Reg Kray gritted his teeth.

'Come back next year, sonny – you may be bigger by then,' shouted the ringmaster as the tent boomed with laughter. This was by now far too much for Reg to take. He couldn't see his brother tormented in this way.

'I'll fight him,' shouted Reg, as he strolled towards his brother in the ring. There was pure determination on his face and the ring went quiet. The professional boxer climbed through the ropes and into the crowds as the ringmaster called the boys together. The fight began.

Arms flew everywhere as the twins punished each other with vicious blows to the head and to the body. Time and time again they lashed out in a frenzy as the onslaught continued, neither giving way to the other. Suddenly Reg understood that there was a way to defeat his brother – simply by playing to the rules of the game. He enjoyed it in the ring, there was no fear for him here and it was down to him and him alone. In this most lonely of places Reg came of age.

Ron didn't like being hit by his brother, who was obviously a much better boxer, but he loved the punching, the ducking and the diving. As the sweat flowed both twins were beginning to learn a lesson and when the blood appeared it was time for the ringmaster to call a halt.

'It's a draw,' he announced, and he paid both boys for their performance. The crowds cheered and the twins loved the adulation of their first real audience. Grandfather Lee was all smiles as they walked back to Vallance Road, but old man Charlie was prepared for the worst. He could see the bloodied noses and the battered faces of the twins – and so too would Violet . . .

Their mother hit the roof when they returned. Their father was proud of their performance, but Violet was scornful in her assessment of the situation. There and then she made the twins promise not to fight each other ever again. The twins knew she was right, they had sensed this when they were thrashing each other with the best punches they could muster, back at Victoria Park. It was time to work together. The next time they would fight side by side, back to back – against *anyone* who got in their way.

When they were 12, the twins got into trouble by firing an air rifle in a public place and were put on probation. But this didn't stop their fights. They were quickly back on the streets with their chains and their knives and the fights soon grew in intensity. The twins were now rulers of the ruins – and no one could stop them.

In 1949 the twins appeared in court. At only 16 they were accused of having beaten and battered a youngster from another gang, using chains and iron bars. There were witnesses to the event, but the twins had already developed certain survival tactics, so the witnesses were scared off and the case was dismissed when it came to the Old Bailey. Even the lad who had been beaten refused to give evidence against them. This would have meant breaking the East End code of not snitching.

'You don't grass,' said Ron – so he didn't.

Shortly after this incident, the twins were again in trouble. Ron had punched a policeman by the name of PC Baynton and had been taken into custody at the local 'nick'. When Charlie arrived Ron's face was bruised and battered. Charlie warned them, and told them he was taking his brother to the doctor, with or without the police's permission. They let them go, but the news soon reached Reg.

Reg went out, scouring the East End for the villain of the piece – PC Baynton. He found him – and hammered him to the floor. Reg was soon in that same cell previously occupied by his brother. But no one came near him. Charlie's warning had done the trick.

At the trial Reverend Father Hetherington spoke up for the twins. He told the court that it was completely out of character for the twins, whom he had known since they were born. 'They are most helpful in the community,' he told the court. 'They have helped me on many an occasion.'

The twins were put on parole – and they walked free. Their father, old man Charlie Kray, was always running away from trouble, trying to hide his head in the sand, saying, 'If they can't find me, then they can't hurt me.' But the twins, Ron and Reg, never worried about trouble. They would never back down or run away – they were fearless!

3.

December 1951: Fighting the good fight

All three Kray brothers fought on the same bill at The Royal Albert Hall on 11 December 1951. It was a record then and it still stands today as an outstanding achievement.

The twins had trained rigorously for the event and were looking forward to their fights, eager to show what they could do in the ring. But Charlie wasn't in good shape – he didn't have the heart for fighting any more. He had only signed on for the match when his manager, Jack Jordan, offered him the princely sum of twenty-five pounds for the evening's work and, as usual, money did the trick. With Charlie it was always, 'Show me the money!'

Charlie was good at his trade, even fighting for the Royal Navy when in the services. He had taken up fighting at an early age. It taught him discipline and it taught him to pace himself – and it earned him respect. The Krays all had fighting pedigree – it was in the blood.

Violet didn't like fighting at all, but she had to accept it. She was Cannonball Lee's daughter and she was used to seeing her father come home at night bloodied from ear to ear. She had to accept it then – and she had to accept it now with her own children.

Old man Charlie, however, was proud of his lads. He even used to sort out their kit before the fights, pressing the shorts and packing up the bundles of clothes – one for Reg, one for Ron, one for his oldest son and namesake, Charlie. It was a ritual to him. Highly polished black boots, clean white socks, blue satin dressing gowns, towels, protective cups and anything else he thought would go down well. They were all carefully prepared and tidied away.

The Kray name was by now well known, both in and out of the ring. Old man Charlie got a real kick out of it. He would swagger down Bethnal Green Road when the fights were on, accepting the acknowledgements of the locals and a drink or two when offered. In this way he was trying to make up for the love missing in the twins' formative years, when he was on the run from the police – a deserter, wanted by the law.

Their father was a cunning and shrewd businessman, but handling children was something that he never wanted in his younger days. They were a handful, those kids, always in and out of the house, always in and out of trouble, always in his hair. But he never harmed them in any way, or mistreated them. He just wasn't there for them when they were growing up. A few visits to the Suffolk countryside to see the family wasn't enough for any of them, but that was what they got. The twins accepted this, but they never forgave him for it and always took their mum's side in any argument at 178 Vallance Road.

It was their father who was the breadwinner. He travelled far and wide throughout the south of England – even to Wales. And he always came home with the bacon. He would literally buy and sell anything, going from house to house pestering his way to goods, unwanted or unneeded. There was a market for anything in those days and old man Charlie Kray was the best in the game.

If old man Charlie was the breadwinner, then it was Violet who took care of everything else. She looked after all three children with pride and dignity and she never let them starve or go short. She also had the family nearby, the Lees, to help her when things were difficult and it was Aunt Rose who was always the first to offer assistance. It was Aunt Rose who became their surrogate father, so the ways of the Krays became dominated by women at an early stage. None of the women liked the fights, but they would never let on, never refuse to let them show their worth. It was a question of honour, just as much for the family as it was for the sons.

Charlie Kray had started boxing early on at senior school and he had been training ever since, three nights a week since the age of 15. It was Cannonball Lee, his grandfather, who rigged up the gym in the upstairs bedroom. He joined the naval cadets at Hackney Wick and even fought off the effects of rheumatic fever to become a champion. Charlie was serious about boxing at first, but later his energies were consumed elsewhere – when wine, women and song became his daily routine. The twins took over the punch-bag and the weights, and by the time they were in their early teens they were accomplished boxers.

It was the sight of a cabinet full of prizes and trophies that encouraged the twins to take up the 'noble art'. Soon they had their own trophies and prizes, enough to make them serious about considering boxing as a way of making a living. Now, on 11 December 1951, all three Kray brothers were to fight as professional boxers at one of London's most famous venues, The Royal Albert Hall.

Jack Jordan, their manager, drove them to the awesome arena in his Riley. He had been their manager for years and he had even managed to get good seats for a family party keen on seeing their boys do the business. But Violet didn't come. The thought of one of her sons being hit and possibly injured was too much for her. She stayed home at Vallance Road, with a cup of tea – and prayed.

The car pulled up outside the side entrance at Exhibition Road and they piled out. Ron was due to fight first, then Reg and finally Charlie. They were all ready. It was now or never.

Ron was quickly dressed for the fight and Jack Jordan led him from the dressing room. Reg and Charlie followed close behind. The atmosphere could have been cut with a knife as Ron trod that red carpet leading to the ring. Reg and Charlie stood behind the curtain – and watched. Soon it would be their turns. The fanfare blared out as Ron entered the ring.

Henry Berry was taking care of Ron in the ring and he tried to give his fighter encouragement. Ron, however, appeared to be somewhat indifferent. He was taking it easy – some would say too easy. In the feverish heat Ron Kray started to sweat.

Smoke filled the hall as the fight fans were eager to get things started. Everything was intense, everything was noisy, everything was getting hot. As the master of ceremonies called out his name, Ron Kray took no notice. His opponent, Bill Sliney, was introduced. The man from King's Cross was due to fight the man from Bethnal Green.

The referee called both men to the centre of the ring.

'We want a nice clean fight,' he told them. 'No butting, no holding, no low punches!' He looked both fighters in the eyes. 'Go to it,' he said. 'Have a good fight.'

Ron Kray strolled back to his corner and the waiting Henry Berry who again offered his fighter encouragement. They didn't have long to wait for the fight to begin. 'Seconds out,' shouted the time-keeper. The bell rang out loud and clear. The fight was under way.

It couldn't have started any better for Ron Kray. He had Bill Sliney down for a count of eight at the start of the opening round. The odds were beginning to look good – when a dangerous clash of heads changed everything. It left Ron's left eye in a bad way and he could hardly see. But Ron wanted to continue – he was strong and wanted to win. Surely that would be enough . . . The doctor entered the ring and took a look at the almost-closed eye. 'Continue,' he said.

The first round ended. Both men were tired; they had fought well. But Ron's left eye was closed now and he couldn't see well. He was unable to judge distance, and being short sighted didn't make it any easier.

'Keep your distance,' urged Henry Berry. But Ron knew what he had to do and was determined to do it.

At the start of round two Bill Sliney came out into the ring, circling to the left, anti-clockwise. Ron now had a real problem, with his opponent going out of vision from time to time. Sliney's corner had given him good advice and it worked well.

'Jab!' they shouted from Sliney's corner as he began to dominate.

'Box!' shouted Henry Berry. But Ron knew that there was only one way to win, and that was through sheer courage. He had to get close and land that killing blow. But throughout the rest of the fight he couldn't catch Bill Sliney. When the verdict came it was close, but they all knew the outcome.

Ron Kray lost on a narrow margin – a close decision on points. That closed eye made all the difference. It was an accident all right – Sliney was a clean fighter, but in defeat Ron had here been made to learn the hard way that sheer will to win was not enough, courage in abundance was not enough, and pride was not enough.

Ron Kray quietly slipped away through the ropes and into the dressing-room. He cleaned up his face as Reg walked out to face Bob Manito. Charlie helped Ron, dreading the time when he would have to take him home – to Vallance Road, and his mother.

Reg went through the same routine. He was ready – all psyched up for anything the south Londoner from Clapham could throw at him. He was undoubtedly the best of the Krays when it came to boxing. He had fought many times as a junior, winning most of his fights on points. He didn't have the knock-out punch of his twin brother Ron, but he had determination and will power, and the skill to go with it.

Reg won every round easily on points. Manito never landed a telling blow and Reg skipped his way out of trouble. He had trained well for the fight. He was fit and clever too. He fought with his mind as well as his gloves.

The decision was unanimous, Reg Kray was the victor.

Reg had listened to Henry Berry and followed his every word, unlike his brother Ron. It may have been the trainer's words that formed the basis of the tactics, but it was the fighting skill of the young 18 year old that had won the day. And Reg enjoyed winning.

Reg was smiling as he made his way back to the dressing room to the cheers of the crowd. Ron greeted him with a hug, as Charlie walked out to face his opponent, Lew Lazar. There was only one thought in Charlie's mind – to get that twenty-five pounds.

Henry Berry knew that Charlie wasn't in good shape. 'If you go down,' he told him, 'then stay down!' Charlie knew it was good advice. But once again there was that Kray pride to contend with. It followed him everywhere. Would it help or hinder him here?

The first round went well enough. Charlie kept his distance and it was fairly even. But round two saw a total change in the fight when Lazar felled him with a left hook to the stomach. Charlie staggered to his feet, but he knew his time had come.

He managed to get up and box on, but not for long. Soon another powerful left hook sent him once more onto the canvas. His trainer was telling him to stay down, to concede victory. But Charlie's pride wouldn't let him. Maybe he could endure it all – and still win? He clung on to the ropes until the bell sounded for the end of the round, before edging his way back to his corner, and his trainer.

'That's enough, Charlie,' Henry told the breathless boxer. 'You've earned your money. Next time, stay down.' Charlie nodded, but could he do it? Could he give up? The bell sounded and he knew that he would soon find the answer.

Yet another left hook to the stomach sent Charlie Kray down for the count. Charlie looked at his corner, then he looked at the referee. But up he came again. That fighting spirit was still there, but was that enough to win? The fight was going all one way and the whole crowd knew it. It was no surprise when the telling blow came. It knocked Charlie to the floor and this time he just couldn't get up, no matter how much he tried. The referee counted to ten. It was the slowest count that Charlie had ever heard. It was over. He had lost – on a knock out! His trainer soon got him back to his seat and got the revival process under way. Charlie even managed a smile as he was sponged down.

The crowd roared their approval as Charlie walked back to the dressing-room. He only had one thought in his mind now, as he strode down that red carpet and out of the hall. At least his brothers hadn't seen his defeat.

Back in the dressing-room all three Kray brothers were laughing and joking when their manager Jack Jordan entered. He had seen it all from ringside and he had been particularly impressed with Reg, he said. He had plans for him, big plans – maybe even championship fights.

When he shook Charlie's hand he gave him the twenty-five pounds. It was all there, no manager's cut as usual. This was Charlie Kray's last fight and they all knew it. And he had earned the money.

The drive back to Vallance Road was quiet. Ron's eye was still closed and Charlie didn't look too well either. They were all thinking of their mum and of how she would take it.

For the Krays it was decision time. Charlie had already told Jack Jordan that he would never fight again, but Ron and Reg had also learned something from the experience. When it came to playing by other people's rules, there was a chance of losing. And the twins didn't like losing. There and then they made up their minds never to box again. Sure, they would train and keep fit. But never again would they fight by anyone else's rules. For the rest of their lives they would make their own rules – street rules!

This was the first and last time that three brothers appeared in a boxing ring, anywhere in the country. The record still stands. This should have told the world, there and then, that these Kray boys were something special, but the word never got out. Things had changed forever, but no one knew it.

4.

March 1952: Privates on Parade

Ron and Reg Kray got their call-up papers for National Service in mid-February 1952. They were required to join the Royal Fusiliers at The Tower of London on 2 March of that year.

They arrived wearing identical blue suits and reported for duty to the Yeoman Warder at the Shrewsbury Tower. The directions given led them past Traitor's Gate to a building opposite the White Tower. This was home to the Royal Fusiliers. A sergeant showed them to the mess where the enlisted men could grab a bite to eat before reporting back for duty.

First they had to collect uniforms and equipment. Then the corporal showed them their barracks and their beds. As he was telling them how to lay out their kit Ron and Reg Kray slowly walked towards the door. The corporal stopped.

'And where do you two think you're going?' he asked. The twins stopped and looked around. The corporal asked them once more. 'I said where are you off to?'

Ron looked at Reg. Reg looked at Ron.

'We don't like it here. We're off home for some tea with our mum!' said one of the twins. The corporal approached them. He was angry, annoyed at being made to look a fool. He grabbed one of them by the arm. That was all the twins needed. With extreme violence the corporal was hit with a single blow to the jaw. The man staggered back against a wall and slumped to the floor. The twins then simply walked down the stairs, out of the building and home to Vallance Road. They showed no signs of nerves, or temper. It was a simple act of aggression, nothing personal.

The police collected them at their house the following morning without a struggle. Ron and Reg Kray were taken by army escorts back to the Tower of London from Bethnal Green police station. They had been out all night, at a dance hall in Tottenham, so they were glad of the rest. They had even told their mum that they would soon be back at Vallance Road.

The next morning they joined the line-up of mischief-makers and others who had been absent without leave. Striking a non-commissioned officer was a serious offence but the army had a problem – who had landed the fatal blow? Was it the twin on the right, or the one on the left – or was it both of them? The proceedings were getting just a little comical and out of hand.

The corporal told his version of the story. The Commanding Officer asked him to say which of the two youngsters had thrown the punch. He stood and stared. 'It may have been the one on the right,' he answered.

The CO walked over to Private Ron Kray. 'Was it you?' he asked. 'Were you the one who attacked the corporal?'

Ron looked at the CO. 'No, sir,' he replied casually.

The CO walked over to Reg Kray. 'Then it must have been you,' he said, staring the youngster in the face.

Reg looked up. 'Not me, sir,' he said.

The CO was furious. 'Well, it must have been one of you,' he shouted.

The twins looked at each other. It was a routine they knew well. 'Did what, sir?' said one of the twins.

'Hit the corporal,' shouted the CO.

'Did someone hit the corporal?' asked the other twin.

'It was one of you!' screamed the CO.

'But which one are you accusing?' asked Reg.

The CO had had enough. He simply read out the rule book, telling them of their duties and of the kind of behaviour expected by the army. They were duly sentenced to seven days in the guard house.

Ron and Reg settled down and made themselves at home. But then and there they decided that army life was not for them. They would get out of the Tower of London as soon as possible. But they had learned a good trick – being twins made it difficult, if not impossible, for the authorities to say who was responsible for any particular incident or crime, and to prosecute them. When Ron hit someone, they had to ask themselves, 'Was it Ron Kray or Reg Kray?' When they were out driving, the twins often swapped driving licences, to confuse the police.

Strangely enough, the punishment cells here were just what they wanted. They needed to show the army that they could handle it all – the depravation, the sleeping on floorboards, the poor food. If they could prove they could take whatever the army could throw at them they could feel there was some justification for the ordeal. It would also toughen them up for the future – all at the expense of the tax payer.

For the first few days they were alone – alone to think, to plan, to dream. On the second day they had a visitor, their father. Charlie Kray had managed to convince the guards that he was their uncle. Their dad couldn't come since he was wanted as a deserter, he told them. The guards allowed him to see his 'nephews'. The boys laughed at their dad's story. They knew he was a good talker, but this was something to tell all their pals.

On day three, a new man arrived. He had come straight from borstal – and he would soon teach the twins a trick or two about being confined against their will. His name was Dickie Morgan.

Morgan had a criminal's philosophy on life: grab what you can, use it and then grab some more. So what if you're caught? The state has to house you, feed you and teach you something. And the more you were taught, the better the chances of getting away with your crimes. 'Enjoy it', was his motto. Soon the twins would adopt it.

Ron and Reg loved his stories, his wicked smile and his knowledge of the criminal way of life. He was to be the first of many who would teach the Kray twins new tricks.

After one week in the guardhouse Ron and Reg Kray were released and put on ordinary duties. Their first act of rebellion on their first day of release was to walk straight out of the barracks, just as they had done before. Only this time, Dickie Morgan went with them. Their first port of call was Morgan's home, a neat terraced house in Clinton Road, down by London Docks. The twins were now entering a new world, one where criminals were the kings and the ordinary people were just mugs – trying to make a living from nothing.

Morgan's family were all involved in crime. His brothers were at borstal and his father had only recently been imprisoned for armed robbery – this was a household of thieves and the twins loved it. Back at Vallance Road they had been protected from the world, but here they openly talked about crime and the benefits it could bring.

Overnight their habits changed. From being teetotal non-smokers, they became ardent drinkers and cigarettes were lit up without a second thought, as though there was no tomorrow. The twins had always used to jog in the morning, as part of their keep-fit training, but suddenly they were out all night, sizing up jobs, robbing merchants – making money from crime for the very first time.

As they visited Morgan's pals all along the Mile End Road, they started to become famous. Everyone knew they were on the run from the law, deserters from the army. And when Ron and Reg introduced Morgan to their own community around Bethnal Green, the twins knew exactly what this respect and regard could bring them among their peers of the East End – power!

But gradually the twins became bored with their new lifestyle. When a new pal arrived at Morgan's home, they decided to do something different. He could drive. So instead of thieving or downing pints at the local pub, they stole a car and took a trip to Southend.

They walked among the holiday makers, eating ice-cream. They walked along the pier and had a drink or two. They even went to the cinema. But once again the twins were after something more. So they bought a postcard and sent it to their CO at the Tower of London. It said simply, 'Having a great time. Best of luck – Ron, Reg and Dickie'.

Eventually, still not really knowing what to do or where to go, they decided to head home. Bethnal Green was the place to be – among friends. But the twins could not stay at home forever. At night they would go out and visit the clubs around Bethnal Green, along with Dickie Morgan and their new pal. They would drink, they would fight – but they were learning quickly and Dickie Morgan could see it in their eyes. These twins were something else – they were different. They were fearless.

Eventually, though, the twins grew tired of being on the run. Soon they were openly defying the police, drinking in the pubs along the Mile End Road – even taking afternoon tea in a local café. They were not looking for trouble – they simply wanted to be arrested and taken back to the Tower. One young local police officer obliged and the twins accompanied him back to the local nick. They were calm, subdued and even friendly. They had escaped the army and had had a great time, but it was now time to fight the Fusiliers again.

The pattern continued. They escaped and were captured, escaped and captured again. More fights ensued; more NCOs were floored by both twins. For a while they were separated, but it didn't help. Soon the army gave up on the Krays.

For assaulting a policeman they were sentenced to one month's imprisonment at Wormwood Scrubs by Colonel Batt, the magistrate at Thames Street Court. When they were released a military escort took them to Wemyss Barracks in Kent, where they were tried for striking an NCO and going absent without leave. They were sentenced by the army to nine months at the Shepton Mallet Military Prison. The authorities were in fact actively conspiring to train the Krays in the ways of the criminal.

The time spent at Shepton Mallet did the twins no harm. It only encouraged them in their new-found ways. The staff of the prison had to be changed time and time again. No one could handle the Kray twins. The only time the twins actually had any fun at Shepton Mallet was when one of the sergeants showed them the gallows, where men were still being hanged. Ron, naturally enough, had to try it out – he loved being centre stage.

Eventually brother Charlie was asked to go down and have a chat with them about their antics in the prison and their violent assaults on the guards – and to try to get them to co-operate. Ron and Reg were adamant. There was only one thing the army knew – and that was a punch in the face. Charlie tried to tell them of his own experiences in the navy, where he excelled both in and out of the ring. But it did no good, no good at all.

All they did at Shepton Mallet was to learn how to beat the system. They learned things from the old professional thieves and con-men they met in the dirty cells – and they loved every minute of it. They even got to hear of future plans from the likes of Charlie Richardson and Johnny Nash, both of whom would later form rival gangs to the Krays.

By the time of their dishonourable discharge, they knew exactly what they wanted to do and even knew who could help them. Their training in the army had been thorough – Ron and Reg Kray wanted adventure and excitement. And nothing would stop them.

5.

Summer 1954: Doing the Business

The seeds of the Krays' empire were sown in April 1954 – and they started at The Regal. It was a 14-table billiard hall, in a bad state of repair and definitely not in the best part of town. It was situated in Eric Street, just off The Mile End Road – and it was easy pickings for the Krays.

The twins had been in trouble and elder brother Charlie knew he had to do something to help – otherwise Ron and Reg would soon be carted off, either in a van or a box. He couldn't turn a blind eye any more when a truck was hijacked and plundered, or when stolen driving licences turned up at Vallance Road. He encouraged them to find something to do, something legal and safe – for the sake of their mum and dad.

What they found was The Regal. But they needed money – and that was something they just didn't have. What they also needed was a deal, but the owner was not interested, so Ron and Reg made him an offer he couldn't refuse. First they started to escalate things on the fight front – more punch ups, more stabbings. Then, when the owner bought an Alsatian dog, they had their pals throw fireworks at it, which sent it crazy. After a two-month work-over the owner submitted and offered the twins a deal – for five pounds a week they could take it over, lock, stock and barrel.

But there was still the money problem – they had to clean the place up; paint it and stock it with drinks and suchlike. This was where young Charlie came in. He lent them the money to buy the paint, sort out new tables, build a bar and organise tables and chairs. For the first and last time he coughed up for the twins. Later on it would be the twins who would always be coughing up for Charlie.

On re-opening, The Regal was an instant success. The money came rolling in and their troubles stopped. The twins were on easy street and they knew it. Gradually they established themselves as businessmen, always on the look-out for easy pickings. Sometimes they would deal in stolen goods and sometimes they would just hide out for a day or two. But whatever they did they made a lot of dosh – and Charlie was getting just a little bit jealous.

It was all too easy at The Regal. No trouble, no problems; readies by the score. Things had to change and change came in the form of a certain Maltese gang who called asking for protection money. It happened late one night when Ron and Reg were tidying up the place, stacking chairs and cleaning up the refreshments bar. The twins sensed trouble immediately as the Maltese gang – with unfamiliar faces but a familiar attitude – approached the new green baize. They played with the billiard balls threateningly.

One of them asked for protection money. 'Protection from what?' asked Ron. He drew a cutlass and lashed out at them. Reg drew a knife and the two brothers ran after the Maltese gang, who fled into the night, never to return.

'They've not got much bottle, these continentals,' said Reg. 'Especially when the knives come out!' The East End was like a firework, waiting for someone to light the blue touch-paper, but the news was out. No one wanted trouble with the Krays, these twins were two tough performers. They were only 21 years of age, but they could handle themselves in any situation. The news soon got around, it even reached crime bosses Jack Spot and Billy Hill.

It was while at The Regal that Ron Kray adopted the nickname 'The Colonel' and started to dress, and to act, as though he was Al Capone. He would organise parties, performances, sometimes even taking people off the streets to come in and perform for their supper. He would bring in animals too – he was rapidly becoming a real local personality. Reg played along, following his twin – and he didn't even care when Ron announced now openly, for the first time, that he was homosexual. But Charlie was shocked.

He knew his brother Ron was different, but a queer, a fag, *gay*? That was unacceptable in Charlie's book and he tried to distance himself from The Regal and his brothers. He sank himself into his travel company, organising tours down to the south of France. It was better for him to get away to the sun rather than stay at home and face the potential heat of the East End – and his brothers.

Ron and Reg took it all in their stride. After all, they didn't really need their brother Charlie's help. All they needed was his money. And now the show was well and truly on the road and the cash was rolling in – by the bucketful.

But protection loomed its ugly head again and the twins were approached by a gang from the docks. It was headed by three men from Poplar – and they ruled the Mile End Road. They were big and brash, and they used to be heavyweight boxers.

They sent a message to The Regal for the twins to join them in a pub along the Mile End Road. It was one of their protected establishments, home territory. The news quickly spread and soon everyone at The Regal knew about it. That Sunday the twins packed up the tables and chairs, just like on any normal day, but this was D-day – showdown time!

Ron and Reg simply went about their business, not saying a word to anyone. All their pals were there, waiting to see what was going on, hoping to get involved. But the twins said nothing, they didn't need or ask for any help. Without a word Ron and Reg put on their jackets – and walked out the door of The Regal.

They continued until they came to the public house – and the meeting with the dockers. There they were, all three of them drinking light ale in the private bar. Soon Ron and Reg Kray stood face-to-face with the three big men. One of the men offered them a drink, but his words were not well chosen.

'Here you are, sonny – you're just about old enough for a shandy!' he said. That was all he said, though. Ron grabbed him and hurled him to the floor. Reg joined in and felled one of the others. Soon all three dockers were on the floor, bloodied and bruised – and gasping for their lives. Reg had to drag Ron from one of them, otherwise he would have got his button there and then.

As cool as you please the Kray twins tidied themselves and walked out of the pub. What they left behind was a mess – bloodied bodies on the carpeted floor. It would be the last time anyone tried to collect protection money from the Krays.

Reg and Ron talked on the way back to The Regal. If this was the best the gangs could offer, then maybe the twins should just walk in and take it all over. It would add a string to their bow and with their growing reputation it should be a piece of cake. Now it would be them who would be demanding protection money.

They devised two lists – the nipping list and the pension list. For the first, one of the Firm would nip into the establishment and walk out with a carton of cigarettes, a case of gin, or what have you. Chicken feed – just enough to sweeten the appetite of the Krays. The second list was the real breadwinner. They would aim for the better restaurants, the clubs, the car dealers. Those with real money would be the target of the pension list, and would be enough to supply the Krays with an income for life.

Nothing describes the pension list better than the following incident with a car dealer. A customer bought a car – a nice, clean, shiny car – but he had second thoughts and wanted his money back. He phoned the dealer and told him so straight: 'just give me my money back or there'll be trouble'. But the dealer paid the Krays for protection, so he phoned Ron. Ron was delighted: a real reason for a shoot-out.

Ron turned up at the site, complete with Al Capone head-gear and tooled-up for good measure. He waited for the time to kill. But the adrenaline was flowing and he knew what he had to do. As soon as the dissatisfied customer turned up, Ron drew his gun and shot him. He never allowed him to say a word. Fortunately, he only shot him in the leg. The man said that he'd told the dealer that at first he'd wanted his money back, he didn't think the car was right for him. But after thinking about it, he thought he had a good deal and was quite pleased with the purchase. He had only come along to apologise.

Ron was furious – and marched off in a huff. Members of the Firm helped the poor man to a nearby hospital and got him treated, telling a concocted story that appeared to satisfy them. They stuffed his coat with money to keep him quiet and he never let on about the incident.

Needless to say, the car dealer never called on the Krays again. In future he would take care of his own business – and guns were banned. It was a lesson to Ron Kray too – never again would he go off half-cocked. Next time he would kill – and no questions asked. Losing face was not what he wanted. Better to kill than to be ridiculed. But it told the world that Ron was capable of killing – and that was enough at the time.

The difference between the twins was illustrated the time Reg paid a visit to a new night spot in the West End of London. When Reg had a chat with the owner, a certain Peter Cook, he couldn't resist mentioning the word 'protection'. Peter Cook picked up his glass of champagne and said nonchalantly 'I don't really think we need more protection than we have at present'. Reg was disappointed and pressed the proposition further. But Peter Cook had an instant reply. 'Did you know we are right next to a police station?' he asked Reg. Reg and his pals beat a speedy exit, stage left – and never went there again. Reg knew when to press home an argument and when to retreat. It was a lesson his twin brother Ron, though, was never to learn.

The Regal was the place to be in or around the Mile End Road. It was a haunt of crooks and criminals of all shapes and sizes. And the Krays made money from them all. Even Charlie couldn't stay away from the place for long. It attracted the attention of the gang leaders as well as the cops who were trying to catch them. Soon the Krays were known throughout London – later they would be known throughout the country, and even beyond.

6.

April 1955: Organised Crime

By the early '50s, the world of the East End had changed. London was in the grips of a violent criminal, a man who would stop at nothing to get what he wanted.

Billy Hill and Jack Spot (real name Comer) had run the underworld successfully for more than ten years from their base in the West End of London. Hill was a thief with a passion for organisation, whereas Spot was the minder who arranged the heavy stuff. They were the very best and everyone knew it. From the Krays to the Richardsons and throughout the entire city of London these men were the un-crowned kings of crime.

But by the mid '50s things were changing and the team of Hill and Spot had a falling out. They disbanded the old guard and formed new allies. Jack Spot turned to the Krays.

Spot introduced Ron and Reg Kray to Epsom Races and to real money. Organised crime has always seen an easy racket in supplying protection to bookmakers. If the bookmakers didn't pay then they would be roughed up. So they ended up paying people like the Krays for protection. Real violence was what gangsters were using and knives and guns became the tools of the trade.

Jack Spot was not a young man and had been badly cut around the face just a short time before by the evil 'Mad Frankie' Fraser who had joined Billy Hill's forces. Getting the Krays on his side was a bit of a coup. The twins were keen to learn and took time off from The Regal Billiard Hall to size up the opposition. They were fast becoming good businessmen themselves and were quick to spot an opportunity. They could already smell the money.

Billy Hill was not a man of violence. He would sooner make a deal and share the profits than risk war. War just wasn't good for business.

But he could see that the whole underworld scene was hotting up. Violence was now the key.

Gang met gang in minor skirmishes, only using knives or fists. They would arrange for a meeting on one of London's eternal bombsites, where rubble still littered the streets and back alleys. But these skirmishes were not the important events – they only showed which gangs were the dominant ones. The big business was making money, not war.

Robberies were executed with bloody efficiency. The stakes were high and crimes of violence were commonplace. The crooks wanted the good life, no matter what. Callous people committed the most violent of crimes. These people knew that once caught they would face harsh treatment in prison. The cat-o'-nine-tails was still around – or the birch was available for serious offenders – and sentences were long. In this dark world of the criminal, brutality bred brutality and there was no one better than Ron and Reg Kray when it came to out-and-out violence.

The twins were playing a waiting game, hoping for a fight where they could show their strength. They began to work for both of the bosses, Hill and Spot. On one occasion Billy Hill phoned them saying that he needed them urgently. They rushed round to his flat, only to find him sitting reading a newspaper. When Reg asked what the problem was, Billy Hill smiled. 'I was only testing you out, to see if you would really get here,' he told them both, tossing a wad of five-pound notes onto the table. 'Take that for your trouble,' he told them. There was five hundred pounds in all, not bad for a quick car ride.

The rest of 1955 went by with skirmishes, but no real gang wars. Every time Spot called on the twins to sort out Billy Hill's mob, Hill managed to call off the fight. Look as they may for trouble, the Krays just couldn't find it. Frankie Fraser had by now joined Billy Hill, so the Kray van was always at the ready and the guns were always loaded. But the fight never happened.

It was now the time of the gun. And it was time for Spot and Hill to beat a hasty retreat. Later, in the summer of 1956, Billy Hill retired to his villa in the south of Spain, and Jack Spot took over a furniture business in the West End. They got out while the going was good and before the killings started.

7.

November 1956: Prison

By the summer of 1956 the Krays had become a force to be reckoned with in the East End. They weren't just crooks any more – they were gang leaders and proud of it.

The Regal was still their base and business flourished, but Ron was looking for something else. He needed the excitement – he needed action. The feud between Jack Spot and Billy Hill had ended in a whimper, with the Krays having no opportunity to show their worth. This was a perplexing time for the twins, especially Ron.

Just when he was beginning to think he would never get his chance, the phone rang. The owner of a club called The Stragglers was having trouble. There was regular fighting there and he wanted it stopped. Reg agreed the terms – a percentage of the club. The deal was done. The owner, Billy Jones, wanted peace. And for Ron Kray there was only one way to get peace – and that was by the gun.

It was an old pal of the Krays, Bobby Ramsey, who had suggested calling in the twins and their reputation did the rest. The gang of Irish labourers who had been terrorising the club soon had had enough of the Krays. They left before the battle could properly begin. Again Ron's quest for excitement had been thwarted in the nick of time.

But the peace just couldn't last. Billy Jones was beaten up one night by a lad called Charlie. He was known to Ron and Reg – and they didn't like him. Bobby Ramsey drove to meet the lad the following night to sort things out, but he ended up beating Charlie to within an inch of his life. A few nights later Bobby Ramsey was attacked by another gang, known as the Watney Streeters.

The Krays planned revenge for Ramsey's attack. Ron used his boys at The Regal to keep a close watch on the lad called Charlie. Sooner or later they would teach everyone who was really the boss of London.

The night came when the rival gang was gathered in a pub in Stepney known as The Britannia. Ron and Reg Kray, Billy Jones, Bobby Ramsey and a whole gang of followers marched inside. It was almost deserted. The rival Irish gang had walked out the back door as soon as they suspected trouble. The only one who resembled an Irishman left in the pub was a man called Terry Martin and he was playing cards with some friends.

Bobby Ramsey thought he recognised this man as one of those present when he was beaten up. That would do quite nicely, thought Ron Kray as he grabbed the man and hurled him through the door and out into the street. Ramsey took over and slashed at the man with a bayonet, bringing him down in a pool of blood. Ron, Reg and the others gathered round to give him a kick or two. Martin was a bloodied mess by the time Reg called them off.

Martin's pals from The Britannia rushed him to the London Hospital while Ron and Bobby Ramsey scoured the streets for the Watney Street gang. They didn't find them, but while they were searching they were spotted by a police car and were pulled over. The police saw that there was blood on Ron's clothes – and saw his gun. Ron's only words were, 'Be careful – it's loaded!'

Martin began to talk – he wouldn't stay silent. On November 5th, Ron Kray was sentenced to three years' imprisonment for grievous bodily harm.

Ron appeared at first to accept his position and seemed to settle in to Wandsworth prison. He met up with his old deserter pal Dickie Morgan and they relived old times. In fact Ron knew many of the faces he saw in Wandsworth and with his regular visits from Reg and Vi, he took it all in his stride.

Reg supplied Ron with tobacco, by fair means or foul. Ron 'arranged' for non-smoking prisoners to keep him supplied with their tobacco rations, so he was soon the top dog, buying his way with the only unofficial currency known at that time in the jails of the country – tobacco. Ron ate special food, he drank special drinks, he did almost what he wanted. In only a few weeks he ruled the roost.

With Ron taken care of and out of harm's way, Reg got down to business. He contacted brother Charlie and asked to meet him in Bow. It was cold and dreary, with the rain falling like a fine mist. Charlie didn't know why Reg wanted to see him – and he didn't know why they had to meet here. But he showed anyway, feeling that Reg would probably need his support now that Ron was inside.

Reg was there, standing in the dim light holding a flashlight. Charlie walked over and they stood there for a moment. 'What do you think?' asked Reg. Charlie looked around the dismal scene. There was nothing here, except an old imposing house with a bombed-out site next door. 'Well?' said Reg again, shining his light all over the building.

'What can I say, Reg?' said Charlie cheerfully. 'It's a building. What do you want it for?' he asked, growing just a little impatient.

'This,' said Reg proudly, 'is our new club!' That was it. The decision had been made and Charlie hadn't even been consulted. Charlie took a second look – and he liked what he saw. There was potential there – and there was the site next door where cars could park, off the main Bow Road. Reg grinned as he stood in the rain.

Charlie was feeling good, too. Reg had money and power, and now with Ron away they could really get down to business. 'But what's that over there?' asked Charlie, looking across the site next door and over to the adjoining road.

Reg didn't even bother to look. 'Oh, that's Bow Street Police Station,' he said casually. Charlie gave him a look. Then they both roared with laughter.

Reg had borrowed his way to the money for the club. He went to see a guy in Park Lane and walked away with a deal – signed, sealed and delivered. But he had the audacity to ask Charlie to put up the money for the drinks, even though it had never cost him a penny. It was a typical Reg Kray way of doing business – why put up your own money if you can get someone else to do it? In fact the money he had borrowed was never paid back – it came from a car dealer and was taken as protection money.

The club, at 145 Bow Road, London E3, opened in the spring of 1957 and Charlie called it 'The Double R Club' in honour of his brothers. Reg didn't object. In fact he liked the name. It had a good ring to it and he could tell his brother Ron that it showed his allegiance; his hopes that his brother would be involved in it later when he was free. It would keep his spirits up, he thought.

The club opened on a Wednesday night, 3–11 p.m. during the week and 7–10 p.m. on Sundays. There was a good looking bar, stretching from one end of the room to the other, all lined with bar stools, straight out of a western. With music every night, Charlie and Reg sat back and watched the money roll in. Celebrities such as Sylvie Burton and Joan Collins came over to see what all the fuss was about – and they brought their showbiz chums with them. The club became the 'in' place in the East End. It had the added advantage of an elderly couple living upstairs on the first floor, so Reg took them on as caretakers. No one would think of trying to rob them.

Reg was happy with the new business, but Ron was in for trouble. It all started when he was suddenly transferred to Camp Hill Prison, on the Isle of Wight. This was a shock to the system for him. In Wandsworth he was kingpin but in Camp Hill he was a nobody. The governor there was liberal minded; the prisoners there were not lifers or long-term criminals. He had no friends – he was alone.

Trouble started almost immediately. With Reg back in London, Ron began to feel the isolation. He kept to himself, ultimately refusing even to leave his cell. He would stare into the mirrors for hour after hour. Soon the authorities feared that he was going mad and Ron even told the governor that 'there were people after him'. The paranoia was there for everyone to see.

Ron felt that they were ignoring him at Camp Hill. So he decided to take action to get attention – in the only way he knew. One day he charged a group of fellow prisoners, hurling several of them to the ground. He made a real mess of the place, throwing chairs around and tipping a table over. He screamed and he cried. He was desperately ill.

He was rushed to Winchester Gaol, where the prison doctor diagnosed 'prison psychosis' and Ron was sedated. He appeared to recover, but then came the news about his Aunt Rose. She had died of leukaemia. Ron went berserk. By late that evening he was incoherent and in a straitjacket.

That night Reg had an awful night's sleep, so too did Vi. They were both dreaming about Ron, he was tied up and being attended to by men in white coats. That morning they received official notification from Winchester Gaol.

The note said simply 'Your son Ronald Kray: certified insane'.

8.

Spring/Summer 1958:

Taking Over the Asylum

Ron Kray was transferred from Wandsworth Prison to the asylum at Long Grove in February 1958. By the summer of that year there were over 1,000 patients there – some of these were Ron's ex-fellow prisoners, some from other state institutions. Not everyone at Long Grove was a criminal, but all were prisoners of the system.

The doctors who were to treat Ron Kray had no previous information about him; no medical history not even a criminal record to go on. They were told nothing of his past, so they treated him like everyone else at the asylum. To them he was just a man who was paranoid and schizophrenic – to them, in a word, he was insane.

Reg and Charlie visited as much as possible, but there was a business to run and things to do. Ron was in the main left alone with his thoughts. He thought about his old pal Frank Mitchell and the problems he had. He was at that time being detained in Dartmoor Prison at Her Majesty's pleasure – for an indefinite period. That word 'indefinite' was bad news to Ron Kray. Having a date for release was what he wanted. It made it easier, he could cross off the days on his calendar. There was something to look forward to, anything was better than nothing.

On one visit Ron was talking to Reg and an old friend, Johnny Hutton, when a fellow inmate walked up and spat in their faces. Ron was quietly eating an apple at the time, not bothering a soul. But that was the kind of place it was and Ron wanted out. He told his brother straight, 'This place is full of nutters!'

Reg was also to learn that this was not the first time such an event had occurred. Previously someone had strolled casually up to Ron and hit him in the face. The man was restrained by the big guards stationed everywhere around the asylum, but it was all Ron could do to refrain from retaliation. He knew that sooner or later, there would be real trouble and his card would be marked forever.

However, Reg and Charlie were pleased with Ron's progress at Long Grove. He had been a model patient, taken his medication and been subdued. But even they knew that this new situation would not last, they had to get him out.

One evening at The Double R Club, Reg and Charlie were taking a few drinks after hours. They were alone with the empty glasses, alone with their thoughts. They had to devise a plan, but what kind of plan – and how forceful could they be without being too drastic? There were guards everywhere, so guns were out. Also innocent people could get hurt and that wouldn't do their public image any good – and Ron was all about image.

'What was that about this six-week rule?' said Reg suddenly. His brother caught on immediately. 'If you get out for six weeks then they have to send you back to the prison you came to Long Grove from, to serve out your time – that is if you don't commit a crime in the meantime,' replied Charlie. But he was still a little puzzled. 'But how is that gonna help us?' he asked Reg. 'We still have to get him out!'

Reg had a glint in his eye. 'No trouble – no trouble at all,' he said. 'I'll just walk in and Ron will walk out!' It was as simple as that, after all they were identical twins and not many people could tell them apart. But would it work? Would the guards at the asylum recognise Reg from Ron? They laughed as the plan took shape. It made perfect sense. Combined with the six-week rule, they had it made. All they would have to do was to keep Ron out of trouble for six weeks . . .

For the plan to succeed they had to make sure Ron's certificate of insanity lapsed, but keeping Ron away from trouble for six weeks was no easy task. He had improved of late, though, surely it would work. It *had* to work!

Reg and Charlie planned it meticulously. They chose the busiest day of the year for visitors. It was a Sunday. A lovely summer's day, with crowds galore. Ron was told about the elaborate details of the plan on their routine visits. But the day of the escape was by no means routine, it was a conjurer's delight – all performed to perfection by Reg Kray.

Charlie stayed back at The Double R Club, so as not to arouse too much suspicion. Only those actually involved in the plan were told about it, and they all knew exactly what to do. Some of the Firm were put on standby with cars at the ready, but they weren't told too much. It kept everyone on their toes and the Krays liked it that way. They even arranged for a caravan to escape to to be put on a friend's farm, way out in the Suffolk countryside, just in case of trouble.

The day arrived and the plan was put into action. The drive to Long Grove in Surrey took around an hour. There were two cars in the convoy. They were all dressed up and raring to go. The excitement reached fever pitch as they neared the huge gates of the asylum. One of the cars was a black Ford, packed with some of Ron's oldest pals. Billy Nash was there, so too was Bernie King and Mick 'The Hammer'. And they had carton-fulls of Ron's favourite cigarettes with them.

The other car was a blue Lincoln, with Reg driving accompanied by an old family friend, Georgie Osborne. Reg was always ultra careful in his planning, so along the route a third car was hidden, just in case.

Visiting time was at three o'clock, so they arrived a few minutes early and parked the cars just outside the gates. There were people everywhere, since almost everyone had Sundays free and they took the opportunity to visit their troubled relatives and friends held at the asylum on this day. Reg and Georgie Osborne would go on the visit, since only two visitors were allowed at any one time. The others would stay in the Ford and wait.

The blue Lincoln parked in full view of the gate-house keeper. But the black Ford was positioned just around the corner, away from any prying eyes. The escape was all set.

Billy Nash, Bernie King and Mick 'The Hammer' chain smoked as they waited in the Ford. They had their excuses ready, just in case they were questioned by anyone. But they didn't have to worry. No one came near.

Reg and Georgie Osborne stepped out and walked along the gravel path leading to Long Grove. Through the beautiful gardens and in through the entrance they went, men on a mission – to them it was the great escape. The adrenaline began to surge as Reg checked his equipment. The blue suit was clean and tidy, the grey overcoat was neat, his hair was cut and his face clean-shaven. Yes, he thought, everything was in place as they entered the building.

Back at The Double R Club Charlie just had to wait. But there was a job to do and Charlie knew his trade. The customers came and went and Charlie was the perfect host. No one noticed any difference in his behaviour, even though his heartbeat was quickening by the minute. Charlie was his natural, cool self.

It was a pleasant summer's day. Rain had been forecast though so no one paid any attention to a well-dressed man wearing an overcoat. Reg Kray was just like any other visitor that day. They continued to walk through the maze of corridors, until they finally reached their goal, the section where Ron was housed. They didn't talk as they entered the visiting room, through door after door, unlocked for them one at a time.

'We've come to see Ron Kray,' said Reg, matter-of-fact and as casual as usual. The guard showed them over to a table near the main doors, where they could wait. The room was packed. They had chosen the right day all right. Both men began to relax.

Reg had brought a photo album with him. He and Osborne looked at the photos and laughed out loud, waiting for the appearance of Ron Kray. They looked around them as they sat quietly in the wooden chairs. They could see the huge windows looking out onto the garden, making the room light and airy. It was comfortable – no problem waiting. Reg was still wearing his raincoat. But they didn't have long to wait.

Ron entered the room, looking like the chairman of the board. He was wearing a blue suit, smart and clean. He was even wearing his spectacles. He soon saw Reg and strolled over to the table. Reg and Georgie Osborne got up and they shook hands. As Ron sat down, Reg got up and removed his coat. Reg was also wearing a blue suit. His hair was the same as Ron's, and when he put on his glasses he looked the spitting image of his twin brother. But no one noticed. They sat down and got busy looking at the photo album.

The general noise in the room rose a notch or two as people talked and chatted about everything and anything. Soon it was tea-time and Ron saw his chance. He took it. Standing up and taking Reggie's raincoat over his arm he pocketed his spectacles and walked towards the door. 'Just going for the tea,' he told the guard. Nothing strange here, it happened every day at Long Grove. Ron took a quick look back at his brother as the guard opened the door. Soon he was out in the corridor.

As Ron walked out of the asylum Reg chatted and laughed with Georgie Osborne. Reg kept burying his face in the photo album and kept hiding his features from the view of the guards, as if it would have mattered. But he knew instinctively that his plan had worked. Now it was all up to Ron.

Ron walked unchallenged all the way to the main doors of Long Grove – and beyond. He strolled down the gravel path, not too quick, not too slow. He thought about freedom and he thought about his twin brother back there in the visitors' room. He smiled. (Many years afterwards I asked him how easy it was to find his way out of Long Grove, since the asylum was known for its maze of corridors. 'Easy,' he told me. 'I just followed the exit signs!')

Ron Kray soon made it to the black Ford and his waiting pals. Even the big iron gates of the asylum couldn't stop him. He was free. As he got into the car he grabbed a pack of Players and lit up. It was party time all the way back to London. And they didn't even need that extra car.

Meanwhile, back in the visitors' room, one of the guards became suspicious. 'You've pulled a flanker!' he shouted at Reg as he raised the alarm. But it was all too late. Ron had flown the coop and nobody could catch him. The sound of the alarm scared everyone. Visitors and patients alike ran in all directions. It took a long time to sort them out and to get round to questioning Reg and Georgie Osborne. Reg was grinning like a Cheshire cat at the goings on. He had done it – he had managed to get his twin brother away from the clutches of the asylum and to safety. But just how long would it be safe, and just how long a six weeks would it be?

Reg told them that he didn't know where his brother Ron had got to, and that he was actually beginning to get worried. He said he was even considering legal action, in the event that his brother came to harm. The authorities at Long Grove knew that it was all part of the act, but they couldn't prove anything. So they had to let him go. Reg and Georgie walked back down that gravel path, laughing all the way, and drove nonchalantly back to London.

On the way he phoned Charlie at The Double R Club. 'It's done,' he told his brother. Charlie poured himself a whisky. Now he too could relax. But Charlie knew that this was really only the beginning, not the end. Six weeks was a long time and nobody could predict the future.

A few days after the escape a doctor at the asylum phoned Reg asking to see him. Charlie and Reg drove down to Long Grove and talked with the doctor at length. The news was not good. 'You must remember that your brother needs help. He is sick and must not be taken off his medication,' the doctor told them. Reg and Charlie started to worry, their faces turned a whiter shade of pale. 'But it was cleverly done, I'll give you that!' he added. 'If you need my help, then you have my phone number,' he told them in parting.

The following weeks saw Ron in Walthamstow and then in that caravan, deep in the Suffolk countryside. He always had company and at first he was all right. But his pills soon ran out and Reg started to lose control of him.

One night, just to keep Ron happy, they arranged for him to visit one of Reggie's favourite watering holes and got him to pretend to be his twin brother. Ron walked in and sat in Reggie's chair up at the bar. Everyone was asking, 'How is Ron?'

Ron told them. 'He's fine, thank you!'

They did the same trick at The Double R Club, with Ron pretending to be Reg. It was proving to be very handy being twins. It had worked well in the past when they were really identical, but now that Ron was ill his appearance began to change. Most of the Firm could see it but others, outside their immediate circle of close friends, could still not tell the one from the other.

Those six weeks couldn't go fast enough for Reg and Charlie Kray. They did what they could, but without proper medication no one could help their brother Ron, whose condition was rapidly deteriorating.

Charlie was concerned and so too was Reg and the members of the Firm. They could all see it – all, that is, except Ron himself. But they did manage to talk him into seeing a psychiatrist in Harley Street. Ron saw the man and they did some tests. The results were not good – as expected, Ron was diagnosed a paranoid schizophrenic. When Charlie asked about treatment, he was told to get his brother back to Long Grove as quickly as possible.

So Ron was rushed by taxi back to the asylum and instant treatment. Fortunately though those six weeks were up so he could soon be transported back to Wandsworth Prison to serve out his sentence there. The escape plan, then, had worked well – they got clean away with it.

9.

October 1960: Clubbing

Esmeralda's Barn was one of the hottest night spots in the West End. And in the autumn of 1960 Ron and Reg Kray, with brother Charlie in tow, made one of the owners, a man by the name of Stefan de Faye, an offer he just couldn't refuse.

Somehow the twins got to hear that the club-cum-casino was practically owned by one man. There was another minor partner though and that was where the trouble lay – the two men didn't get on and couldn't agree a strategy for the business. One major shareholder, they thought, would be no match for the Krays – and they were right. At 50 Wilton Place, in the heart of Knightsbridge, the Krays would have the perfect base in the West End and for Charlie Kray it had one special thing going for it – it was legal. The phone number even had a good ring about it – Belgravia 3040.

The beginning of that year, however, had started badly for the Krays. Reg had managed to get himself into Wandsworth Gaol. He had been out assisting a Mr Shay, a pal of Ron's who had been using his name in business deals. Since he had been paying Ron for the privilege then Ron didn't mind – in fact he wanted more of the same. So when Mr Shay asked Ron and Reg for their help, it came as a formality.

But this kindly fellow then did a personality U-turn. From friendly chap, he turned overnight into an aggressive villain. He went to a travel goods shop in Hampstead where he had seen a briefcase he wanted and he did a deal with the owner. The owner, a Mr Podro, had played cards with Shay on previous occasions and he let Shay take the briefcase with him – with payment to follow in a few days. But when Shay came back he brought the twins with him.

'You've charged me too much,' shouted Shay. With the twins to back him up poor Mr Podro couldn't say very much – their fame had reached the whole of London and beyond by then. Shay then lashed out at the man hitting him in the face and screaming blue murder. 'I'll be back in a few days,' shouted Shay, 'and I want a hundred pounds for my trouble!'

When Shay returned to the shop, this time with only Reg alongside him, the police were there to arrest him. Ron was nowhere to be seen, luckily enough for him. So poor Reg had to go down for 18 months – and all because he did Shay a favour. Neither he nor Ron knew what Shay was up to. If they had, then they wouldn't have gone along with it.

With Reg inside, Ron was free to wage war. There were minor skirmishes throughout London, but soon Ron's attentions were drawn to a certain Peter Rachman, a slum landlord from Notting Hill. He had a team of rent collectors, who collected on demand – or else. But Ron's old pal Dickie Morgan, who worked for Rachman, told Ron that he could be on to a nice little earner – so Ron wanted to meet the man face-to-face.

Rachman refused to meet Ron Kray though. This was a big mistake. One night, at a Soho casino, Rachman and some friends were playing at the tables, when Ron Kray walked in followed by an army of Kray enforcers. When Rachman went downstairs to the rest-room the enforcers followed. Soon enough, Rachman was sitting in his Rolls Royce, waiting outside the club. Ron walked out, opened the door and jumped inside. 'Where to?' asked Rachman. 'Vallance Road,' replied Ron. Ron Kray had got his meeting.

They agreed a deal over a cup of tea and a chat with Violet Kray. Rachman handed over £250 in cash there and then and wrote Ron a cheque for £1,000. The next day the cheque bounced – and Rachman had disappeared. But by this time Ron didn't care, for he had heard about the deal with Esmeralda's Barn. His own casino – now that was something else!

They were given the tip by an old friend of Charlie's – a Commander Diamond. He lived in Knightsbridge, just around the corner from the casino and he had heard on the local grapevine all about the problems between the two owners. And since he didn't like either one, he thought he would give Charlie the nod – maybe it would be the foothold that Charlie had always wanted in the West End.

Commander Diamond even suggested arranging the meet at his flat.

Since he knew all the rumours and stories concerning the two men, he thought he could be of some help in pulling off the deal. A club around the corner, owned by his pals the Krays, would give him that extra security – and that frisson of danger.

The Commander was a wealthy man. He owned a Rolls Royce, lived in the best part of town, went everywhere, did everything. He was a man of means. And he knew the West End social scene better than most.

The meeting was arranged and the Commander looked forward to the showdown. Charlie arrived at the flat with Leslie Payne, Ron's business manager, and Freddie Gore, their accountant, in tow. Leslie Payne, in particular, was eager to be in on the venture. He was a man who smelled money – especially someone else's. No one told Stefan de Faye and Mr Burns, the other owner, who they were due to meet. They were simply informed that there were people who were interested in either joining them in the management, or even possibly taking over full control of 'the Barn'.

Charlie and the others arrived early, to be prepared for the meeting. Burns and de Faye arrived on schedule and the negotiations got underway. The two owners of the Barn were not prepared for dealing with the Krays. This became obvious to Charlie as he introduced himself, Payne and Gore to the two men who appeared timid, yet relaxed – completely oblivious of what was about to happen to their business.

'We know all about your problems,' said Charlie. 'And we know you're going nowhere fast. In fact you're making a loss.'

Burns and de Faye looked at each other. They didn't say a thing. They couldn't.

'We could, if we wanted to, just walk in and take it over – purely legal, of course,' said Charlie in his own well-rehearsed business talk. Charlie waited for a sign. It didn't take long.

Burns was furious. 'Do you East Enders really think you can come over here, to the West End of London, and tell us what to do?' he ranted and raved.

But Charlie was equally angry. He didn't like being told that he had no right to be in the West End. 'I told you – we could do what we wanted to, but we are prepared to make you an offer for Esmeralda's Barn – completely legal and above board, and a fair one at that.' He spoke, holding back the anger he felt inside. Now it was sit-back time – the negotiations were about to start.

This Burns character, however, was in no frame of mind for this kind of talk. 'You can't run a business in the West End!' he said.

Charlie didn't like the stress he put on the 'you'. The room went quiet. Even Commander Diamond knew when to be quiet, he was no idiot after all.

Eventually Charlie broke the silence. 'I don't like your attitude,' he told Burns. He then went on to extol the virtues of folk from the East End, to tell of his background, of his mum and dad and of their trials and tribulations.

Burns and de Faye sat motionless. The Commander watched. Payne and Gore remained silent. The atmosphere could have been cut with a blade.

'To be perfectly honest,' he told the two men, 'I feel like knocking you two to kingdom-come – but I won't.' He then turned towards Leslie Payne and the dumbfounded Freddie Gore. 'My friends here will explain the details.'

But Charlie hadn't finished. 'We are willing to give you £2,000 for the Barn. You'll be paid tomorrow – in cash!' He then looked towards the Commander who was showing signs of a smile. 'And if you don't like my proposition, then we'll just take it over anyway – all cosher, perfectly legal. But you'll get nothing!'

Charlie rested his case.

The two men spoke quietly with Payne and Gore, while Charlie took a welcome drink with Commander Diamond. They chatted quietly, looking in the direction of the seated men who were obviously talking money. They knew they had won.

The following day The Krays took over Esmeralda's Barn without a shoot-out, without even any objection The brown envelope with the £2,000 was handed over and that was that. The Krays now owned the Barn, one of the most lucrative club-cum-casinos in London. And all without the normal threats that associated a Kray deal.

Esmeralda's Barn was on several floors with a discothèque, a gambling casino, a club and bar – and there was even a lesbian bar too. Ron and Reg felt quite at home, in a glitzy way. This was where they felt they belonged, with the glamour and the money. For the Krays this was a new beginning.

Being in the West End also had a number of other advantages. One of these was that the Krays could extend their protection rackets from their new base. The gambling tables at the Barn were bringing in some

£1,600 a week, a lot of money back in 1960. And the proliferation of casinos throughout the country helped to make easy pickings for the Krays. Soon they were collecting £150 a week from a dozen or so West End clubs. The Kray bandwagon just kept rolling. It seemed that nothing could now stop Ron, Reg and Charlie.

This was the swinging '60s and the stars soon started to appear at Esmeralda's Barn. Eric Clapton was one of the first. He had just started his solo career at the time, having just left his group The Yardbirds. Eric Clapton became a regular at the Barn, so much so that Reg often told people in later life that one of his favourite albums was *Slowhand*, one of Clapton's most famous recordings.

Everyone and anyone headed for Esmeralda's Barn – it was one of the places to see and be seen in London. The Everly Brothers came calling, so too did the artist Lucien Freud, and Honor Blackman was a regular. The Krays were now in good company.

When the Krays wanted their photographs taken, it was one of the up-and-coming photographers of the day who was asked to do the job. None other than David Bailey was good enough for Ron, Reg and Charlie Kray. (He was even asked to photograph the wedding of the year in 1965, when Reg married Frances.)

The Krays added more clubs to their list during the '60s. When their reign of terror was over in 1968, they had shares in more than 40 clubs throughout the country. They were wealthy enough, they had everything that violence and the threat of violence could provide. But they still had no plan, no overall vision of what they were after.

If Charlie had had his way, this clubbing idea would have had first priority. It meant money – and Charlie loved money. But Ron wouldn't let them do it that way, he had other ideas. Reg wanted to settle down, run the clubs along with Charlie, but Ron said 'No!' And when 'the Colonel' (as he was called) said 'no', then it *meant* no!

10.

July 1964:

The Case of the Brighton Peer

'Where the fuck is Enugu?' asked Ron Kray. Leslie Payne did his best to explain amid the laughter, but 'Africa' was not a good reply. Payne had already been sold the idea – he saw this deal here as his path to riches and glory. Ron Kray, enjoying the joke at Payne's expense, could still see something in the idea. Everyone knew that the Richardsons had a gold-mine in Africa. And what was good for the Richardsons was good for the Krays.

Payne was always on the lookout for something that would improve his image with the Krays and the idea appealed to his sense of grandeur. Three thousand houses, a shopping mall and even a hotel – there was surely money to be made somewhere. The only problem was how to sell it to the Krays – and in particular to Ron Kray.

He was a dreamer, a schemer – and a crook. He knew instantly that he had to provide the Krays with a sound financial bottom line, to ensure their participation and create for himself a place in the history of crime. He soon worked out a plan. With so many companies vying for position and involvement in the work he reckoned that it should be easy to get 'commission' payments or backhanders from those taken on and he openly talked about the bundles of cash, all in brown envelopes, that were simply awaiting collection there.

Ron loved the idea. Immediately he dispatched Payne to Enugu to scout out the land and to contact would-be participants. On his return Payne outlined the deal and proposed that some sort of figurehead be taken on board, to make the whole affair look cosher. Someone should be brought in, without knowledge of the intended rip-off, but it had to be someone in the public arena, someone with charisma to carry it off and to get other investors involved – someone who was a household name.

Ron Kray knew of just such a man – Lord Robert Boothby.

The Krays had previously heard the name of Boothby through an acquaintance by the name of Leslie Holt. Holt was a cat burglar and ex-boxer. It was in his early days in the ring that he had met Boothby and a homosexual involvement started almost immediately. Since Ron Kray was a crook and a homosexual, he too knew Leslie Holt – in fact they were already bosom buddies. Surely, thought Ron Kray, Lord Boothby would be interested in the scheme in Enugu and would become involved on a charitable basis – it would be houses for the poor in Nigeria and, unbeknown to him, money for the Krays in London.

A meeting was set up by Holt at Boothby's flat in Eaton Square, West London, a place where he also carried out his private business functions and charity work. Ron Kray was accompanied by Leslie Holt, a friend by the name of 'Mad Teddy' Smith – and a photographer, Bernard Black. Smith was only there for the ride – but he too had a gay lover, the Labour MP Tom Driberg. Ron Kray had made his plans carefully and dropping a few names around wouldn't do his case any damage, he wanted to keep it cosy and discreet. He needed leverage, and he thought he could get it with Holt and Smith.

Black took a series of photos, all taken with the approval and permission of Lord Boothby. He had nothing to hide (apart from his homosexuality) – so photos for the family album were not a problem. As they discussed the project Boothby took it all in and appeared to take interest. He had other charitable projects in mind, so he told them that he would consider the venture and see whether or not he had sufficient time available in his calendar.

A few days later Lord Robert Boothby phoned to say that he could not, unfortunately, find the time for the deal – and he wished them well. That, according to Lord Robert Boothby, was that!

But Bernard Black the photographer was in need of some urgent cash – and he approached the *Sunday Mirror* with a deal they just couldn't refuse. On 11 July 1964, he handed over a roll of photos – the ones he took at Eaton Square. The following day the paper ran with the headline: PEER AND GANGSTER. They didn't name names, but told of a gangster's relationship with a peer of the realm. Black immediately asked for his photos back. The *Sunday Mirror* refused.

On Tuesday, 14 July, Sir Joseph Simpson of Scotland Yard issued a statement in *The Times*. It read as follows:

> I have today asked senior officers for some enlightenment on newspaper reports that:
>
> 1. I have ordered an investigation into, among other things, allegations of a homosexual relationship between a peer and a man with a criminal record.
> 2. I shall give the Home Secretary details of reports submitted by members of the Metropolitan Police resulting from this investigation.
> 3. An investigation embracing relationships that exist between gangsters, a peer and a number of clergymen has taken place and that blackmail is alleged.
>
> None of these statements is true and beyond this fact it is not my intention to make any report to the Home Secretary.
>
> My duty as Commissioner of Police in serious criminal cases is to put the facts before the Director of Public Prosecutions, for him to decide whether prosecutions should take place.
>
> In saying that I hope it will be understood in the press that I am not going to disclose information about the many inquiries being conducted into various aspects of underworld life. Inquiries of this kind are in fact going on almost continually.

The *Mirror* followed up their exclusive on 16 July with the heading THE PICTURE WE DARE NOT PRINT. Details were added, but again, names were not revealed. The whole nation was in suspense.

The storm had to break sometime though, and it did so in Germany, where the magazine *Stern* told it straight. Lord Boothby was confirmed as the Peer and Ron Kray as the gangster.

Lord Boothby, on holiday in France at the time, phoned a friend in London – Tom Driberg, MP. They needed help and they needed it quick. Driberg called a friend – none other than the Prime Minister of the day, Harold Wilson. Wilson was outraged. He instantly realised the damage that could be done in the press so he asked Gerald Gardiner QC and Arnold Goodman to find a solution. Somehow Driberg and Boothby had to be put in the clear, off the hook and away from danger.

Their answer was for Boothby to write to *The Times*, where he would deny all allegations outright. This letter was drafted and accepted by Boothby. It was published on 1 August 1964 and read as follows:

Sir, On July 17 I returned from France and found, to my astonishment, that Parliament, Fleet Street and other informed quarters in London were seething with rumours that I have a homosexual relationship with a leading thug in the London underworld involved in a West End protection racket; that I have been to 'all male' Mayfair parties with him; that I have been photographed with him in a compromising position on a sofa; that a homosexual relationship exists between me, some East End gangsters and a number of clergymen in Brighton; that some people that know of these relationships are being blackmailed; and that Scotland Yard have for months been watching meetings between me and the underworld thug and have investigated all these matters and reported on them to the Commissioner of the Metropolitan Police.

I have, for many years, appeared on radio and television programmes; and for this reason alone, my name might reasonably be described as 'a household name', as it has been in the *Sunday Mirror*. On many occasions I have been photographed, at their request, with people who have claimed to be 'fans' of mine; and on one occasion I was photographed, with my full consent, in my flat (which is also my office) with a gentleman who came to see me, accompanied by two friends, in order to ask me to take an active part in a business venture, which seemed to me to be of interest and importance. After careful consideration I turned down his request, on the grounds that my existing commitments prevented me from taking on anything more; and my letter of refusal is in his possession.

I have been since told that some years ago the person concerned was convicted of a criminal offence, but I knew then and know now nothing of this. So far as I am concerned, anyone is welcome to see or to publish any photographs that have ever been taken of me.

I am satisfied that the source of all sinister rumours is the *Sunday Mirror* and the *Daily Mirror*. I am not homosexual. I have not been to a Mayfair party of any kind for more than 20 years. I have met the man alleged to be a 'king of the underworld' only three times, on business matters, and then by appointment in my flat, at his request and in the company of other people.

I have never been to a party in Brighton with gangsters, still less clergymen. No one has ever tried to blackmail me. The police say that they have not watched any meetings, or conducted any investigations, or made any report to the Home Secretary, connected with me. In short, the whole affair is a tissue of atrocious lies.

I am not by nature thin-skinned; but this sort of thing makes a mockery of any decent kind of life, public or private, in what is still supposed to be a civilised country. It is, in my submission, intolerable that any man should be put into the cruel dilemma of having to remain silent while such rumours spread, or considerably to increase the circulation of certain newspapers by publicly denying them. If either the *Sunday Mirror*, or the *Daily Mirror*, is in possession of a shred of evidence – documentary or photographic – against me, let them print it and take the consequences. I am sending a copy of this letter to both.

Your obedient servant
Boothby
House of Lords, July 31

It was an outrageous lie. Boothby had always been keen on boys. He had, in fact, often said, 'I'm not sure if I like the boys better than the girls, or the girls better than the boys'. Driberg was also an out-and-out gay, but he was an old established MP and Wilson feared that any sensational revelations regarding his sexual leanings would be bad for any forthcoming election. They both had to be saved.

Boothby, the bisexual, continued his association with Leslie Holt, long after the meeting at Eaton Square. He also relished the attraction of being involved with a gangster – and Ron Kray was the biggest and best he could possibly find. On one occasion Ron introduced a boy to

Boothby, saying 'You will do anything Mr Boothby wants – or I will hurt you badly!'

The letter to *The Times* worked – and Lord Robert Boothby became richer by a £40,000 libel payment. Some time later, when Charlie Kray was in urgent need of some cash, he visited Boothby at his London flat. 'It's all gone, dear boy,' said Boothby. 'Gambling debts, you know!' Charlie knew all about Lord Boothby and his gambling habit, since he had seen him gamble at every Kray establishment in town.

'It was all down to Wilson,' Boothby told his friends. 'He got me out of it.' Lord Robert Boothby got away with it, by careful planning or sheer luck. In future he was a little more careful about who he invited into his flat and the photographers weren't so pleasantly catered for any more. He had outlived his nine lives.

Because of the denial Scotland Yard had to shelve information so painstakingly gathered over the previous two years. It set their case back immeasurably. The Krays could continue, Boothby could continue – and the press would be a little more wary about saying anything about a 'household name' in the future.

No one could touch the Krays and now Ron was a 'household name' – something that he had strived for since early adolescence. But what of the others involved in the case?

'Mad Teddy' Smith was also getting himself into trouble, by being involved in the same case of extortion as Ron and Reg, but Leslie Holt had flown the coop. He teamed up with a Dr Kells, who found him clients for his cat-burgling skills. These robberies continued for a number of years, until Scotland Yard caught on to the two men. The doctor knew that the police were onto him and hadn't decided what to do when Leslie Holt inadvertently gave him the solution that he so badly needed. Holt told the doctor he'd been having some trouble with one of his feet. Dr Kells offered to operate on it for him. It was no trouble and wouldn't take long . . .

Leslie Holt died on the operating table in 1979. The doctor was tried for murder, but acquitted. So the man who had introduced Ron Kray to Lord Robert Boothby, the man who was pictured in all the photographs taken at Eaton Square, was dead.

No one really knows what happened to 'Mad Teddy' Smith. He disappeared in 1968, shortly before the arrest of the Krays. There were rumours at the time that Ron had killed him and certainly there was an argument when they took a trip to the coast. To Scotland Yard he became just another name on another list – the one headed 'These people were possibly killed by the Krays'.

Perhaps we will never know everything, but the Krays' killing fields did exist, somewhere on the Essex–Hertfordshire border. The ones they couldn't burn in the incinerators or cart off in a coffin were all sealed in oil drums, filled with lime and buried in a field. Boothby had played a most dangerous game with the most dangerous man in town – but like Boothby, Ron Kray got away with it.

11.

Summer of 1964: Safari

The Krays continued with their scam in Africa. Throughout the summer of '64 Leslie Payne made many a routine trip to Nigeria, to size up the venture and to collect the backhanders he required. He even set up a company called GAS to handle the transactions. But sooner or later the bubble was bound to burst.

Ron made the trip several times to Enugu. Sometimes Charlie went with him, sometimes it was Leslie Payne and Freddie Gore. On only one occasion did the twins venture to Africa together. One of them had to stay home, to take care of business and to keep the element of fear alive. They had their dreams all right, but they knew where to find the bread and butter of everyday life. Their home turf was London and they never forgot it.

Payne had been lured into Africa with dreams of riches and power, but to the twins it was just another nice little earner and nothing more. It started well, the money came rolling in, but when Leslie Payne let the whole thing go to his head, then the project was doomed.

Back in the spring Leslie Payne had started well enough. He had it all worked out. He had some £120,000 due from contractors who wanted to be in on the project. The first brown envelope had contained £5,000 in readies and there was to be plenty more where that came from. The Krays were on to a winner, but they hadn't reckoned on the greed of Ron's financial adviser.

Further trips and more promises of wealth had Leslie Payne's head spinning. Even Charlie couldn't control his ups and downs. Charlie had been asked by Ron and Reg to take a keen interest in GAS. He was never a part of the project, never on the board of the company, but he enjoyed the luxury of the hotels and he enjoyed the prestige of the visits. At times they were even escorted around Enugu in a chauffeur-driven Rolls Royce with motorcycled police to lead the way. It was just up Charlie's street and he loved every minute of it.

Payne set up offices in Mayfair, under the Carston Group of companies – the Krays' trading front, developed from an idea inherited from the Richardsons. Payne was in complete control of the company – and he had full control over the cash.

By mid summer things were beginning to hot up again. The Krays decided to send a deputation to Enugu, to size things up now that the Boothby scandal had hit the headlines world-wide. They were finding it difficult to get the right sponsors engaged in the project, even though by now it was viably sound.

The men chosen for this important assignment were Charlie Kray, who was basically acting as minder for the party; Leslie Payne, who was in control of all finances surrounding the deal; Freddie Gore, the GAS company accountant, and Gordon Andersen, a Canadian who dealt in insurance.

The flight was just like any other flight to Kano in Northern Nigeria. It was hot. The VC-10 landed to shed passengers, to take on some more and also to re-fuel for the next hour's flight to Lagos. All was routine. But when they got to The President Hotel, the reception was not the cordial one they were used to, not at all.

Charlie was no happy mobster as he sat at the bar in the lounge of the hotel. Had they really been put off by the Boothby affair? He couldn't see it. These were business people and whatever the Krays were doing, it was sure to be of great benefit to Nigeria. No, it was something else – something that was going on down here in Enugu. But what?

On a previous trip Leslie Payne had received £5,000 from one of the contractors. Everything was hunky-dory, no problem until the great white hunter, Leslie Payne, decided he could run a construction project better than the professionals. It was a bad move on the part of Payne, and it doomed the deal forever.

Charlie confronted Payne about the reason for their miserable welcome. 'What are you playing at?' asked Charlie. Payne told him not to worry, it was only a small-time contractor. He would soon have it sorted out. 'Don't worry, have a drink or two. Take it easy and I'll work it out.' This was not what Charlie wanted to hear. Payne acted like God – and Charlie Kray knew they were in for a rough time.

The actual problem was minute. It was about where to begin the project, now that the monsoons were over. It was simple enough for any organised contractor, but Leslie Payne thought he knew best. It was a big mistake to make. And with Reg and Ron back in London, Payne didn't have the muscle he needed.

Charlie's fears were confirmed when he heard Payne arguing in the lobby of the hotel. It was the local Nigerian contractor who had given Payne the first £5,000 for his involvement in the project. He wanted to get started, but Payne had other ideas. The talk got louder and louder. Eventually Payne blew his top. Leslie Payne – a big man, refined and with an almost aristocratic air, leant over the diminutive Nigerian and told him that he, the white Englishman, knew best. It was all too much for the Nigerian.

'I want my money back' he told Payne. Payne laughed, a raucous belly laugh if ever there was one. Charlie tried as hard as he could to calm things down but to no avail. All the diplomacy in the world could not rectify the damage done by this great white hunter.

The Nigerian stood firm. 'No. I just want my money back,' he said again. He turned and headed for the door. Then the Nigerian turned to face them both once more. 'My cousin is the chief of police,' he said calmly. Then he walked through the doors and out into the warm Enugu air.

Charlie looked at Leslie Payne. 'What on earth have you done?' he asked the big man. Payne just about turned and walked off. Charlie was left there , the only man in the lobby. Suddenly he felt very much alone. The omens were not looking good and he could think of a dozen or more places where he would rather be. This was not his home turf and he didn't have his brothers there to take care of troublemakers. He shivered as he edged his way back towards the bar.

As he drank he thought of his brother Ron. Ron had told him of the time he had visited the local jail here. (He was 'interested in sociology and rehabilitation', he told them.) His impression of the jail was not good. 'Dartmoor's a holiday camp compared to that place,' he told them when he got back to London.

Why had it gone so wrong, and on his watch? What would Ron and Reg have to say about it when he got home? But first things first, he thought. Maybe what Ron had said about the jails was all a load of bull, something said in the heat of the moment. Charlie Kray was soon to find out.

He heard the sirens long before the cars arrived at the hotel. Three police cars arrived, full of armed police – and one civilian, the Nigerian contractor. Charlie's worst fears had come true. They soon had the members of GAS rounded up in the lobby. Leslie Payne and Freddie Gore were there, so too was an English surveyor, who had arrived on another flight. Gordon Andersen, the Canadian, joined Charlie Kray at the bar. Fortunately for the two of them, they were not officially a part of GAS.

When Leslie Payne could not stump up the missing £5,000 the police took them away to the cars. The three Englishmen ranted and raved, but no one was listening to them. Charlie rushed outside to see what was going on. 'Where are you taking them?' he asked.

He didn't like the answer – the local prison at Enugu.

The simple fact that Charlie Kray was not a part of the GAS company turned out to be their salvation. With Charlie on the outside they had a chance of freedom. Without him the three men would surely rot in this Enugu jail. Leslie Payne, Freddie Gore and the surveyor all settled into the bleak, dark, stinking prison cells – and waited.

Charlie came to visit them that evening, to check up on news with the prison authorities and to tend to the needs of his pals. He found the place as bleak as it had been described back in London. Being tropical, Enugu was a good place to live – if you were a bug. And the cells hadn't been painted for years.

Leslie Payne was in a bad way. He whinged and croaked about the facilities, the food, the treatment – everything! The others were waiting more calmly. They knew that Charlie was the one to take care of things. Surely his pragmatic approach would save the day.

Charlie confirmed that he would be getting a message back to the twins in London as soon as possible. He wasn't sure how it would be done, or when, but soon they could expect some action.

When he left the prison in the early hours of the morning he noticed a blackboard with a list of the prisoners written in chalk. Some of the names had been crossed out.

'I see some of them have been let out,' he said casually to one of the guards.

'Yes,' said the man 'they got out all right – in wooden boxes!' Charlie didn't like it in Enugu Jail.

Eventually he found a field telephone and phoned London via a relay station in Lagos. The twins were furious – how could Payne jeopardise their earnings in this way? Ron was so mad that he told Charlie that they would all catch the next plane to Enugu and sort out the police once and for all. Charlie was shocked. 'No,' he told his brother. 'They'll throw us all in jail. They've got guns down here!'

Charlie managed to calm Ron down, to get him thinking along the right lines. Ron gave the phone over to Reg to sort things out.

Charlie told Reg the whole sordid story. At first Reg laughed. He had been trying to get rid of Leslie Payne for years, so maybe the Nigerians had done him a good turn. But Payne ran the accounts, and that meant he had the money. One way or another they had to get Payne back from Africa, otherwise they couldn't lay their hands on their own cash. Sure, the best way was to repay the £5,000. But they had already spent some £25,000 setting up the scam in the first place. Reg was not in a good mood when he hung up the phone.

He phoned the Nigerian High Commissioner in London. It was all true – and if they didn't act quickly then Charlie could also be in trouble as an accessory. There was only one option still open to them. They had to raise the money there and then and send it as quickly as possible down to Enugu, so Charlie could repay the contractor.

It was a Saturday, most of the Firm were out on the town enjoying a drink or two. It was not easy to get everyone together for a briefing, but they managed to do it by early evening. At first they thought of dipping their hands into their own pockets, but the twins realised that they just didn't have that kind of money at hand. Even Dolly, Charlie's wife, said she didn't have any money at home and Leslie Payne's wife said the same. But they had to get it from somewhere.

Luckily for the twins they had their pension list and their nipping list – those protection rackets. Ron took over as he sat at a large table in the Crown Public House, just around the corner from Vallance Road. Ron took on his guise as the Colonel – and he gave everyone their orders. A list had been prepared. Ron wrote a figure against each name and it was the job of the Firm to go out and get it. And they shouldn't come back if they didn't have it all – in full! Some had one hundred pounds against their name, others five hundred. This was urgent – their brother was in trouble. And if they needed support, then Ron would be at the end of the telephone line. That generally did the trick when it came to protection. No one wanted to quarrel with Ron Kray. But that night, the phone never rang once. The money came pouring in. At first a trickle, then in abundance. Soon they had more than enough for Enugu. Reg counted it up bit by bit until he had the five thousand pounds in readies. Now all they had to do was to get it to Nigeria.

It took two days for the money to arrive. Charlie had already found a friendly solicitor who explained to him that it had to be paid over to a judge – all proper and above board. The solicitor even said he would go with him, just to be sure that he found the place.

Off they sped through the jungle of Enugu, along a narrow track and into the deep, dense undergrowth. Charlie began to fear for his life. If they were attacked or robbed in this neck of the woods they would never be heard of again. He had to put his full trust into the hands of the solicitor. Charlie had never had such an agonised trip in his life.

At last they found the judge's house and the money was paid in full. Five thousand pounds was in 1964 a large amount of money, so Charlie was strangely relieved when it left his possession. With the release papers in his hand, he headed for the jail.

Things had gone from bad to worse for the Englishmen there. They just weren't used to these conditions. The lack of clean clothing, food and proper drinking water was causing chaos in the jail. Summertime in Enugu is *not* the time to be in prison.

With their morale shattered the Englishmen gathered themselves together. They were in tears when Charlie arrived to release them. Leslie Payne, in particular, was by now chronically depressed and on the verge of a nervous breakdown. But Charlie had the paper with him, the paper that proved that the money had been repaid and was on the way to the contractor who had complained to the police. It was all over – bar the shouting.

They collected Gordon Andersen from The President Hotel and had their luggage thrown into the boot of one of the police cars. With sirens blaring they sped off in the direction of the local airport and the small light-aircraft that would take them to Lagos. The pilot had been told to delay departure, since these were special guests – guests who would never, ever, be allowed back into the country.

They were ushered into their seats for take off. Once in the air they were sure of freedom. But once in the air Charlie knew that their African experience was well and truly over. No one spoke as they flew to Onitsha. No one said a word as they landed at Benin City and as they flew into Lagos. The three Englishmen had been in jail for three long days. They were glad to be free, but they had to look forward to the wrath of the Krays when they got back to London. Charlie had saved them, but even he would not be spared from the scathing words of the twins once back in the East End of London.

The Krays were now out of Africa. Their dreams there had ended in a nightmare, the bubble had burst.

12.

April 1965: Getting Hitched

When Reg Kray was 27 years old he met the one and only true love of his life – a beautiful young girl of sweet 16. Her name was Frances Shea and she was the daughter of one of their employees. He was besotted with her at first glance. Reg, together with his twin brother Ron, was the fast-rising leader of the London underworld – she was a ravishing redhead, pure and innocent. But it was a match that no one either understood or wanted – except for the lovers themselves.

Reg was now a director at Esmeralda's Barn. He had an office in Park Lane, drove a Mercedes and had dosh galore. He was also becoming a bit of a playboy with Frances constantly alongside him, taking the place of his twin. Ron was now getting worried about his own relationship with his brother and it was this troubled relationship, not the one between Reg and Frances, that came to dominate their lives.

Ron asked Reg to bring Frances to the Barn, ostensibly to meet Lord Effingham, one of the directors, but also, for him, Ron, to meet Frances. Reg turned up with Frances, who was keen to meet the Lord, but when she met Ron Kray something scared her. There was something about his eyes, his personality. She could see that he totally dominated his twin. He was constantly quicker on the uptake and quicker with a put-down. There was no doubting the fact that Ron Kray was the master – and Reg Kray the slave.

Reg would seek solace in the countryside and at Steeple Bay in Essex, where the family had a caravan. Reg and Frances would drive down for a few days' solitude – to be alone without the constant interruptions from Ron. Once by themselves their thoughts turned to other things – more important things. They both fell madly and deeply in love.

At only 17 she was whisked away to Milan and Barcelona by her lover.

Frances' father hated the attention Reg paid to his daughter, but he was between a rock and a hard place – after all, he worked for the Krays, helping to run The Regency. Even at this early stage, Reg had started proposing. He wanted marriage – but she wanted to see the world. She denied his advances, at least in front of her parents. But she took the holidays away from home. It was a time to forget the problems of the poor East End and time to see the sights of places like Holland and the South of France – and to hear the chatter of the continent. She loved it.

It was a strange meeting of hearts. With her swept-back hair and long eyelashes, Frances was a pretty picture compared to the rugged good looks of the former boxer. Reg treated her like she was on a pedestal and showed her the utmost respect. In fact some said he found it difficult to touch her. Some said that even after a few years of courtship they had never slept together. Reg never talked about sex though – only of his love for the beauty from Bethnal Green.

Violet was soon greeting the youngster at 178 Vallance Road. Frances enjoyed her time there with the Kray family, but never when Ron was home. Perhaps she saw the trouble that lay ahead – peering into his deep eyes. She could also see the power hold that Ron exerted over his twin brother and how Reg would always take his brother's side, even though she was sure he knew that it was wrong. She didn't like it one bit. And the simple fact of knowing that Ron was a homosexual made the brothers' relationship even harder to take.

At home in Ormsby Street things were also getting harder by the day. Neighbours were beginning to notice the cars and the chauffeurs and it all spelled trouble. They recognised the gangster who came to call. Everyone knew the Krays and the gossip was impossible to stop. The news soon spread far and wide: Frances Shea was Reggie's girl, make no mistake about that. And anyone who paid her too much attention or mistreated her in any way was in for a serious makeover . . .

At first it was fun, being a gangster's moll. But soon the laughter changed to tears, as she tried to come to terms with all the problems of being a teenager in the '60s, even if her dreams were full of bright hopes for a brilliant future. Reg didn't understand her dreams. He only cared about himself ultimately, and about the way he was perceived by those around him whom he admired and feared. She was Reggie's dream – a kid out of her depth in the quagmire of the East End underworld. She tried to understand him, but he never really tried to understand her.

But the event that really set the Sheas against Reg Kray happened in

1962, when Reg ended up getting sent to jail. They didn't want their daughter to have a jailbird for a husband. It was only a six-month term, but it was a stretch too far for the Sheas. They could see the writing on the wall – but they couldn't do a damn thing about it.

Reg Kray was soon out of jail and back on the streets though, and into her affections once more. Reg never intended to disappoint Frances, far from it – but the Kray lifestyle got in the way. Ron was always in the background, urging his brother on. Reg played between the two of them, taking care of business for Ron and taking care of things for Frances. He never felt comfortable in his new role.

At first things worked out pretty well superficially. Reg bought himself a new Crombie overcoat and a respectable briefcase and started acting like an insurance salesman. Charlie was overjoyed – at last he could see a real gambling empire, the kind of thing he had always dreamed of and wished for. But Ron didn't take to the new briefcase, calling Reg names and ridiculing him in front of everyone.

Reg kept it going for a while. It was just what Frances wanted and it was really what Reg himself wanted. But again, they had that twin brother to contend with. And as Frances had already seen, it was always Ron who won the battles between the twins. Frances began to lose her dreams of riches and her hopes for stability – her fears really started taking hold.

One evening, at Esmeralda's Barn, Frances was witness to one of the worst arguments ever between the battling brothers. They were both drunk and they pulled no punches. Frances had never seen this side of Kray family life before and it petrified her. Ron ended the slanging match by walking out that evening, saying that his days in the West End were over.

Reg took over the Barn and began running the business sensibly and correctly. Charlie was there to help too. Business boomed. New customers were lined up for protection rackets and new casinos opened, with the assistance of the Krays. Now it really was an insurance business – and soon the American Mafia would be banging at the door asking for help.

Frances now took a back seat. She was Reggie's girl all right but now she was also a part of the set-up, a part of the organisation. And she didn't like it. No more was she high on that pedestal, that girl of Reggie's dreams. She was simply an established part of the environment – a part of the Firm.

Reg showered Frances with gifts. There was the usual expensive jewellery, the fine stylish clothes, anything that would make her stand out in a crowd. She was there to be adorned, not adored. Soon she tired of it. Frances could now really see the down-side and she wanted out.

But it was not easy. She had become tagged with the label 'Reg Kray's girl' and no one was interested in helping her. When she went out alone she never spoke to anyone. If she did, then they were soon warned off. Everyone knew the arrangement and no one could change it. Frances left Reg a number of times, but she always had to go back. There was nowhere else to go.

She soon began to hate the big flash cars and the big bouncers and bodyguards who followed her everywhere. And Reggie's drinking made it worse. Reg Kray had always been a heavy drinker, ever since his so-called army days, but now he became dependent on the stuff. And when Reg drank, he was intolerable.

But as time went by, gradually Frances settled into a routine. She tried to convince herself that the only way to survive was to marry Reg once and for all. Surely, she thought, *that* would change everything.

Frances agreed to marry Reg when he was held on remand at Brixton Gaol, for his part in the McCowan case – but only on the condition that he and his brothers were acquitted. She got her wish and during the celebrations at Vallance Road, Reg, once again, told them all of his love for his wife-to-be. He gave her more presents – a gold pendant, a car, an engagement ring. This was it – and it would all be done with style.

Soon they decided to talk to Father Hetherington, whom the Krays knew well. He had recently been moved to Ealing, in West London, but when Reg and Frances drove over to see him he refused to marry them. He didn't give his reasons, but he just didn't think it right. So they then talked to the young Father Foster, who had taken over from Father Hetherington at Bethnal Green. He agreed to marry them – no words of warning, no conditions, no problem.

The East End turned out in their droves to witness the wedding of the year on 19 April 1965 at St James The Great Church in Bethnal Green. All the old pals were there and the whole Kray and Shea families turned up for the street party. The Krays were ecstatic; the Sheas sombre. All the Krays wore the appropriate costume, but Elsie Shea, the mother of the bride, wore black. Reg never forgave her for that unkind gesture.

Even after they were finally married the problems continued.

Frances had wanted a quiet wedding but Reg had to invite the entire East End of London. Frances had wanted a simple family affair, but Reg wanted all the razmataz of their club scene with Rolls Royces in abundance and David Bailey taking the photographs.

As Reggie's wife, Frances took on a new role. She had new clothes and a new life. She also got a new car. But when she managed to get an instructor to teach her to drive, Reg became jealous and threw the man out of the house. 'And don't come back!' he shouted after the instructor. When Frances decided to take up her old job as a secretary, Reg intervened. 'No wife of mine will work!' he shouted at her. It was a situation that Frances would regret for the rest of her short life.

It was Reg who was the breadwinner, and Frances was not allowed to play her part. When they went out together, they met Reggie's friends and not hers. When they had a chat with people the talk was about the local criminal goings on – who had committed what crime – not who had been sleeping with whom. Her dreams had become a nightmare again. She had awoken to the reality of going from a gangster's moll to a gangster's wife. She was only 21.

The honeymoon was a nightmare. Reg was drunk most of the time and Frances complained continually about the food. She longed for the bangers and mash of home, but Reg longed only for home and the territory he knew so well. Athens was a delight, but it did nothing for their love-life. News was already rife in the East End that Reg couldn't get it up. He was a 'no-show', he couldn't have sex, even with his own wife.

Reg knew he was in a bad situation – and it got worse by the day. No sex, no virility, no passion. He was a spent force in an underworld who prided themselves on doing what a man does best. It was no good – he was up shit creek without a paddle.

13.

Summer/Autumn 1965: Bonds

By the summer of 1965 the Krays had already managed to establish well-founded, deep-rooted connections with the US Mafia through the Philadelphia capo, Angelo Bruno. This relationship started when Bruno asked the Krays to protect his establishments in London and it blossomed throughout the early '60s, when Bruno used his connections to pass on extra business to Ron, Reg and Charlie Kray.

Bruno was an important man in the Mafia ranks. Apart from running organised crime in Philadelphia he also ran Atlantic City – traditionally a part of Philadelphia as far as Mob business was concerned. Atlantic City rivalled Las Vegas as gambling capital of the USA and it helped to make Angelo Bruno a most respected and honourable man. Whereas all Mafia families were allowed into Las Vegas, only Angelo Bruno ruled Atlantic City.

So it was on this basis that Bruno achieved his enviable status and a friend of Bruno's was a friend of the Mob. Another factor that made him an important go-between for Mob business was the fact that he sat on the infamous *commissione* together with the likes of Vito Genovese, Carlo Gambino, Joseph Colombo and Joseph 'Joe Bananas' Bonnano (all of New York), and Salvatore 'Sam Moony' Giancana of Chicago, Stefan Magaddino of Buffalo, and John Scalish of Cleveland. These were some of the most powerful mobsters in the world – and they all had, through Bruno, connections with the Krays in London.

It was Bruno who organised the protection for American stars who came over to England for shows, shopping or holidays. And it was Eddie Pucci, Bruno's chief bodyguard, who handled the business on behalf of Sam Giancana – the boss of Chicago, and the capo who controlled organised crime in Hollywood. Pucci's business partners in England were the Krays and their Firm.

Eddie Pucci was a man who worked for organised crime in general – but for the highest bidder in particular. There was another factor that made him an important go-between for the Krays – he was also in charge of protection for none other than Frank Sinatra. An ex-American football player, Pucci was a big man in both senses of the word – and his word carried weight. He became a good friend of the Krays, even introducing them to the Meyer Lansky set-up of George Raft's Colony and Sporting Club when it opened in Berkeley Square.

With his successful experience of the Krays firmly established in his mind, Angelo Bruno had no hesitation in introducing the twins to the team of Mafia associates who were looking for a way out of a most difficult problem they had – how to get rid of $2 million in instantly negotiable bearer bonds, without losing money on the deal. Their plan was to sell these bonds on the European Undercover Exchange – and who better to handle the deal than the Kray twins in London.

The Mob couldn't sell these bonds in the USA because the Bobby Kennedy administration was actively trying to catch them with a task force. If they sold them in the USA, then their sources would be exposed, the business would be over before it had begun and Kennedy would win.

The solution to their problem, then, was to use the Krays as go-betweens. They or their associates would sell the bonds in Europe in exchange for half of the proceeds. With the amount already held in the USA, the Krays knew they were on to a good thing. But they had just one small problem: they weren't bankers. They needed help.

The man they chose was an American. His name was A.B. Cooper and he had a small bank in the City. He had just the right credentials for the Krays – he had been involved in money laundering, gold smuggling, even in weapons deals. This bald American, who stuttered when nervous, drove around in a black Rolls Royce, normally accompanied by a small dog. He bragged of homes in Switzerland and elsewhere. His bank was private too – no public dealings and positively no police involvement. It was as undercover as they could get. Cooper was also adept at forgeries – there would be plenty of those needed for attaching to the bearer bonds, which would from time to time be supplied without certificates of origination.

The Mob decided on a trial-run, to see if the Krays were up to the job. The venue was Montreal and the prize was $25,000 of stolen bearer bonds (all, on this occasion, with certificates of origination, so they wouldn't have to involve Cooper in falsifying documentation). Ron was delighted. This was big business – the American way. And Ron knew just the man to go to Montreal to collect the bonds – his business manager, Leslie Payne.

Payne didn't like the idea at all, but he couldn't say that to Ron Kray. He couldn't let on that the whole idea of meeting the Mafia on their own turf made him shiver. And the plan of bringing the bonds back to the UK in his briefcase was abhorrent to him.

But Payne agreed to the deal and made his way to Montreal. Don Ceville, the capo of that city, met him at a motel, just outside of town. They greeted each other and the deal was done. Payne received a package – $25,000 in US bearer bonds.

Payne arrived back safe and sound – with the bonds in his briefcase, as planned. No one stopped him at customs and he walked through without any bother. Charlie Kray was there to meet him and the two men drove slowly back to the East End.

Charlie phoned Ron and Reg to let them know that Payne had arrived safely and that the goods were in hand. 'How's he taking it?' asked Ron. 'Maybe we can use him again?' Charlie thought for a moment. 'I don't think so. We'll have to find someone else next time,' said Charlie. 'When he told me about the flight and walking through the customs I thought he was going to shit himself!'

Ron and Reg had a talk about the whole thing – what they needed was a man of steel, a man they could trust, someone from their own family. They chose the only man who could possibly fit the bill – Charlie Kray. From now on, Charlie would be the courier – he would go wherever the Mafia wanted him to go, he would do whatever they wanted him to do, and he would say whatever they wanted him to say. Charlie was now a Mob man.

In August of 1965 important news reached the Krays via an old friend. It was the Canadian Gordon Andersen, one of Charlie's fellow conspirators involved in the failed Nigerian venture. He had interesting information for Charlie. 'There's more bonds waiting for collection in Montreal,' Andersen told him. 'I have spoken with Don Ceville and he wants them collected urgently.'

Charlie had a meeting with the twins, who decided to send a delegation over to Canada. Charlie Mitchell, a bookmaker, was included, so too was Bobby McKew, a printer, Charlie's old pal Gordon Andersen and of course Leslie Payne. These men were not simply chosen because they could help to carry the load, but because the twins wanted to widen their business with the Mob. The chosen few were business people alright, but they were also crooks.

Charlie agreed to lead the expedition to Canada – in fact he was looking forward to it. He loved the high-life and the champagne and he loved being away from the twins. Somehow his life was easier and simpler when they were not around. This was Charlie's big opportunity to show that he could handle it, to prove that he was their equal.

The trip to Montreal was fantastic. Fortunately for this delegation from London there was a party of 'Playboy Bunny Girls' going over to Chicago for training. With Charlie Kray on board the training started on the flight. The five drank their bubbly and chatted with the girls – and that was only for starters. They were all looking forward to meeting Don Ceville and learning the Mafia ways and means.

Their arrival at Montreal went smoothly, but what awaited them at passport control was all but polite and welcoming. When they showed their passports they were all asked to go to a waiting-room. There were irregularities, they were told. The Royal Canadian Mounted Police were there in abundance, something that shocked Charlie – and some of them were carrying machine guns.

'What's going on?' asked Charlie, and he tried to get information – any information. Gordon Andersen had done the trip many times before and he had never previously encountered such a show of force. 'There's something terribly wrong,' he told Charlie. 'But Don Ceville is here – I caught a glimpse of him in the hall. Don't worry, he'll sort it out.'

Charlie was, nevertheless, a worried man. When the police came and told them that they were all being taken to the 'Tombs' (the prison just outside Montreal), Charlie's worst fears were confirmed. The police were there for them and no one else. Someone must have talked – but who?

As the police cars sped through town, taking their new prisoners to their awaiting cells, Charlie had time to think. Ron and Reg were far away, so they couldn't help him here. But Don Ceville *had* seen it all, so maybe there was hope . . . The first sight of the prison made him really wish that he had never agreed to the trip. This was hell on earth – and there had not even been a trial.

Once inside the towering gates, the five men were lined up and told to empty their pockets. Charlie Kray first, then Gordon Andersen, then Charlie Mitchell and Bobby McKew – and then a shaking, cowering Leslie Payne. For Payne this was a real nightmare. He had only just survived the turgid torment of imprisonment in Enugu, Nigeria. His saving grace then was that Charlie was there, outside and free. He saved him then, but now Charlie too was imprisoned. So who would save him now? That first night was frightening.

Early the next morning a jailer rattled on the bars of the cells. There were no walls, just bars, so they could all see each other and talk to one another if they wished. But no one had spoken, no one had said a word. 'There's someone here to see you' said the giant-sized uniformed man, as he unlocked the doors to the cells. They were all shown into an adjacent room – and there they waited.

A few minutes later a woman entered the room and the jailer closed the door behind her. She was smartly dressed, young and pretty. 'I've been sent by Mr Ceville,' she told them. 'I am your lawyer.'

The five men looked relieved. Leslie Payne reached out and shook her hand. 'Please help me,' he said pitifully. 'I don't belong here.' Charlie Kray dragged him away and placed him back in his chair. Payne was weeping.

The young woman opened her briefcase and looked at some papers. 'They can't prove anything,' she said at last. 'But they can keep you here for a long time.' She looked at the bedraggled men – and stared at Gordon Andersen. 'You are a Canadian, are you not, Mr Andersen?' He nodded. 'So they cannot detain you – you are free to go.'

Charlie thought for a moment, before replying. 'So how do the rest of us get out of here?' Charlie was nobody's fool. He knew the authorities couldn't have much on them, so there had to be a way out.

'If you want to stay in Canada, then you'll have to go through the process – and that could mean months in jail,' she told them casually. 'But,' she added with a grin, 'if you just want to go home, then I can get them to deport you.' She looked at the group of unshaven Englishmen. 'You can never come back, but you'll be free!'

Charlie Kray stood up and walked around the room. 'Fuck them – *fuck them all*,' he said through clenched teeth. 'I want to go home!' he added, turning to the pretty woman and the others.

Gordon Andersen thought for a moment. 'I'll go with them,' he said. 'But I'll be back.'

The formalities of the proceedings were over in no time and the five men were all piled into separate cars and driven to the airport. The police escorted them all the way, and even stayed in the airport lobby, just to make sure they couldn't sneak back into Canada – as if any of them really wanted to. All the way back to London Charlie Kray kept to himself. He didn't talk to any of them. He kept thinking: who was behind it all? Why did it happen? And what would the twins say?

The whole experience had been something new for Charlie Kray – he had never been in jail before. He made up his mind there and then never to be put in that situation again.

Charlie told the sordid tale to his brothers as soon as he arrived back in the East End. 'I think it was Mitchell,' said Charlie. 'He either wanted to embarrass us or he wanted the business for himself – or both!' Ron and Reg were worried. How would this look to the Mob in New York and how would they behave towards their new recruits? Fortunately for the Krays, the Mob were used to this kind of thing. Arrest, imprisonment, deportation – it was all in a day's work to the Mob.

Just a few days later Don Ceville flew into London. With him he had a parcel – a 'gift' to the Krays. Ron, Reg and Charlie Kray were back in business. It was bonds and they were on the move again. Cooper supplied the necessary forgeries and Charlie flew to Hamburg to cash them and bank the money. He even sent the money back to the UK over the usual banking system.

Ron asked him about this when he got back home.

'That was cheeky,' said Ron.

'Well, I thought it would be safer that way,' said Charlie, sipping his beer. 'I didn't want to risk getting it stolen!'

The Mob set up safe routes to Europe, so that this kind of slip-up could never happen again. And Charlie was made chief courier and collector. He had a great time in the latter part of 1965 and into the following summer. He loved staying at the best hotels, drinking the best champagne, shacking up with the best hookers in Europe. This was his best time. The twins enjoyed the money, but it was Charlie who enjoyed the lifestyle of travelling to Paris, Hamburg, Geneva, Amsterdam and Frankfurt.

Gordon Andersen was made responsible for getting the money into the USA and Canada. (Being Canadian, he had no problems getting into North America.) Charlie, however, wasn't now allowed into the country, but he didn't care that much. The memory of those few horrible days in the 'Tombs' would stay with him for ever.

Bobby McKew soon inherited a fortune and settled in South Africa. The other outsider in the team, Charlie Mitchell, went back to bookmaking, eventually getting himself killed at his home in Spain. Drugs cartels were suspected, but no one ever faced prosecution.

So the team had changed. Charlie acted as courier, Andersen moved the cash, Cooper forged the certificates of origin – and Ron and Reg lived high on all their efforts. Leslie Payne was still around, but Charlie never again had any kind words to say about him – and eventually Ron lost faith in his business manager.

The final straw for the Ron Kray–Leslie Payne partnership happened in Paris in late autumn. It was Reg who made the phone-call to Charlie. 'We've got some business to discuss, Charlie – you have to go to Paris. Can you come over straight away?' The phone went down with a thud, as Charlie grabbed his car keys and strolled out of the front door and made for the car. 'Paris,' he kept thinking to himself – 'that's just the place for a little excitement.'

Charlie arrived at his mum's house, in eager anticipation of the trip to France. He loved the style, the elegance, the nightlife there. Ron and Reg were already there, drinking their tea and talking shop.

'Laurel and Hardy will be going with you,' said Ron suddenly. Charlie was taken aback.

'I don't need them,' he told his brothers. 'They'll only get in the way.' But Ron stood firm.

So it was agreed – Leslie Payne and Freddie Gore, the accountant, would be going with him. Charlie didn't like the idea of them being there, but he had no choice. He phoned his travel agent to make the bookings at The Claridge Hotel, just off the Champs-Elysées – and then asked them to confirm the flights from Heathrow. It was simple. Nothing was left to chance.

Leslie Payne had smuggled those bonds in from Canada, so he had proved himself in the eyes of Ron Kray. Charlie had been imprisoned on his way to meet Don Ceville in Canada, so he too had shown his true worth. But Freddie Gore had never really been involved, he wasn't really one of the Firm. But he knew too much about their business and the source of their wealth. Ron Kray had chosen Freddie Gore himself to bring the bonds back to London. And Gore had agreed.

The trip to Paris was easy. They were three businessmen visiting the French capital and no one questioned them on arrival. The cab took them to the hotel – and all they had to do was to wait to be contacted by the Mob. They were told to expect two wise-guys called Artie and Tony.

They arrived at the hotel mid afternoon and by the evening they had not heard from the Mafia. Freddie Gore thought they should get the next flight back, so too did Leslie Payne. 'No,' said Charlie. 'We'll give them some time. Why don't we go out and enjoy ourselves tonight?' Charlie drew out a wad of cash. They all agreed. A night out in Paris was quite acceptable.

As they talked in the lobby of the hotel, Charlie was paged.

'*Mr Kraaaay*,' said the boy. 'Mr Kraaaay, please take the nearest phone.' Charlie strolled over to the desk and asked for the phone.

'Yes?' he said. 'OK, let's meet in the foyer in 30 minutes.' He hung up and rejoined his associates, who were by now both curious and wide-eyed.

'That was Artie and Tony,' he told them. 'They'll be here in half an hour.' Charlie walked over to the bar. He was followed silently by Payne and Gore. It was time for a drink. After all, they only had to collect some papers. They could be out on the town in an hour or two.

Time passed slowly. Neither Payne nor Gore was very chatty, so Charlie enjoyed himself by looking around the room – at the gold chandeliers, at the luxurious decoration, at the girls.

Soon Artie and Tony arrived. There was no mistaking the Americans. They looked as though they had just come off the latest gangster film set. Charlie grabbed the bonds, all tied up in a paper bag, and rushed up to his room. He had to hide them, but where? He decided on putting the bag behind the wardrobe. Surely no one would look there? Soon he was downstairs with his pals. 'How about a night on the town?' said Charlie. The Americans smiled. 'It's on us. But you'd better lead the way,' said Tony. 'This is our first trip to Europe,' said Artie. 'But it won't be our last!'

The night was great. Charlie couldn't remember going to bed. He also couldn't remember putting the bonds under his pillow, but they were there the next morning so he bundled them up and put them in his bag. Freddie Gore and Leslie Payne were already down at the breakfast table. Gore looked at him as he approached.

'Have you got the bonds?' he asked.

'Yes,' said Charlie, as he pulled them out of his bag. Leslie Payne was grinning like a Cheshire cat.

'Can I take a look?' he said, as he caught them mid-air. 'I wonder how much there is?'

Charlie ordered breakfast and coffee too – lots of it. Payne suddenly went as white as a sheet.

'What's up?' asked Charlie. Leslie Payne looked at him.

'There's $250,000 worth of bonds in that bag,' he said.

Payne smiled. So too did Charlie. Freddie Gore was quiet, he just put down his knife and fork and sat there motionless.

'I can't do it!' he said at last. 'I'm an accountant, not a smuggler!' Charlie grabbed the bonds and gave them to Leslie Payne.

'No,' said Payne. 'I can't do it,' he whispered. 'That wasn't the deal!'

Charlie took the bonds and placed them in his briefcase. 'You're no good, either of you.' he told them straight. 'I'll do it – and I'll tell my brothers all about it.'

None of them spoke on the trip back to London. At the airport Charlie walked through the customs area, only to be asked to place his bag on the desk.

'What you got here, then?' asked the customs man.

'Dirty laundry,' said Charlie, opening the case. 'Here, take a look!' The customs man grinned and sent him on his way. It was as easy as that.

That night he hid the bonds in a secret hiding place in the bathroom. But the next morning there was a phone call from Artie.

'You'll have to get rid of them, Charlie' he told him down the line. 'They're just too hot to sell, so get rid of them as best you can.' Charlie didn't know what to say. 'Don't worry' added Artie. 'There'll be plenty more!'

Charlie took and the car and the bonds and headed over to his mum's house. 'I've got a few things to burn,' said Charlie, as he started a fire in one of the dustbins, using a can of petrol. 'I won't be long,' he told his mum, as she ran to make the tea.

Charlie counted as he let the bonds drop into the dustbin.

'$10,000 . . . $20,000 . . . $30,000 . . .'

Bonds to the value of $250,000 – all burned and worthless. As his mum approached with the tea, Charlie was almost in tears.

'I thought you were going to save that for later, Charlie!' said his mum. Charlie looked at her. There was a smile on her lips and a glint in her eye. Charlie didn't understand a word.

'You haven't forgotten, have you Charlie?' she said at last. 'It's November 5th. Guy Fawkes' Night!'

Later that month, the Mafia showed they were as true as their word. More bonds arrived and Charlie did the business every time. He never had to burn any more bonds. Charlie Kray loved money. He loved to use it and enjoy it, but he hated to throw it way. The bond deals were the best deals the Krays ever did – they made them a fortune.

14.

March 1966: Button Man

Ron Kray had been in a bad mood for months. He wanted something to happen – and happen fast. Things hadn't worked out as he had planned lately. The meeting with arch rivals, the Richardsons, at the end of the previous year, ended in shambles. Nothing had been sorted, everything was left unsettled. The Astor Club in Mayfair may have been mutual territory, but they all lost their cool – and that slag George Cornell had insulted him in front of everyone. 'You fat poof!' he had said, right out loud so they could all hear. It couldn't go unpunished. Ron had to maintain control and he could only do that one way – with pure and unadulterated fear! Ron was still taking his pills, but they weren't helping.

The Richardsons had done well across the river. Charlie Richardson had run a successful business for years. The scrapyard made dosh and lots of it – and the Krays knew it. His brother Eddie ran a wholesale chemists – he was about as straight as a man could be. But on the side they dealt in devilry. Long-firm frauds, fruit machines, extortion and protection – these were their endeavours after dark, when dirty men did their dirty deeds.

Through these enterprises the Richardsons grew rich. Charlie in particular was a shrewd businessman. His speciality was buying surplus stocks from the government – any kind of metal and scraps. He sold these to everyone and to anyone – as long as they had the readies. The family also had interests in South Africa, where they owned a goldmine.

Legitimate business, though, wasn't enough for the Richardsons. They lived double lives, in a fantasy world, hidden behind a façade of regular business activities. They kept their hands clean by day – and got them bloodied by night, when their torture chamber opened to take care of mischief makers and no-hopers. To the Richardsons, torture was the name of the game. Their victims suffered all kinds of ill treatment and foul play. Fingernails were ripped off, teeth pulled out with pliers, hands nailed to the floor – testicles were even electrified. They were a hard bunch, the Richardsons and their gang – and again, the Krays knew all about it.

It was rumoured throughout London that the Richardsons even had a contact at Scotland Yard, who tipped them off when the law was closing in, or when the long firms were under suspicion. The brothers from Lambeth lived good middle-class lives, with offices in Park Lane. The Krays hated the sight of them and wanted them out of the way.

But the Richardsons had some real heavies to assist them. One was 'Mad Frankie' Fraser – and another was George Cornell. These two were the enforcers, the main men in this team of torturers and cut-throats. Fraser looked after the debt-collecting, while Cornell managed pornography and slot machines. But Cornell's main speciality was the long-firm fraud – and getting rid of evidence.

On one particularly dark night in Shoreditch, Cornell had been asked to tidy up after the closure of a long firm. The order had come to 'hit the floor'. Everything had been sold, lock, stock and barrel – and all for cash. The directors were already on their way out of the country, but the Richardsons had to be sure it was a clean job. And so they called for the expert, George Cornell.

He set about his task with glee. First there were the sales ledgers, then the stock-control books, the receipts and the invoices. They all ended up on the floor being burned. But Cornell was the conscientious type – he wasn't finished yet. He drove back to his lock-up south of the river and collected some sticks of dynamite. Once back in Shoreditch, he quickly rigged it for firing. As he drove off home he snatched a look in his rear-view mirror – as the whole building went sky-high!

Frankie Fraser and George Cornell were known throughout London as two of the toughest, roughest crooks in the game; they had reached the height of their fame, rivalling even the Krays as the hardest of the hard-men. So when one of the Richardson henchmen wanted to play silly-buggers, Ron was only too willing to comply. That the henchman was the Krays' enemy number one, George Cornell, only made the game more attractive. Ron was eager to play.

Billy Haywood was a thief. Together with his pal Billy Gardner, he ran a spieler in Lewisham. It gave them a good living and gangsters were not allowed. Thieves, however, were allowed in and many came to talk and chat and to plan deals. Thieves kept to themselves. They didn't like gangsters, who they thought wanted to take everything away from them.

Eddie Richardson, together with Mad Frankie Fraser, visited the club and asked for protection money. Haywood and Gardner weren't interested, so Eddie Richardson and the much-feared Fraser, (also known as the 'dentist', since he liked pulling teeth out with pliers), left empty-handed.

Fraser had a reputation to live up to, as the hard man of the East End, so he phoned Haywood to invite him and Gardner to a meeting at Mr Smith's, a gambling club in Catford on 8 March. Haywood had already been warned, so he and Gardner and a group of pals turned up at the club heavily armed. Fraser, with Eddie Richardson and a dozen or so members of the gang, including Cornell, were already there. They too were heavily armed.

The shooting had to start sooner or later, but it happened sooner than anyone had imagined. Eddie Richardson said only a few words and that was it. Shots were fired everywhere. All the gang members dived for cover and soon there was blood and guts all over the floor of the club.

Dickie Hart, a member of the Kray gang, but who was by chance with the Lewisham gang that night, fired at will. He wasn't very accurate, but he did manage to hit one of the Richardson gang. Fraser saw the incident and managed to shoot and kill Hart – but not before Hart had managed to shoot Fraser in the leg.

When the police arrived all they had to do was to go around and pick up the bodies. There was no resistance and even the 'dentist' went peacefully. The battle scene at the back of the club, where the police took away the mutilated bodies, was a blood bath. The police found weapons everywhere. There were guns, iron bars and knives. The gangs had with them anything and everything that could be used to kill or maim.

Incredibly though, only one man was killed, and that was Dickie Hart. George Cornell got away in the chaos of the fight, hoping to live and fight another day.

George Cornell was only 38 when this happened. He had been in jail a number of times for violent crimes, and he had served a three-year stretch for threatening a woman with a knife. He knew the rules of gang warfare, and his gang leaders were now in custody, so why did he risk being at The Blind Beggar on the following night, 9 March 1966?

Cornell was the only Richardson gang member to escape from the Mr Smith's fiasco of the previous evening, all the others had either been arrested or taken to hospital. Just why he felt he had to go and have a drink on the Krays' turf is anyone's guess. Maybe he was visiting someone in the hospital just across the street, maybe he was just looking for trouble. He was a loner and not, as yet, really an established part of the gang. He was a mean man who had built a reputation of being a tough customer to deal with and Charlie Richardson, his new boss, was not one of his favourite people.

The East End has a grapevine all its own — and it had a way of reaching the Krays. They quickly learned that George Cornell was alive and well and whooping it up in The Blind Beggar saloon, on nearby Whitechapel High Street. This was sheer bravado on the part of Cornell, who had only recently called Ron Kray a 'fat poof' in front of friends and foes alike. This intrusion on Kray turf was a direct provocation — and Ron Kray decided to do something about it.

Ron made his excuses and left The Widows, the pub on Tapp Street just around the corner from Vallance Road. The twins used this small, cosy establishment as their local. It was where Ron and Reg would often enjoy a drink with some of the members of the Firm. He just told Reg he was going to drink elsewhere. He took his driver John 'Scotch Jack' Dickson and his minder Ian Barrie with him for the ride as he rushed home to 178 Vallance Road to check out his arsenal. Soon he had chosen a number of guns — including his favourite, a 9 mm Mauser handgun. He shared out the artillery, put the Mauser in a shoulder holster, and they went on their way.

They were there in no time. As they approached they saw Cornell's Vauxhall parked outside. Ron Kray's moment had come. A quick look around showed it wasn't a set up.

Dickson was told to remain with the car, which they parked outside with its engine running, while Ron and Ian Barrie fitted themselves up. The minder strolled slowly through the passageway and up to the private bar at the back of the pub. He stopped and reached for the handle. On a nod from Ron he opened the door and Ron Kray stepped inside. It could have been straight out of a western.

Ron Kray spotted George Cornell immediately. Only a few feet away, he was drinking with an old friend, Albie Woods. Both men knew they were in for trouble, they both had their own ways of protecting themselves.

Cornell rose from his stool and stared at Ron Kray. Albie Woods tried to hide himself in the darkness. If Cornell was scared, then he didn't show it.

Ian Barrie was the first to react. Without a word being said he fired a few shots into the ceiling of the pub. Ron took a couple of paces and stood face-to-face with Cornell, who sneered back. 'Well look who's here,' Cornell said without a flinch.

Albie Woods was over in the corner trying to disappear. Ian Barrie could just wait and watch as Ron Kray drew his 9 mm Mauser and aimed it at Cornell's head.

No one really expected Ron Kray to shoot and kill George Cornell there and then – in a public house, with witnesses. The barmaid had only just put a new record on the juke box. The Sun Ain't Gonna Shine Any More sang the Walker Brothers as George Cornell slumped off his stool and onto the floor. Albie Woods, hiding underneath the bar, was now face-to-face with his pal who was lying on the floor with a bullet in his forehead.

Ron Kray pocketed his gun and together with Ian Barrie, he strolled away from the scene of the crime and out onto Whitechapel High Street. Albie Woods was quick to act. He phoned the hospital for help and tried to console his old pal as best he could, but it was a hopeless task. Blood was pouring from his brain. So next he had to phone Cornell's wife, to give her the bad news – there was nothing left to do.

John Dickson drove Ian Barrie and Ron Kray back to Tapp Street and to home territory. He still wasn't aware of what really went on back there at The Blind Beggar. The whole Firm took a trip to Stoke Newington to a pub called The Coach and Horses. And only then did Reg get to hear about it. Ron Kray, once they were carefully stationed in their private upstairs room, gave his gun to one of the Firm, saying 'Get rid of that!' He then went on to tell Reg all about the shooting.

Cornell was quickly rushed to the nearby hospital (where he had actually been visiting a friend earlier that evening – one of those injured at Mr Smith's the night before). But it was too late. He died shortly after arrival. Ron laughed when he heard the news – so too did the Firm. But Reg didn't like it one bit. He knew it meant trouble, but he also knew that he couldn't stop his twin brother. If Ron wanted to kill someone, then he would do it.

Now the whole Firm knew that this was his 'button'. There was no turning back. Ron was later to tell his pals, 'I was loving it. Fighting, scrapping, battling – that's what I'd come into it for in the first place.'

They quickly dispatched someone to warn off the witnesses. Freddie Foreman was the man chosen to do the intimidation – and he was good at his work. Members of the Firm applied the pressure elsewhere where it was needed – and no one talked to the police.

Later on that same evening the police raided a flat in Lea Bridge Road, where the Krays and the Firm were having a drink. They took the twins in for questioning and even arranged for a quick impromptu identity parade. But the barmaid who was called in to identify the murderer had already been frightened off. 'He's not here,' she told the police.

Later, the following week, Cornell's wife went over to Vallance Road and threw stones through the downstairs windows. 'You're bloody murderers!' she cried.

In 1993 I visited Ron Kray in Broadmoor and asked him about the killing. 'Just how did you feel that day, Ron?' I asked him.

He looked right through me as he said with a glint in his eye – 'Bloody marvellous!' He continued, re-living every moment. 'I had killed a man and everybody knew I had killed him,' he told me. 'Now there was no doubt that I was the most feared man in London. They called me the Colonel because of the way I organised things and the way I enjoyed battles,' he said. 'It was a name I loved. It suited me perfectly.'

At about the same time that I talked to Ron, the police were asked to drag the River Lea, near the flat where the Krays had partied that evening. Hidden in the mud and slime of the river they found an artefact of interest to them – the 9 mm Mauser handgun used by Ron Kray to shoot and kill George Cornell that night in 1966. Today it looks its age, having rusted in the water for all that time. But it can't tell the real tale – it can only remind us of the killing and of its historical significance. John Ross, the curator of Scotland Yard's Black Museum, calls it one of their most prized and cherished possessions.

Ron Kray had now re-written the rules of combat. Killing was now on the agenda – and he enjoyed it. No more was there stalemate, where neither side would show their hand; no more would anyone question Ron Kray's willingness to exact the ultimate punishment. He had found his button – and everyone knew it!

15.

Spring 1966: The George Raft Story

George Raft was once one of the highest earners in Hollywood – he was a legend. Although the Krays met showbiz folk of all kinds, there were not many who made a lasting impression on them. One man who did was Raft. He had been an icon of the silver screen all their lives. He had impressed Ron Kray in particular, with his screen persona, his image of the gangster, his look of authority. George Raft had been working in Cuba for Meyer Lansky, but now he was on his way to London to open a new club on behalf of the American Mafia.

George Raft was born on 27 September 1895 in New York. Initially he was a boxer, but his footwork in the ring soon got him work as a dancer. He came over to London in the early '20s and toured the country on the boards, but his career really took off when he entered films in 1929. In 1932 he made the film *Scarface*, which made him a star.

By 1933 he was the highest-paid actor in Hollywood, but he didn't always make the right choices, turning down the part of Rick in *Casablanca*, which meant Humphrey Bogart took it. His career took a slide from around this time and a move to London in the early '50s didn't help. Ultimately he returned to Hollywood to make guest appearances in other films.

In his autobiography, published in 1950, he spoke of working with the Mob and in organised crime. Somehow Meyer Lansky got to hear of his plight as an out-of-work actor and invited him to join some old friends as owners of The Sands, in Las Vegas. His partners were none other than Lansky himself; Frank Costello, the New York Mob boss – and his old friend Frank Sinatra.

By the time he got to Cuba he was fronting the business, but not actually owning any part of it. He was down on his luck, but the Mob had a use for a good gangster – they needed him in London.

A phone call told the Krays where and when they could meet up with Raft. The Mafia needed protection for their new club in Mayfair and there was no one better than the Krays to handle the business. And there was no better front man than George Raft. A meeting between the two just had to be arranged.

The meeting had been arranged by the gentle giant Eddie Pucci. Previously an American football player of some renown, Pucci was now a goafer for the Mob, setting up deals and organising protection for the US stars who came over to London. Pucci knew his game and he knew the Krays. He knew that Ron and Reg Kray were just the right team to handle protection for the racketeers. They had been doing business with Angelo Bruno for some time, protecting his establishments in London – and business was good. Pucci knew the Philadelphia Mafia boss well – even handling his protection as a bodyguard some years earlier.

All three Kray brothers arrived early. As they stood outside the club (which was not yet open for business as it was still being decorated) they glanced around the rich setting of Berkeley Square. 'Typical,' said Charlie as he waited by the main doors. 'Trust the Yanks to pick this spot!' he added, as Ron and Reg sized it all up. The twins smiled – it smelt of money.

The doors opened and Eddie Pucci was there to greet them. The hugs and handshakes over, they moved into the club which was a hive of activity. Workmen were coming and going all over the place. Some were painting, some laying carpets – all were working hard, since the Mob always demand value in exchange for their ill gotten gains.

'Where is he?' asked Ron, as he hurried down the stairs. Ron had been looking forward to this moment for some considerable time – and he knew his host wouldn't let him down. This was Hollywood come to Berkeley Square.

Reg and Charlie followed in his wake, taking in the luxury of the casino, the club, the bars – this was just their kind of place and it was ripe for the picking.

'He's here,' said Eddie Pucci. 'You'll meet him in a minute.' The goafer was all smiles as he spoke quietly to Reg Kray. 'We want you in with us – for a share of the take.' Reg nodded in agreement – the deal was done there and then and they hadn't even met the star of the show.

Making their way through the confusion of the work in progress, they eventually arrived in the bar where they came to a huge oval table.

George Raft rose, holding his right hand out in friendship to greet them. He was everything Ron had hoped for. He was the best-dressed man in the place. This was the big time – and for once Ron Kray was speechless.

The star had been well prepared. 'I hear you'll be joining us,' he said, shaking hands with an ecstatic Ron.

The club was named after the actor – but in fact it was owned by Meyer Lansky and a syndicate of Mafia pals. But the Krays didn't care about ownership – it was who they worked with and who they dealt with that mattered to them. George Raft's Colony and Sporting Club was just one of many casinos owned around the world by the US Mafia and it was run by the best in the business. Dino Cellini had been entrusted with the casino and Alfred Salkin had been given responsibility for the management of the club. They were the best in the game – and the Krays knew it.

It was early spring, 1966, and the ageing actor had just been given a 12-month visa for the UK. While the club was being prepared he had managed to get some other business organised – like commentating on boxing matches for a US television station. It was all above board and accepted by the British government and immigration authorities. George Raft was soon to make a regular appearance in the gossip papers – even making the front page on several occasions.

The Mob had no difficulties making George Raft the Chairman of the Board. They quickly found him a suitable penthouse flat and a Rolls Royce was always at hand to take him around the sights and to help him organise Mob business. They even supplied a dog to keep him company.

But the gangster of the movies never had any problems attracting company. He may have been some 70 years old, but he was fit and well and extremely competent when it came to socialising. He had made a go of Cuba and now he was looking forward to the same in London. George Raft had never been shy of work – even for the Mob.

As Raft and the twins got to know each other, the Krays were absorbing the real meaning of Mob business. This place was plush and posh – just the place to be seen and just the place for the Krays and their photo shoots. Ron, in particular, was looking forward to making new acquaintances, learning from organised crime and having a few snaps taken of himself alongside George Raft.

This turned out to be one of the hottest night-spots in town. Stars gathered of an evening to see and be seen with one of the greatest American actors of all time. Joan Collins and Richard Harris quickly became regulars, so too did many other up-and-coming British actors, all eager for the limelight. When it came to running clubs and casinos, the Mob were experts.

One of the funniest moments at the club was when Richard Harris got blind drunk – and asked the twins to step outside. He was planning to teach them a boxing lesson. Instead though, he fell flat on his face and Ron asked someone to sober him up. Harris couldn't remember it afterwards, but the Krays never stopped talking and laughing about it. Luckily for Richard Harris, he caught Ron and Reg Kray in a good mood.

It was Charlie Kray who was given the job as representative of the Firm – and Charlie knew the game inside and out. He had money in his pockets and the best clothes money could buy. He had made the big time – and nothing would get in his way. Being a pal of George Raft's was the icing on the cake.

But there was trouble looming for the Krays. All those photos in the newspapers and the magazines, all those celebrities and all that glamour – this was rapidly becoming too much for the frustrated detectives at Scotland Yard. With the US Mafia behind them, the Krays were getting too big for their boots.

But the Krays couldn't give a damn about Scotland Yard. They didn't care about what they did and how they did it – just as long as they weren't caught. Ron and Reg took care of the family business and Charlie continued to drink at the Colony Club.

Charlie was the one who showed George Raft the places to go in London. The chauffeur took them to East End and West End alike, as Charlie showed him the pubs, the clubs, the restaurants and the dives. Charlie even took him to see the Repton Club, where all three Kray brothers had trained in their days as boxers. The actor made a quick stop-over to see the great boxing champion Rocky Marciano here and he was so impressed with the club that he made them a gift of a juke box.

As he strolled around the club he told them that music had been a great benefit to him in his younger days as a boxer and a dancer. It was a gracious gesture and completely out of the blue. In fact the manager of the club didn't know about it until the chauffeur pulled up outside the club one day in his Rolls Royce – with the juke box in the boot.

This was gradually becoming a routine for Charlie Kray. Almost every evening something would happen – as if on cue, and tailor-made to suit the tastes of the Krays. One such evening started, as usual, with a couple of drinks and a chat with George Raft. 'There's some of my old friends here tonight, Charlie,' said George Raft. 'Come and meet them – they're over at the tables.' They put their drinks down and strode across the plush red carpet and over to the gaming tables. Light from the golden chandeliers cascaded around the casino as Charlie neared the players – amongst them a well-known face.

'Charlie,' said the best-dressed man in town, 'let me introduce you to Charles Bronson.' George Raft was casual, but respectful. And when the Mob introduces one of their pals, then it's best to shake hands and smile that smile.

Charlie knew the face well and he vigorously shook the actor's hand. But there was no time for a longer chat – his host had spotted another guest, and another introduction was on the cards.

'And this is my friend Richard Jaekel,' continued Raft as he looked around the tables packed with gamblers and on-lookers alike. Another handshake and another few kind words and it was again time to move on.

'What's next?' thought Charlie.

'Another couple of pals for you to meet,' said George Raft. 'This is Telly Savalas and Donald Sutherland.' Charlie reached out and welcomed the actors to London. Not that Charlie knew their faces that well, but they were pals of the great George Raft and that was good enough for him. It was his duty to welcome these people from across the pond – and it was a matter of pride.

Charlie drank his drinks and chatted his lines. Now it was someone else's time to talk. 'There's so many actors here tonight,' he said at last. 'It's like a friendly invasion, just like during the war.' His new pals were laughing. 'What's going on?' he asked at last, trying not to look a complete fool.

'We're makin' a movie,' said Telly Savalas, downing his drink. 'I believe they're gonna call it *The Dirty Dozen*.'

So that was it. The chat naturally got around to the location of the film. The producers had found an old army barracks out in the country. 'Do you know it?' asked Savalas. 'It's called Shepton Mallet!' Charlie knew it only too well, since he had visited his brothers there when they were imprisoned for desertion. He quickly changed the subject.

Later on in the evening Ron and Reg turned up to meet the stars. Reg chatted to Robert Ryan who had just arrived, Ron had a chat with the jovial Lee Marvin, while Charlie mixed with the rest of the actors.

Reg was very impressed with Robert Ryan. 'He had huge hands,' he told me once. 'He was such a big man – and those scary eyes could see right through you.' Now, that coming from the brother of Ron Kray, was serious praise indeed. 'Once, at the Colony Club,' Reg said, 'Don Ceville, the Canadian Mafia boss, had a row with him. Robert Ryan stood up and towered above the little capo. You should have seen him scamper away, just like a lost rabbit.' Reg loved the story – and he loved those days at the best joint in town.

But the glory days were not to last for George Raft and his pals. When his work permit and visa came up for renewal, the authorities refused him permission to stay. He was soon on his way home, back to the States. They said he was 'undesirable' – but no one stopped the Mafia bosses coming and going at will. So why evict such a likeable and well-known man; someone who did no real evil and did so much good? Well, the reason was never given. But Scotland Yard were overjoyed. They had put an end to the photos and they hoped they'd put an end to the friendship between the Krays and the actor.

Their friendship lasted for the rest of their lives, though – and the Krays all recalled the great actor, his gracious gestures and his words of wisdom. 'Don't watch television,' he once told them. 'Get out and meet people – it'll keep you young.' The Kray brothers remembered these words until the day they died.

With George Raft gone, the Colony Club ended too. Without the chairman of the board there was no reason for things to carry on and the place went from bad to worse. The celebrities turned their back on the casino and the money stopped overnight.

Suddenly there was a void in the media. Raft and his Rolls Royce were gone and with him the chauffeur and the dog. There was something missing in and around the nightspots of London. The greatest show in town was no more – the showman had left the arena. But there were other stars around. One of the brightest ones was another of his old pals, Frank Sinatra, who would next make the headlines too – but for all the wrong reasons.

The Krays were now into the realms of celebrity big-time. They had mixed with the best and they had come up smelling of roses. George Raft died in 1980. He had been diagnosed with leukaemia some time earlier and died peacefully at the age of 85. Stars had come and gone, but none shone brighter for the Krays than George Raft.

16.

Autumn 1966: Sinatra

Frank Sinatra was always connected. He was always there when needed by the Mob, always available to act as go-between. He even came to London to help cement relationships between the Mafia in the USA and the Mob-run clubs and casinos, all protected by the Krays. Ron, Reg and Charlie Kray were his guests at many a bash – but it was only Reg Kray who met him up close and personal.

Sinatra's connection with organised crime started early on in his lavish and outrageous life. They were there when he needed help – the kind of help epitomised in the film *The Godfather* when the director of a movie wakes up to find the severed and bloodied head of his favourite horse in the bed next to him. The horse's eyes stare at him as he awakes from a blissful sleep. He rushes to the phone and tells the Mob that he will, after all, give their pal Johnny Fontaine the role he wants in the film.

It has been suggested by many that this was an interpretation of how Frank Sinatra got the job on the film *From Here to Eternity* starring Burt Lancaster and Deborah Kerr. Sinatra was a fading star at that time but the Mob helped their old pal back to health and wealth – and he never forgot them. Apart from the club gigs that revived his career, Sinatra received an Oscar for his part in *From Here to Eternity* and the Mafia had a true ally in 'old blue eyes'. The Mob have always been good at making an offer you couldn't refuse.

One offer Sinatra couldn't refuse was a part of the action at The Sands Hotel, Las Vegas, which he co-owned in the early '50s with the Mafia 'Mr Fix-it' Meyer Lansky, the Mob boss of New York Frank Costello, and his old pal from Hollywood, George Raft. Frank Sinatra owned other properties in and around the strip here, including The Riviera (where I had the good fortune to stay some years ago). It was plush and glitzy, a Hollywood dream in a Mecca for gamblers, and Frank Sinatra gambled plenty. But this was one man who could afford it – if only because of his connections.

Later, in 1959, he used these same connections in Las Vegas to fund-raise for John F. Kennedy when he was running for President. He organised spectacular showbiz events at The Sands, together with his pals Sammy Davis Junior, Peter Lawford and Dean Martin. Peter Lawford became so involved that he married into the Kennedy family – later even setting up secret meetings between Marilyn Monroe and Jack Kennedy, without the knowledge of the rest of the Kennedy clan.

But these events in 1959 and 1960 were designed to enthral – to make a star of the would-be President. It worked. They toured throughout Nevada, staying at other Sinatra hotels, such as the Cal-Nev on the California–Nevada border.

One of Sinatra's pals, Sammy Davis Junior, was not pleased when one particular guest made an appearance in Las Vegas. It was the Chicago Mafia boss Sam Giancana. Davis had been in debt to the Mob for years. It was only his close connection with Sinatra that had kept the wolves at bay. Now they were closing in for the kill. But Frank Sinatra was able to deal with Giancana, a personal friend from the old days. And Giancana needed Sinatra more than Sinatra needed Giancana.

Sam Giancana had already had a meeting with Murray 'The Camel' Humphries (who was in charge of the Mob-controlled unions) and Jack Kennedy's father Joe. The deal was simple. If the Mob could help Jack become President, then the Mob would have a foothold in the White House. All they needed was a go-between, someone everyone could trust. That man was Frank Sinatra.

Sinatra moved easily between the east and west coasts. Money was transported, messages taken, deals done. It worked. Jack Kennedy became the President of the United States of America. But when Sam Giancana went to visit Kennedy in the White House soon after the inauguration, the door was closed firmly in his face. Giancana was not a man to rebuff – he was already planning his next course of action.

The first phone call went to Sinatra. If anyone could repair relationships, then surely it was this celebrity pal of the President. But Sinatra was snubbed. Joe Kennedy ordered Sinatra's phone calls to be diverted to his office, or to Bobby Kennedy's – no calls from Sam Giancana or Frank Sinatra were to get through to the President.

When Giancana let it be known that he had tapes of conversations between Monroe and Jack Kennedy, Joe flatly denied impropriety. He knew that the tapes were real enough, but he also knew that releasing the tapes to the public would show the power of the Chicago mobster.

Sam Giancana was a very powerful man in Al Capone's Chicago – and elsewhere in the USA. He was the Mafia boss of Hollywood, through his previous association with Bugsy Siegel and the ever-present Meyer Lansky, the business brain behind many a Mob move. He was also on the *commissione*, a group of Mafia capos, whose task it was to sort out trouble between the families. This trouble-shooting operation had worked well, ever since it was developed by Charlie 'Lucky' Luciano, and it was full of powerful men, including Vito Genovese and the Krays' pal Angelo Bruno.

The only man who could thwart Giancana was Frank Sinatra. When he heard in 1962 that Marilyn Monroe was in danger, he invited her to stay with him at his home in Palm Springs, even asking her to marry him so he could protect her from any harm at the hands of the Mob. But she saw no danger and she went back home to Hollywood. On 3 August 1962 she died in her home. Sam Giancana had ordered the hit – some say he did it himself, since he and Monroe had been frequent sleeping partners.

Rumours have always been rife about who made the decision to kill Monroe. Was it the White House who asked for assistance from the Mob? Or did the CIA establish the contact and order her killed by Mob assassins? Perhaps we'll never know – and in any case, she took her secrets to the grave. Only Jack Kennedy knew about their pillow talk and he wasn't telling anyone – certainly not his wife Jackie.

With Frank Sinatra in the wilderness, the Kennedys changed tack. Joe ordered his son Bobby, the Attorney General, to go after the Chicago Mob boss. Bobby Kennedy set about his task with glee – he had a hatred of organised crime and had always disliked his father's close association with the Mob, dating back to the bootleg days in Chicago. His task force was organised to cross state boundaries – to go where no FBI agent had gone before.

Sam Giancana didn't like being snubbed by the Kennedys. But he was a patient man, willing to wait for the right time to exact his revenge. And he knew that with a womaniser like Jack Kennedy, he wouldn't have to wait long.

In 1963 Frank Sinatra was in trouble – someone had kidnapped his son, Frank Junior. The police didn't take the case seriously – many thought it a Sinatra publicity stunt – so he called on his Mob pals for help. The kidnapping had taken place at one of Sinatra's own hotels, the Cal-Nev, where Frank Junior had been staying, while singing and performing for the fans at the nearby Harrah's Casino with the Tommy Dorsey Band.

A ransom note was delivered and Sinatra raised the necessary readies in double-quick time. After a swift search of the area the Mob soon found Frank Junior walking aimlessly in the mountains. And they found the three kidnappers, who were all handed over to the police. Surprisingly enough, they also found the ransom money – intact.

Frank Sinatra denied reports that this was a publicity tactic, but he couldn't deny asking the Mob for help. His involvement with organised crime was well established and well documented, but even he didn't know what was about to happen to his old friend the President, Jack Kennedy.

On 22 November 1963, in downtown Dallas, Jack Kennedy was shot and killed as he drove in an open car in a procession through the streets. The man set up for the killing was a former army misfit, by the name of Lee Harvey Oswald, who had been involved in the failed Bay of Pigs mission in Cuba. He had also been to Russia and had a Russian wife – he was perfect for the fall guy.

Some say that the deal was done through Naval Intelligence, who were not very pleased with the new President – and that the man they'd got for the job was none other than the Kennedy adversary Sam Giancana. Even the man who killed Oswald on prime-time television was an old employee of the Chicago boss – a man by the name of Jack Ruby. Ruby was obliged to do the killing – and to be seen doing it. This was one killing the Mob *wanted* the world to see. Now, at last, Oswald couldn't spill the beans about the whole sordid affair. Soon the history books would say that a single shooter did the killing, but the Mob know the real story – and so too did Sinatra.

He hadn't been able to help Monroe and he couldn't stop them killing Jack Kennedy. Frank Sinatra just wanted to forget the whole business, but he couldn't. He had work to do and that normally involved the Mob in one way or another. And when he came over to London in 1965 he asked the Krays for help, as bodyguards.

Eddie Pucci was the man who set up the arrangements for Sinatra's visit – and the Krays were taken on as minders for the star. Frank Junior came over with his father, and he stayed on to do shows in the

UK after his dad returned home to Hollywood. Frank Junior was wined and dined throughout the country but always in the background were Ron, Reg and Charlie Kray.

The following year, Eddie Pucci promised the Krays an audience with Sinatra. The star was over in London performing at The Apollo Theatre. The Krays would protect the star and they would protect his good name, all in return for a meeting with the singer himself – and the gratitude of the Mob. Eddie Pucci had even arranged for front row seats for them and the entire Kray family – the best seats in the house. The best ones that Mob money could buy.

The show was a sell-out and the audience was enthralled by Sinatra's performance. Violet especially was looking forward to the reception after the show, where she would be meeting one of her all-time favourite performers in the flesh. But it was not to be this time around. Eddie Pucci approached them during the intermission and told them straight. 'It looks as though Frank Junior has been kidnapped again, back in California. It looks as though he'll have to go straight home after the show.' The Krays were shocked. They were eagerly awaiting the moment when they would be shaking hands with the man himself, but they were also pleased that it hadn't happened on their watch. Now *that* could have been disastrous for their future Mob involvement.

The kidnapping was, it turned out, a farce. It was a college prank that got out of hand. There were no threats, no demands for ransom, there was no fear of instant death. Frank Sinatra was pleased, too, that there was no Mob involvement and that his place within their society was as safe as ever. So much so, that he was once again asked to try to patch things up between Chicago and Washington.

The only time any of the Krays actually got to meet Sinatra in person was in 1967, when he came over to London to perform and he paid a visit to the Colony Club, run by fellow actor George Raft. The two had been business partners in the past and they had remained friends through the years. It was a casual visit, to meet up and have a few drinks after a show – and Reg Kray was there to meet him.

Eddie Pucci introduced Reg as one of their 'valuable English friends'. Sinatra was pleased to meet him of course, but he was tired and had really only come to see his old pal, the movie gangster. So Reg moved aside and let the two men talk about old times, people they knew, things they had done all those years before.

By the following year Bobby Kennedy was also dead – at the hands of the Chicago capo. (The Krays were arrested this year too, and put into jail.) Frank Sinatra had played his last card in the Kennedy game – and he had lost. Even Eddie Pucci couldn't win for ever. In 1972 he was shot and killed while playing golf in Chicago. Eventually Sam Giancana, the man who knew all the Mob secrets, was also killed with a bullet in the head. Only their ghosts can recall the real truth about the Mob–Kennedy association, but the Krays were there all right – and they talked about Frank Sinatra for the rest of their lives.

When Reg Kray was finally buried in 2000, the refrain was heard loud and clear around Bethnal Green.

I did it my way, sang the King.

17.

December 1966: The 'Mad Axeman'

On the 12 December 1966 the 'Mad Axeman' Frank Mitchell escaped from Dartmoor Prison. To say 'escaped' may, however, be a little over-dramatic – in actual fact he casually walked out of the gates of one of Her Majesty's top security prisons and disappeared into the mists of the moor and away to freedom.

It was another madman, 'Mad Teddy' Smith, who had suggested the caper to the twins. Smith was, amongst other things, a playwright, and his imagination often got the better of him. He had a difficult time telling reality from fiction.

The plan was to break Frank Mitchell out of Dartmoor as a protest about his treatment. It would be, according to 'Mad Teddy' Smith, a bit of a coup and it would be good public relations for the twins. The 'Mad Axeman' had already phoned the twins for help and Ron in particular was interested in doing something, especially something big like breaking a man out of 'the moor', as Dartmoor was known.

'Mad Axeman' Frank Mitchell was a giant of a man with big hands and big feet – everything about him was big. He earned his nickname from the occasion when he had grabbed an axe and threatened an elderly couple with it, demanding new clothes for his getaway. He was 37 years old and was serving a sentence of 18 years for robbery with violence, while on the run from Broadmoor. Only two months earlier no one would have thought this probable – since the governor, Dennis Malone, was eagerly trying to get a release date for Mitchell to aim at. But the Home Office were dithering and the delay became too much for Mitchell to take.

Mitchell had been birched, flogged and generally tormented and tortured during his 20 or so years of imprisonment. He had seen most jails in the country and most asylums for the mentally imbalanced but Dennis Malone, in his reports, stated that

Mitchell has continued to progress and improve. He has made
every effort to demonstrate his reliability and the absence of
risk to the public. The prison chaplain added 'I sincerely believe
that Mitchell will make a great effort to justify the trust placed
in him.'

One of seven children, Frank Mitchell was also from London's East End.
In fact he was a good pal of the deserter Dickie Morgan, so he was
known to the Krays well before they actually met him. He had always
been in trouble with the law. He started it all by stealing a bike when
he was nine. Breaking and entering followed later and various stretches
at borstal. Not even the army could tame him, and like Ron and Reg
Kray he was given a dishonourable discharge.

Frank Mitchell was always running away. He ran away from borstal,
from the army, from prison, from the asylums. As big and as strong as
you can imagine, Mitchell didn't like the authority he found
everywhere. He soon turned his animosity towards the jailers and the
guards of the prison service – and this didn't endear him to the system.

Mitchell was clever too. When he escaped from Broadmoor, he did
so by making keys to fit the locks of the institution. And believe me (I
have been there) you need a *lot* of keys to get out of Broadmoor. His
idea was to use the same trick Ron used later on: by staying out of
trouble for six weeks he could be sent back to his original prison to
serve out his term.

He had met Ron Kray when he was in Wandsworth Gaol, so Ron was
interested in his case. At weekends the twins would organise whip-
rounds for Mitchell and other prisoners – and they would send them
the money. Ron had even managed to get Mitchell out of custody on
one occasion by paying for his brief, who eventually won the case.

But once in Dartmoor Mitchell began to change. They treated him
well and the authorities at the prison only had kind words for him. 'He
has come a long way,' wrote the deputy governor, Donald Ward. And
in 1965 he was made a part of the Honour Party, a group of trustworthy
prisoners who were allowed out under supervision, having given their
word not to escape. 'I have seen him disappearing into thick mist in the
morning and not looming up out of it again until teatime. This is real
progress,' Ward said.

The Home Office refused every attempt by the staff at Dartmoor to
get a date fixed for his release. They pleaded for a term – a week, a

month, a year. They urged the Home Office to give him something to aim at. But all to no avail.

Initially his letters home were full of hope. But by 1966 they were full of despair. By early 1966 Ron and Reg Kray were his only visitors.

Ron, along with Albert Donaghue, drove down to see Frank Mitchell just a few weeks before the planned escape. Mitchell told them both: 'They're messing me about, Ron. They offered me this deal – if I behaved myself I would get a date. But now the governor's gone.' Dennis Malone, the governor who had built up such a good reputation for Mitchell, had retired in the November and Mitchell thought he would have to start all over again.

On the day of the escape Albert Donaghue and 'Mad Teddy' Smith drove down to Dartmoor and found the designated meeting place. Frank Mitchell had already been informed of the plans by telephone (since he regularly roamed the moor, given complete freedom by the guards). He was a huge man and had once been certified insane, so he wasn't a man to argue with either. Mitchell knew exactly where the telephone box – the pick-up place – was. As 'Mad Teddy' Smith faked making a phone call to avoid suspicion, the 'Mad Axeman' Frank Mitchell slowly walked over the hill and to freedom.

Quickly the 'Mad Axeman' got changed from his prison gear into something more suitable, since they were afraid of road blocks once the escape was discovered. Soon he was in the car and the three men drove towards London. While they drove they listened to the radio, in the hope of hearing news about the escape and of any police road blocks. But they heard nothing – nothing, that is, until they were already safely in London and on home territory. The escape had been a complete success.

But the twins had under-estimated the newsworthiness of the story. For once Ron Kray's sense of media manipulation had let him down.

Soon Mitchell had written a letter to *The Times* protesting about his harsh treatment at Dartmoor Prison and suddenly it was all turning into a farce. The problem for the twins was that the whole underworld knew of the escape and of the predicament that Ron and Reg Kray had got themselves into. It looked as though they were losing their grip; their reputation was on the line.

To keep Frank Mitchell happy at the Barking flat, the twins brought in a hostess, in the shapely form of Lisa Prestcott. But the 'Mad

Axeman' fell in love with her; something that no one could have anticipated. It only complicated an already complicated situation.

Something had to be done, quickly. Frank Mitchell wanted to escape completely and to take his hostess with him, but what would the twins have to say about that kind of a scenario . . . ?

According to Albert Donaghue at the trial in 1968–69, the twins decided to cut their losses by getting rid of the 'Mad Axeman' once and for all. They just didn't know how to handle the situation, so their recourse was to kill the problem by killing Frank Mitchell.

Ron, Reg and Charlie Kray all had a meeting to decide on tactics. They invited Freddie Foreman over too – maybe he could find a way out of their predicament. Foreman's idea was to get rid of the problem by killing Mitchell and dumping his body at sea. The Krays agreed – and the money changed hands.

Albert Donaghue was told to get the 'Mad Axeman' outside the flat and into a van. Mitchell didn't like the idea of going anywhere without his new love, but he was persuaded that she would follow once he was completely safe and out of the country.

Unknown to Mitchell, there were three other occupants in the rear of the van, already in position and armed. They were Alfie Gerrard; a South-London villain by the name of Gerry Callaghan – and 'Hard man' Freddie Foreman. None of the three were members of the Firm, since the twins wanted to keep the plan a secret from their own gang. To be seen disposing of a problem in this way would have done nothing to enhance their reputation.

Mitchell got into the van, which was parked on the Barking Road. Inside he was told to sit by himself on one side, opposite the other three men. As the driver Albert Donaghue drove off the first gunshots rang out loud and clear from the back of the van.

Mitchell wasn't dead though, so the three unloaded their guns into the huge man. He was still groaning as another bullet entered his brain. The 'Mad Axeman' Frank Mitchell died at the hands of his 'rescuers'.

Lisa Prestcott, back inside the flat, heard the shots and was convinced that they would then come after her next. But no one paid her any attention.

Donaghue stopped the van and got out. He couldn't stand the stench of death. He walked away from the van, half expecting to be killed himself. But it didn't happen.

Later Donaghue reported back to the twins that the job was done. It is well reported that Reg Kray wept when he heard the news. The date was 24 December 1966: Christmas Eve.

When policeman Nipper Read pulled Lisa Prestcott in for questioning about the 'Mad Axeman' after arresting the twins in 1968, the police car drove towards Tintagel House instead of towards Scotland Yard. Fearing that these were Krays' killers who were wanting to murder her, she pulled herself free from her captors and almost threw herself off a bridge over the River Thames. Eventually, though, she was convinced by the policemen that they were genuine and they continued the ride.

Donaghue was later asked by the twins to deliver one thousand pounds in cash to Freddie Foreman as a payment for the killing. Recently Foreman has openly admitted to killing Frank Mitchell, but since he has already been acquitted of the murder, then he cannot by UK law be tried again for the same crime. So a guilty man still walks the streets.

And so it was that the Krays caused another killing in 1966, but this time they didn't pull the trigger themselves. They were now being openly encouraged by the US Mafia to use hit men, something that didn't exactly appeal to their sense of honour and respect. To the Krays, men should be men – and they should be seen to be so.

18.

June 1967: Suicide

Problems for the newly weds Reg and Frances started from day one of their marriage. When they got back from their honeymoon in Greece, they couldn't move into their new flat in the West End – the decorators were running behind schedule. So instead they moved in with the Sheas in Ormsby Street, Bethnal Green.

This caused friction between the Krays and the Sheas, since Reg was out all night occupied with his business and club interests. There were always rows with the in-laws, especially the mother-in-law, who never pulled her punches. She would wait up at night, just to moan and groan at her daughter's new husband when he got in. In her opinion he was neglecting his wife and his family responsibilities. The simple fact that her own husband now worked for the twins never entered her head.

When the day for the move out of Ormsby Street arrived Reg was overjoyed. At last he could be alone with Frances with no prying eyes – and none of the Shea family around to make sarcastic and snide remarks about his duties as a husband. But the couple didn't like the flat. Frances was too far from home and couldn't see her mum and dad. Reg didn't like it either. All that pomp and circumstance of the West End just wasn't his style. So it seemed a move back to the East End was imminent.

Unfortunately for Frances, the place Reg chose was none other than Cedra Court. He had a very important reason for choosing this particular block of flats – his twin brother Ron lived there. Whether Reg actually intended to participate in his brother's orgies was not clear at the time. But he did – and Frances knew all about it. How could she not fail to notice the comings and the goings, the men and the boys, Ron and Reg back together again, with his brother Ron exerting the influences of old?

Ron was delighted. He had his twin back again and he started to control him, just as he had done throughout their lives. Frances was the only one who had come between them – and so now he would try to control her too. But Frances was strong willed. Only eight weeks after her marriage, she was back home at Ormsby Street with the Sheas, regretting things and cringing at any mention of the name 'Kray'. Reg was refused access to his wife. They didn't want to know him – and they wanted him out of their daughter's life for good. So they set about getting the marriage annulled. Frances had made a terrible decision when she decided to marry Reg Kray – and now she wanted out. But the Krays were not the kind of people who gave up easily and Reg soon pestered her with gifts – anything to keep her as his wife, anything to satisfy the gossip makers who were all talking about his lack of manliness, his lack of prowess in bed and his apparent lack of sexual drive when it came to women.

Eventually Reg did win his wife back – but it couldn't last. Over the following few years Frances became despondent and frail. Her parents told everyone who was willing to listen that her new husband had supplied her with drugs, that he had kept her locked up in her room, that he couldn't get it up. And throughout these years her mother told everyone: 'My daughter was a virgin when they married – and she's still a virgin now!'

Reg was furious at being labelled 'lacking in bed'. To counteract this he arranged for several women to take him to court, accusing him of fathering their children. They all lost their cases, but Reg paid them off handsomely. After all, they had saved him from an ignominious fate worse than death – his reputation was intact, at least for the time being.

But the problems were still there. Frances became a responsibility Reg didn't need, although from time to time she moved back in with him at Cedra Court. He had business to take care of and his pretty wife was no help at all. In fact she was taking up his valuable time when he was wanted elsewhere. 'Throw her out!' urged his twin brother. 'She's no good for you.' Reg just didn't know what to believe.

The dream marriage had now become a nightmare. Frances had bad dreams regularly, as she became more and more depressed – she even had a premonition that she would die young. She couldn't take it any more, so one night she tried to commit suicide. It was a plea for help. The doctor prescribed pills of all shapes and sizes – but nothing improved her situation. The uppers didn't work and the downers got her even more depressed. Finally she went back home, once again seeking an annulment of the marriage. But time was running out for the pretty redhead from Bethnal Green.

Ron did everything he could to make her stay away this time. He didn't want to see her, hear her name – or even remember the marriage. For him, it was just as though the past few years had never happened. And he laid on the parties and the orgies as though there was no tomorrow. But Reg wouldn't give up on Frances. Maybe it was because of the image that he tried to promote – being a married heterosexual just like any other so-called 'normal' male? Maybe it was because of the gossip that surrounded his name. Either way, he made one last effort to make things work by taking Frances away from everything for a holiday and Frances reluctantly agreed.

On 6 June 1967 they went to a travel agent's and bought the tickets. Frances was excited about the holiday, so much so that she wanted to look good – and this meant a trip to the hairdressers. But she wasn't pleased with the result. Reg tried to calm her down and to encourage her, but it did no good.

Later that evening Reg asked a woman friend to call round to see if Frances was all right, but this woman was too busy to go – so no one went to the assistance of Frances Kray. That same night Frances took an overdose and died in her sleep. At 23 her life was over.

That night had not been good for Reg Kray. He had dreamt of Frances and instinctively knew that something was wrong. At 6 a.m. he hurriedly drove over to Wimborne Court, to Frankie Shea's flat. It had only been a few hours earlier that he had driven Frances back there after collecting those tickets for the trip to Ibiza – a second honeymoon of sorts and time in which to settle their differences and to make a new start. But when he got to the flat he didn't want to disturb her sleep, so he left without a sound and paid a visit to his barber's just around the corner. Her brother found her dead when he took her a cup of morning tea.

The Shea family were the first to visit Frances' body. Only after they were all gone did Frankie Shea try to phone Reg to give him the news. But he couldn't find him. He was driving down the street at that very moment. He saw the cars and the family and stopped to ask why. But somehow he already knew what had happened. She had tried committing suicide before – only this time she had been successful.

Reg was still legally husband, since the divorce had been put on hold, so he knelt by her side all day, her listless body motionless on the bed. Reg looked around the flat. He couldn't find a note. The other times when Frances had apparently attempted suicide there had always been a note, so Reg was sure about one thing – as far as he was concerned she didn't mean to kill herself.

The drinking habit took hold. Reg drank and drank until he could drink no more. The gin didn't help. Nothing helped. And still the Sheas blamed him for it all. He was still in love with Frances and he just couldn't believe that she was dead. Everywhere he went he saw Frances. Everything he did reminded him of his lovely wife. Everything was bleak for the crime boss of London.

At the inquest Reg Kray formally and tearfully identified his wife. The post-mortem showed that she had died from a massive overdose of phenobarbitone, taken that last fateful night. Someone spoke of personality disturbances, others of a suicide just waiting to happen. The coroner gave the verdict of 'suicide while the balance of mind was disturbed'.

The funeral was a splendid affair. Ten limousines carried the mourners and wreaths were sent by every single member of the Firm. It was held at Chingford in Essex, where Reg had paid two hundred pounds for a large plot. The sad occasion got under way with the Kray and Shea families split again in the ever-increasing family feud. It was the first time that Reg had had to face the music alone, since his brother Ron did not attend the funeral. Mum and dad were there with brother Charlie, but it just wasn't the same. He didn't have the support of his twin brother (who had been told not to attend by Charlie, fearing police involvement). Reg Kray was confused and in agony. But the grief subsided long enough for him to drive to the Shea residence and collect all his letters to Frances and the jewellery that he had given her over the preceding seven years. Was this then really the action of a grieving husband?

The funeral attracted the attention of the Metropolitan Police, who appeared in force. This was exactly what Charlie had feared and the ever-present cameras flashing in and around the church, the cemetery and the funeral parlour made sure that once again the Krays were in the news. But for all the wrong reasons.

Reg had wanted Frances buried in her wedding dress, but the Sheas managed to have her body dressed in other clothing just to make sure that the hated dress didn't touch her skin. They even managed to get the wedding ring transferred to her other hand. And all the time they were still trying to get the marriage annulled.

Father Hetherington agreed to perform the ceremony as a favour to Reg. He even tried to patch things up between the Krays and the Sheas – but to no avail. He had feared that things wouldn't work out between Reg and Frances – and that was why he had not been available for the wedding. He had been right all along.

Reg turned to gin and to guns. He drank more and shot a few people just for good measure and he put it all down to the death of Frances. But maybe it was all due to his own shortcomings as a husband and his own family relationships.

Recent revelations help to explain their relationship and the failed marriage. Reg Kray admitted on his death bed that he was indeed homosexual, in his letter to *The People*. Exactly how his new wife Roberta took the news is unclear.

So no wonder the marriage didn't work. Whether or not he was homosexual before his long internment has not been established for definite, but it looks as though there were certain tendencies well before his marriage to Frances in 1965. So did Reg marry Frances to protect his image? Did he hide behind the skirts of his wife, to hide his true sexual identity?

Ron and Reg Kray were truly twins – in every sense of the word. There are not many cases in history where both twins were homosexual. At last Reg showed his true colours. The Shea family were right after all.

19.

Summer 1967: Stars

By the summer of 1967 the Krays were used to mixing with celebrities of all kinds. Some of these stars became good friends, others just acquaintances. They met them because of the clubs they ran and because of the business arena in which they worked. They had met some of the greatest – stars such as Judy Garland, Frank Sinatra, Barbara Streisand, Tony Bennett, Johnny Ray and Nat King Cole. And one of their very special friends was that screen legend George Raft. To talk of the stars they knew is to talk about a who's-who of show business. Even in later years they were fêted by the stars – artists such as Jon Bon Jovi, and boxers such as Mike Tyson would send them best wishes on their birthdays. But it is the stars of yesteryear that the Krays remembered best and talked about through all those years of imprisonment. One of these stars was Judy Garland.

When Garland came over to the UK it was generally Reg who looked after her. 'Judy Garland made us welcome at her party,' said Reg once, reminiscing about the old days at the height of the Kray empire. 'In the early hours of the morning she sat there on the floor and broke out into song – all her old songs.' He had been used to mixing with the great and famous US showbiz personalities who were sent over to the UK with just a little help from their friends the Mob. When the Mafia in the USA wanted their pals to get the best protection and assistance that money could buy, they always turned to the Krays. But Judy Garland was different from the rest.

'I took her to parties in the East End,' Reg told his friends. 'I liked her.' When Frances died, it was Judy Garland who came to the rescue by offering to let Reg stay at her home in Hawaii. Reg was shattered that his wife had taken her own life and he was almost prepared to give up a life of crime for Judy. She appeared to be most vulnerable at this stage of her life and would cling on to Reg's arm in almost any given situation. Reg Kray would still have pleasant thoughts about these times later in life.

Ron saw the attention paid by Judy Garland to his brother – so he stayed well away. And in any case, he didn't like seeing her drink herself silly – and he hated the drugs.

Early in the '60s Reg had taken a shine to Judy, but after his marriage to Frances he withdrew whenever she approached. Reg refused to show her any affection and was strangely embarrassed when in her company. He even became reluctant to embrace her in public places, especially when the photographers were around and when Frances was there.

But Reg continued to show her the town. It was, after all, his duty and Reg Kray did his job well. He took her to both the East End and West End, with Judy singing her heart out in various clubs and pubs all over the capital. Judy even sang songs on request when they visited Kray pubs in the East End of London.

She was a favourite of all three Kray brothers and they have talked a lot about her over the past 30 years. Even at the trial in 1969 Ron Kray shouted at Lord Justice Stevenson: 'I could be dining with Judy Garland, instead of being stuck here in The Old Bailey.' Ron may have disliked the boozing, but he couldn't fault her performances for his friends, his family – and for the Firm.

But Judy Garland wasn't the only star to fall for a Kray. Barbara Windsor, the bubbly star of the *Carry On* films, also fell madly and deeply in love with Charlie Kray.

Charlie enjoyed the romping and the sex, but there was one little hurdle he had to overcome – he had to make sure that no one told her that he was already married with kids back at home. His wife Dolly was no longer the apple of his eye and the roving Charlie had already had girls by the dozen. In fact being the older brother of the Kray twins made him a catch for many a bright-eyed young lady throughout the '50s and '60s. If there was one thing Charlie Kray loved more than money, it was having a young beauty in his bed.

The attraction to Barbara Windsor was obvious. She was well proportioned, blonde and she sparkled like the stars. She was so easily recognisable that men would whistle at her and would stand and stare – she loved the attention. Charlie enjoyed it too. It made him feel proud to have one of the screen's brightest stars on his arm.

Barbara had made her mum a promise not to go out with married men and Charlie had heard about this from a pal. He made up his mind there and then to bed the lady — and keep the secret if he could. The romance lasted quite a while, long enough for Charlie to have marvellous memories about it for the rest of his life. Later, when he was in prison, it was remembering these times that kept him sane, kept him going, kept him from committing suicide.

One of Charlie's favourite stories was of when Barbara was filming in the London docks with Joan Littlewood. They were having trouble with some dockers who were asking for protection money. Barbara remembered Charlie and his brothers, Ron and Reg Kray.

'What can we do?' asked Joan Littlewood. 'They are holding us up — and they are holding us to ransom!'

'I can't do anything,' said Barbara with a grin. 'But I know a man who can!' She was soon on the phone to Charlie Kray.

'That's all right sweetheart,' said Charlie. 'Leave it to me!'

He was on the phone in a flash and the word went out that the Krays were 'protecting' Barbara and the whole film crew. The dockers apologised immediately. 'We didn't know,' they said. 'Why didn't you tell us?' they stuttered. 'How can we help you?' they asked again and again.

Joan Littlewood was so pleased that she asked Barbara to phone Charlie again. This time she said, 'Ask if we can pop by and thank him personally.' Barbara phoned and set up a meeting at The Kentucky Club, just off the Mile End Road.

'I look forward to it,' said Charlie. 'I'll introduce her to the twins — they'll love to meet her.'

The night came and Barbara was looking forward to it. This just wasn't a business trip — this was getting together with her lover. This was serious romance — and mixing romance and business didn't bother her.

They entered the club and met Big Pat Connolly who ushered them into the club and straight to Charlie.

'Hello darling,' he said as they kissed. Then his eyes strayed towards Joan Littlewood — and a hand stretched out in greeting. He shook her hand warmly and kissed her on the cheek. This was his turf — and he was in full control of the situation.

Ron and Reg were in the club that night and after Charlie had been introduced to the stars, they made their way over — all dressed up and right on cue. There were hugs and kisses all round as they greeted each other like old friends. Ron and Reg made Joan Littlewood feel at home, so much so that she had a great time drinking and reminiscing about the East End and talking about her latest film with Barbara, *Sparrows Can't Sing*. Then, suddenly, she had an idea.

'We need a club scene at the end of the film,' she told them. 'We haven't found anywhere suitable yet, but I think your club is just perfect.' The twins didn't know what to expect. It came like a bombshell to them. 'Can we do the shooting here?' Littlewood asked politely.

Ron was quick to reply, and he had just the right words, as usual. 'Well I don't know,' he said, eyes sparkling in the dim light of the club. 'We don't usually allow shooting in here.'

It was a scream. Joan Littlewood understood immediately what he was on about. Everyone in London knew the Krays and everyone knew about their use of weapons.

'We'll throw a party here after the première,' said Ron. 'If that's all right?' Joan Littlewood had no objection – in fact she was overjoyed.

'That's perfect, Ron,' she said. 'We're holding it just across the road, so it won't be too far for Princess Margaret and Lord Snowdon – they are the guests of honour.'

Ron and Reg were already rubbing their hands – royalty at The Kentucky! What a coup! Charlie was all smiles as he chatted with the bubbly blonde. He just couldn't take his eyes off her. The rest of the evening was one big party.

The film premièred and the party at The Kentucky was a great success. George Sewell, one of Charlie's drinking pals was there. So too were Roy Kinnear, Roger Moore and James Booth. Barbara and Joan were a delight, making everyone welcome to the club and the Krays mixed with everyone. The only disappointing thing about the whole event was the fact that Princess Margaret and her husband Lord Snowdon ended up not turning up for the evening's entertainment.

But the party was a success for the gangsters as well as for the showbiz folk. Freddie Foreman, a man who killed for the Krays, was mixing with the stars. Other mobsters were there too (closely vetted by Ron and searched by Reg). The Krays were mixing and partying with the stars – and they were loving it.

Another fine lady much admired by the Krays was Diana Dors. Diana had known them for years, ever since she started acting – and it was Charlie who was the connection. He admired Diana, who had started in such a humble way, just like the Krays. Alan Lake, her husband, was a great pal too – Charlie could think of nothing better throughout his early years of release than going to their home for the weekend as an honoured guest.

Charlie took Diana to see Ron when he was in Broadmoor. Diana and Charlie sat face to face with Ron in the visiting hall, drinking their non-alcoholic beer. Ron was in great form that day, talking about the old days and talking about what he would be doing after his imprisonment. Diana burst out laughing.

'I don't know what it is, Ron,' she told him. 'But you've *got it*. If we could put it in a bottle then we'd all be millionaires!'

Such stories abound when talking of and writing about the Krays and their famous celebrity friends. One of my favourite stories is what happened to Richard Harris at one of their clubs. He was a frequent visitor and was always welcome. But one evening he got terribly drunk and started to shout at the twins.

'Come on!' he screamed at them. 'Come outside now and I'll show you who's tough!' He was falling around the room – and falling right into trouble. But Ron and Reg knew all about his drinking and they took it with a pinch of salt.

'Get him outside,' said Ron to one of the minders. 'And don't let him back 'til he's sober!' he added quietly as they were on the way out the door.

When Richard Harris heard the following day what he had done, he rushed to see Ron and Reg Kray. 'I'm so sorry,' he told them. 'Can you ever forgive me?' he pleaded. He had nothing to worry about though. Ron and Reg bought him a drink and all three of them laughed it off.

Later on, when Charlie was released from his seven-year stretch, he spent many an evening with Richard Harris. Whenever he brought up the goings on of that evening, the actor would cringe and shake his head. He was one person who actually got away with threatening the Krays and he thanked his lucky stars. Many others weren't so fortunate.

Today we all know the Krays from photographs taken during their reign of terror with celebrities of the day. They were, in a way, quite like the Mafia leader John Gotti, who went out of his way for publicity. They thought it enhanced their position as top dogs of the underworld – and they thought they were untouchable.

Everyone knows the Kray brothers if not because of their deeds, then because of those photos. Indeed, it is surprising to find so many good photos of Ron and Reg Kray still around in the archives. Some of the most recent finds appear in this book – check them out and see for yourself how their image changed through the years.

The Krays have become stars – and with their deaths has come a certain immortality. It is the photos that give them this. The Krays are the epitome of the gangster, mixing with the stars and shining brightly for everyone to see. Like their old pals George Raft and Frank Sinatra, they were a part of the show; part of the bill.

20.

October 1967: 'Jack the Hat'

The death of Frances caused a severe deterioration in the psyche of Reg Kray. Ron dominated him more than usual now that Frances was out of his life and the only way that Reg could get through each day was to drink. At first it was to get over the death of his young wife – but then it became a habit. Ron had won the battle of the minds and Frances was out of his brother's life – forever.

But Reg just couldn't forget – and he couldn't forgive. In the main he couldn't forgive himself for not seeing it, for not being there for her, for not understanding her plight as a gangster boss 'moll'. He had put her up on a pedestal and then he had shot her down in flames. It wasn't Ron who caused her death – it was him, Reg Kray, and no one else.

Reg was in a daze. He spent his time boozing and talking about Frances. Everything he did reminded him of her – and every time he took a woman to bed he remembered his wife and he remembered the pain he had caused her. Reg didn't have problems with other women – he didn't care for them, he didn't love them. Frances had been different.

Things went from bad to worse as Reg tried to look for something to take his mind off things – and the only way to do that was to shoot his way out. He had his back against the wall and it was time to move, to show he was the equal of his brother in toughness and brutality. It was time to kill.

The first man he shot was a friend called Frederick. If he was willing to shoot his friends, then what about his enemies? The Firm and other gangs now began to fear Reg more than Ron, who had already achieved his 'button' and therefore had nothing to prove. Everyone knew he was a killer; everyone knew he was a paranoid schizophrenic.

Frederick wasn't exactly expecting to be shot. Some months earlier he had said something not too pleasant about Frances but he was sure that Reg had forgotten all about the incident. Unfortunately for him, Reg Kray had a long memory and he wouldn't let sleeping dogs lie.

One evening, after a huge drinking session, he got one of the Firm to drive him over to Frederick's house. A woman opened the door with a hoard of screaming children in tow. Reg caused a fuss – swearing at the woman and trying to enter the house. The noise attracted the attention of her husband, who approached the top of the stairs leading down to the hallway. As he strolled quietly down the stairs Reg Kray drew a gun. The children hid behind their mother and their mother hid herself in the darkness of the hallway as best she could. Reg raised his gun and fired.

Frederick fell down the stairs. He had been shot in the leg and was in agony as the blood started to flow and melt into the carpet. Reg was dragged away and into the car. No one had expected the shooting, but they knew they had to get Reg away and let him sleep off the effects of the booze. As soon as Reg was tucked away in a safe house, Charlie was called on to pay Frederick a visit.

Charlie drove over to the house expecting the worst, fearing that Frederick was dead. But Frederick was only wounded and Charlie quickly found a friendly doctor who could repair the leg and help Charlie to repair the situation. As they put Frederick back to bed, Charlie stuffed some notes into his hands. 'No talking, no police,' was all he said. It was enough. The police were never informed of the shooting.

Ron heard about his brother's night out and once more applied the pressure. 'You can't kill anyone – you haven't got the bottle!' he would scream.

Reg continued to carry a gun – and he continued to shoot people. But every case was covered up by the Firm and in particular Charlie, who earned himself the nickname 'the Undertaker'. Relationships between the brothers were at their lowest level. Never before had they had to deal with Reg like this: he was now constantly drunk, day and night. The Firm were used to Ron and they had learned how to appease him and to control him. But Reg was different. They were twins, all right, but sometimes they seemed as different as chalk and cheese.

By October of 1967 Ron had decided that they needed to get rid of Leslie Payne. Payne knew too much. He knew their Mafia connections, he knew their crooked games and he knew how they got their money. Ron had totally lost confidence in his one-time loyal business manager.

It was decided the only thing to do was to kill him. Then he couldn't talk to the police, he couldn't tell of their scams and he couldn't embarrass the Krays.

The man he chose for the job was pill-pusher and pill-taker Jack 'The Hat' McVitie. Thirty-eight years old, McVitie was a real villain. He had an unpredictable streak that made him uncontrollable, and he was prone to sadism and masochism. After carrying on with another man's woman once, he had his hands smashed to warn him to 'stay away'. But it didn't help. Only a few short weeks later, with hands still bandaged, he was back on the streets looking for action.

McVitie was feared by women. Once he had thrown a woman from a car speeding along at 40 miles per hour. Her back was broken. She was too scared to talk to the police – she knew McVitie would kill her. She never talked to 'Nipper' Read and she never told the truth about her ordeal. McVitie was an outcast, on the fringe of the London gangs. This, then, was the unlikely man Ron Kray had chosen for the killing of Leslie Payne.

Ron and Reg had a meeting with McVitie. They gave him the money, a down payment of a hundred pounds with another four hundred to follow, after the event – and they gave him a gun. Two weeks later though, the job was still not done and the twins were beginning to worry. When Reg handed over another fifty pounds to McVitie Ron went berserk. Ron was right to be furious, for soon he and his brother became the hunted – and not the hunters.

In late October Jack 'The Hat' turned up at The Regency, shotgun in hand, looking for the twins. 'I'm gonna shoot the bastards!' he screamed. As luck would have it, the twins weren't there that day and Jack walked away, the unused shotgun still in his hands.

On 28 October the whole Kray family were gathered for Violet's birthday bash at a pub in Bethnal Green, when some news on the East End grapevine reached the twins. Jack 'The Hat' McVitie was due any moment at The Regency. Reg left the celebrations at around 11 o'clock and went on the prowl.

At The Regency Reg settled down for the wait, but McVitie never showed. Reg continued to down the drinks and was soon pleasantly intoxicated. With no McVitie to confront, he gave his gun to Tony Barry, the manager of the club. 'Keep this for me.' he told him as he left the club and returned to his mum's party.

Ron decided on urgent action. Immediately he sent Ronnie Hart, their cousin, over to The Regency to get Reggie's gun back. 'Tell Tony Barry to bring it back himself,' he told him. A party was quickly arranged in a flat in nearby Everling Road in Hackney. It was a place they often used, so everyone knew it and no one would be suspicious. Ron then sent Tony and Chris Lambrianou out to find Jack 'The Hat' and bring him to the flat, telling him there were girls and booze galore.

Tony Barry arrived with the gun and then quickly left. He wasn't about to get himself involved in a shooting. Reg now had his gun and was beginning to get his courage in the form of the booze and words of encouragement from his brother. 'Now it's your turn,' he told a bewildered Reg. 'It's time to get your button!'

Jack 'The Hat' McVitie was not difficult to find – and he didn't appear to worry about being invited to a party by members of the Firm. When Tony Lambrianou parked his Ford Zodiac outside the house, McVitie was the first one down the stairs and into the basement flat. Tony and Chris Lambrianou followed close behind. There was no way out for 'The Hat'.

Ron Kray was the first to greet him. 'Fuck off, Jack,' he shouted as McVitie rushed past him and his 'boys' and into the sitting room. 'Where's the girls?' screamed McVitie in response. Suddenly it all became very clear. This was no party and no friendly gathering. This was a set up.

Reg Kray stood face to face with Jack 'The Hat'. They stared intensely at each other, neither saying a word. Ron shouted at Reg to kill him there and then. 'Shoot him!' he screamed. Reg pulled out his .32 revolver and pulled the trigger. Nothing happened. Jack stood there for a moment, not believing what was happening. The members of the Firm also stood in silence. They were used to Ron carving people up, or even killing them. But this was Reg, the businessman of the two – the *sane* one.

Reg tried and tried again. Each pull of the trigger produced a 'click' and nothing happened. Jack 'The Hat' soon realised his predicament. He rushed for the back door, but was stopped by the Firm. He even put his hand through a glass window, trying to get out of that basement flat. There was nowhere to hide.

McVitie shouted his head off as he tried to subdue Reg Kray. But it didn't help.

'Be a man, Jack' said Reg Kray as he pocketed his gun.

'I'm a man, but I don't want to fucking die like one!' he blurted out, hoping for a reprieve. But McVitie knew there was no escape. Reg Kray had already grabbed a kitchen knife and held it up, ready to plunge it into the face of his adversary. The end was nigh.

Reg Kray stabbed McVitie in the face and neck. He did it again and again, until blood poured from the wounds and soaked into the carpet of the sitting room. Jack 'The Hat' McVitie slumped into a heap on the floor – he was dead.

Ron Kray told his 'boys' to leave, they had seen enough. Tony Lambrianou was told dispose of the body. The only one then left at the flat was Albert Donaghue, who was told to get rid of the blood whatever it took. The twins wanted no sign of blood and no sign of a corpse. No body: no crime.

Tony Lambrianou and his brother Chris drove the bloodied remains of McVitie down to Kent, where a friendly fisherman fed the body to the fishes. It was a regular way of getting rid of bodies, along with the pig farm, the incinerator, the funeral parlour and the garden centre. Charlie Kray, the 'Undertaker' was sound asleep at the time, otherwise he most certainly would have been asked to dispose of the body.

At his trial Charlie Kray was accused of disposing of the body of McVitie. He may have been good at getting rid of bodies successfully, but McVitie's was not one of them. When the police eventually got around to searching the flat, they found minute traces of blood under the newly-carpeted floor. Albert Donaghue was no good at cleaning and the link to McVitie was established.

Throughout the first 20 years of his sentence Reg Kray would not admit to the killing of Jack 'The Hat' McVitie. He even tried to get other members of the Firm to take the blame and confess to the killing – but no one did. It was a senseless murder by a man driven almost insane by booze and by the loss of his wife. There was though, in the end, only one man to blame for the killing – Reg Kray himself.

21.

1967-68: The Killing Fields

Did Frances know about the killing of George Cornell by Ron Kray? Did she know that her husband Reg had given the order for the 'Mad Axeman' Frank Mitchell to be killed at the hands of Freddie Foreman and his pals? Did she know what was to come – the killings that Scotland Yard could never prove, but that formed the real reason for the brothers' 30-year sentences? And was this the real reason for her suicide?

There is a farm that has now become a legend, a place that is talked about in many a bar by many an elderly petty crook who all swear blind that they were there. 'I ran the pig farm,' says the little well-dressed fat man. 'We got rid of the bodies for the Firm – the pigs didn't mind where the meat came from.' This man, who I will call 'Willy', is still around and still doing business. Like many of the Krays' pals they were never caught, never prosecuted and never had to pay for their crimes. But Willy knows the truth. He is a man of substance and he has far too much to lose to let his story be made public. His tale is safe with me, though, and I will not be revealing his true identity. I have no wish to join the ghosts of the Kray adversaries who were torn to pieces by first the Firm and then the pigs.

'I can show you the place on the Hertfordshire–Essex border,' said 'Big Al' recently, just before he took the flight to Spain. He had decided that the time had come to tell it straight, to let those skeletons speak at last. 'There's bodies there, all sealed in oil drums and filled with concrete,' he told me. It's no wonder that the garden centre, now on the site, has difficulty planting deep-rooted shrubs and trees here. 'I'll take you there if you like,' he said with a murmur. Somehow, though, it didn't appeal to me. Knowledge is a fine thing, but too much knowledge can sometimes get you killed.

The funeral parlour, Merricks, in Bethnal Green was another favourite location. 'Bodies were piled up two at a time in the coffins,' said Big Al, 'and then carried by the biggest heavies they could muster.' The funeral would take place as usual – none of the mourners ever knew about that extra body in the coffin.

On one occasion the men behind the scenes – the backroom boys of the funeral trade, decided to play a prank on a member of the Firm. The corpse of a petty crook, freshly shot, was tied up in a chair and a book placed in his hands. The darkness of the back room hid the white face of the victim and the crouching prankster behind him. As a Firm member entered the room, he looked around at the coffins. 'Where's the body?' he asked. The corpse raised its hand and pointed. The man looked in the direction of the raised arm – and then back at the seated man. The corpse slid off the seat and onto the floor, a gaping bullet wound in his head. The man ran from the room as the hidden jokers laughed themselves silly.

Al has been living on these stories for years. They're told to young and old alike – in fact to anyone who was bothered to listen. But he is telling them publicly for the first time now that all three Kray brothers are dead. Has he something to gain? I think not, since he isn't sticking around to take the flack and doesn't want anything for the information. Where there's smoke, then there's normally fire.

Question: Where do you hide a stone? *Answer*: On the beach, with all the other stones.

Question: Where do you hide a body? *Answer*: In the funeral parlour, with all the other bodies.

I have also been told of how the Firm used to get into the churchyard before a funeral and put an extra body in the ground. With a coffin planted on top there was little chance of discovery. Ron always used to say, 'If they can't find the body – then they can't prove the crime!'

Tony Lambrianou has admitted that they used incinerators at hospitals to dispose of unwanted human remains and body parts. There is one story that suggests that Ron Kray was the real Hannibal Lector, having eaten a man's liver before it was due to be burned, but this doesn't appear true to character. It is more the stuff of the movies than real life. But once again, who can really say whether it is true or not?

So how many people did they actually kill? Everyone 'in the know' has told me a number; how many they thought Ron and Reg disposed of in total. Their best guesses total well around the 30 mark, one for each year of their sentence.

When Ron shot a youngster he had picked up from the street, after having sex with the lad, it was Charlie who disposed of the body. Ron thought he was stealing money from his wallet, so he casually killed him. Charlie could well have taken it to Merricks for disposal in the usual way – and maybe that is why they called him 'the Undertaker'.

Amongst Kray murder devices found by the police was a crossbow complete with arrows; a briefcase with a cyanide syringe inside; the source of the dynamite used to blow up vehicles; the Mauser 9 mm used to kill Cornell, and a vast array of other weapons – including machine guns. Most of these items are in Scotland Yard's infamous 'Black Museum', but they are not available for public viewing. Just like the files held on the Krays, these items are kept secret and away from any prying eyes.

The killing fields are still there. The bodies still lie in the oil drums and the drums lie under the ground somewhere on the Essex–Hertfordshire border. The doubled-up bodies have never been found. Neither have any of the other Kray victims' corpses. Maybe some day the authorities, or other interested parties, will seek to go where no one has gone before – to the last resting places of the victims of crimes as perpetrated by the Krays and their murder machine.

22.

April 1968: NYC

By the beginning of 1968 the Mafia in New York were busy setting up operations all over Europe. They found it easier to organise Mob business over here and run it themselves. This was common practice, sending their own people over instead of using native henchmen and more unreliable sources, but the UK was the exception rather than the rule. Here the Mafia used local crooks, local gangsters and local knowledge.

Since the Cornell killing in March 1966, though, the Mob were reluctant to use the Krays. Ron was uncontrollable and a loose cannon as far as they were concerned. But Ron wanted back in, he wanted to be a part of the Mob business world-wide – and the only way to impress was to go over to New York and see them up close and personal.

Bond deals were now scarce, although the celebrities still came over from the USA and the Krays did their part in protecting the Mob's clients. Reg wasn't worried but Ron wanted more than the home-spun deals. He would say whatever and do whatever to get to the States.

It was the banker A.B. Cooper who suggested the trip. Reg poured scorn on the idea right from the start. 'We've got criminal records as long as your arm!' he told his brother straight. 'It's fucking useless to try!'

Ron made a cup of tea as they relaxed at Braithwaite House where their parents lived. Mum and dad were staying at Ron's place in the country, The Brooks in Suffolk, so they could talk candidly about the prospects of a trip and sort things out between them.

'Cooper says he can fix it,' said Ron. He sat down and waited for Reg to reply, but his brother was silent. 'He has contacts in Paris. They can arrange it for us,' he continued as he sipped his tea. Reg couldn't be quiet any longer.

'There's no way we can get to America,' he said casually, not wanting an argument, but wanting to make his point. 'They'll never let us in.'

Ron stood up and made for the door. He stopped and looked back at his twin brother.

'Cooper says I can. But it don't matter much.' Ron Kray had victory in sight – and he hated to lose. 'If he can fix it, then okay – but if he can't then I'll have a nice weekend in Paris.' Ron walked to the door. As he grabbed the handle he turned back to face his brother. 'But if I want to go to America then I'll fucking go to America.' He slammed the door behind him.

Over the next few days plans were hurriedly made for the trip. Reg would be staying home. They had been out of the country together before and had regretted every minute of it. Someone had to stay behind – and that man was Reg.

Ron asked his pal Dickie Morgan if he'd like a trip to New York. He said simply 'Why not?' and that was it, the plans were made. Cooper, Ron and Dickie Morgan would take the plane to Paris, from where Cooper would arrange for the necessary visas. It was simple, it was foolproof – and Ron Kray couldn't lose.

Ron made his plans. He would meet with Meyer Lansky and the top bosses of New York and maybe there would be time for a trip to Philadelphia to see Angelo Bruno. George Raft was high on his visiting list too – and there was always Eddie Pucci. One way or another Ron Kray was going to have a great time, no matter what.

The flight to Orly was just the start. Ron was in a good mood – after all he had considered his options well. He had reckoned it out logically. If they couldn't get the visas then they would have a great time in Paris and then go home, but if the visas were a sure thing, as Cooper had suggested, then he would go to New York and meet the Mob. And since no one outside the family knew where he was going, he wouldn't lose face.

It was too late the evening they arrived to visit the US Embassy, so they met a friend of Cooper's for dinner. He was French, but spoke perfect English having lived in the USA for some time. They had a great time talking of criminal deeds past and present.

Back at their hotel, The Frontenac, they retired for the evening – the next day was to be a big one: would they get the visas or not?

The taxi ride to the Embassy was over in a flash and they were all soon inside. Cooper walked straight through the lobby and into the throng as though he owned the place. Ron was impressed. He saw the

ABOVE: Reg and Frances, in happier times, before their marriage in April 1965.

INSET: Reg and Billy Hill – taken at Billy Hill's villa in Tangiers, when Ron and Reg fled the country after the Cornell killing in 1966.

BELOW: Leslie Payne (far left second row) hedged in by Ron (above) and Reg (right). Charlie is in profile (top right). Also present are entertainers the Clarke Brothers (bottom right) and boxer Terry Spinks sits next to Reg.

ABOVE: Reg in Milan.

INSET: Reg with his first scrap car.

BELOW: Reg in the boxing ring –
18 years old and a possible contender.

LEFT: Reg ready for action in the gym above the Double R Club.

BELOW: Ron having a drink with Barbara Windsor.

ABOVE: Ron in New York,
dining with the Mafia.

RIGHT: Reg on the phone –
his favourite photo.

ABOVE: Charlie, Ron and Reg at Billy Hill's flat, in the back room at the bar.

BELOW: Ron and Reg as youngsters.

ABOVE: The Krays, partying. Charlie (second left) is next to Ron; the big Eddie Pucci is holding hands with Shirley Bassey and Reg is in between them.

BELOW: Ron with Frank Sinatra Junior – ready for a quick exit.

RIGHT: Reg with a tribal chief in Enugu, Nigeria.

ABOVE: Ron trying to keep cool in Lagos, Nigeria.

BELOW: Club man Paul Raymond, singer Lita Rosa and Ron Kray.

marines with their bright, shiny swords and buckles and he saw the ease with which Cooper handled people. They were soon standing in front of a door. There was no sign, but according to Cooper it was the visa section.

They straightened their ties and brushed themselves down. Cooper opened the door and they walked right in. There was one woman, sitting at a desk over in the far corner of the room, eating a sandwich. She looked up as they entered.

'Can I help you?' she asked politely.

'We've come for the visas!' Cooper barked back. There was silence for a moment.

'Visas – what visas?' she asked.

'The ones for my friends here,' said Cooper almost losing his cool. 'I phoned from London some days ago – they should be ready by now!' Cooper was pushing his luck. His attitude had changed. He was being aggressive and forceful.

'That's impossible right now,' said the woman. 'You'll have to come back tomorrow,' she told them. She went back to her sandwich.

Cooper stood right in front of her. 'I have explained this before, but if you want I'll do it all over again.' he said, pulling himself together in his 'be kind to the fools' mode. 'My friend here, Mr Kray, has family in New York. If he can't get there in time, then his uncle may die. This will cause the US government much embarrassment and it will cause me much irritation.'

Cooper was quiet for a moment, collecting his thoughts. 'If you would please look through your files, then you will see that this has all been organised in advance – we would like the visas now!'

The woman rose from her seat and moved over to a cabinet. 'What were the names?' she asked.

They were out inside 30 minutes, visas in hand, with New York as their next stop. They made straight for the nearest café to celebrate, laughing and joking about the ordeal with the visas. 'I thought we'd never get them,' said a giggling Dickie Morgan. After a few quick drinks at an outside table, Ron had an idea.

'I have to phone Reg,' he said as he rose and made for a phone at the entrance to the restaurant. It didn't take long to get through and Ron started throwing praise in Cooper's direction.

'It worked a treat,' he told Reg. 'Cooper had it all worked out, as I told you.'

Reg was quiet for a while on the other end of the line. 'I still think it's a trick, Ron. No one can do that without connections – and I mean *real* connections in high places,' he told his brother.

'I know that – I'm no fool. But if I can get to New York then I can handle the rest,' said Ron in a matter-of-fact way. 'But you were right about Cooper,' he said. 'there's more to him than meets the eye.'

Ron Kray rejoined his pals and the party began. In the morning they would be heading for the USA.

The next morning came and they were soon on the flight to New York. 'We are meeting little Joe Kaufman at JFK,' said Cooper as he checked his briefcase and his US dollars. 'He has arranged the hotel and set up meetings with the capos.'

Ron was happy. He knew Joe Kaufman and his wife Marie very well, since they had been over to London many times – they'd even holidayed at one time with Charlie and his wife. 'I want to meet Meyer Lansky too,' said Ron, sipping the champagne. Ron and Dickie Morgan chatted throughout the flight, leaving Cooper to cat-nap. Dickie was an old pal and he knew how to keep Ron's spirits up, not that he needed to now that his dream visit to New York had become a formality.

On landing the three men strode through the immigration building and reception hall. 'Now don't say too much,' said Cooper, looking around him. 'Keep it simple – and only answer the questions. Don't volunteer information!' Cooper was the first in line.

Cooper talked casually with the immigration people, out of ear-shot of Ron and Dickie Morgan. It worked. Soon they were all through and collecting their luggage.

'That was so easy,' said Morgan, as they laughed their way from the building. 'I just can't believe it!'

Cooper looked into Ron's eyes. 'It was easy because it was fixed!' he said in a whisper. 'The Mob have connections everywhere.'

Joe Kaufman was there to pick them up and they were soon on their way into New York. Ron and Dickie Morgan were overjoyed. Kaufman's car was luxury itself and the ride through Manhattan was a dream come true to Ron. Soon they were approaching their destination, The Warwick Hotel.

On the way Kaufman had passed on best regards from Angelo Bruno, Ron's pal and Mob boss of Philadelphia and Atlantic City. Kaufman also told him that he was trying to set up a meeting with the Colombo family. Ron had previously spoken of the urgency of meeting these

Mob people, or 'wiseguys' as they are known. Now he had beaten the system. He was there in New York – and nothing could take that from him. Meeting the Mob would be a bonus.

Kaufman phoned Ron the following morning at The Warwick. He told him that he had managed to set up a meeting with Frank Ileano, a lieutenant in the Colombo family, at a house in President Street, near Prospect Park in Brooklyn. Little Joe Kaufman arrived on time and they sped off in the direction of Prospect Park, across the Brooklyn Bridge. Those famous places that Ron had only seen in the movies were now coming alive in front of his very eyes.

Ron and Joe Kaufman were alone in the car. Morgan had been given some readies and told to go and shop for souvenirs and Cooper, the banker, was nowhere to be seen. He had just told Ron that he had work to do – and that was that.

They arrived safely in President Street and found the house. It was well known to Joe Kaufman – he had been there before. Ron was introduced to the man on the door, 'Crazy' Joe Gallo.

Once seated inside, 'Crazy' Joe introduced his brothers Al and Larry and they settled down to wait for the Colombo lieutenant – a most respected wiseguy. It didn't take long.

Into the room sprang Frank 'Punchy' Ileano, hands outstretched in welcome. Ron had been cleared by Angelo Bruno as a precaution, and now they were free to talk. The introductions over they got down to business.

'I think there is something you should know' said Frank Ileano in a serious voice. 'You are being tailed by the FBI.'

Ron couldn't believe it. 'But no one knows I'm here!' he said.

The Colombo man looked him in the eyes. 'Where's Cooper?' he asked solemnly. Ron couldn't answer. But the facts were plain to see.

'So. What do we do now?' asked Ron. He had to do something to fill in the seven days on his visa – and anything was better than nothing.

Frank Ileano made some phone calls and set up some meetings for Ron. He couldn't get to see Meyer Lansky or any of the other big bosses of New York, but there would be plenty to do and many old friends to see. The rest of Ron Kray's time in New York City was spent as a tourist, seeing the sights and meeting old pals – wining and dining the night away. He loved it.

Cooper showed up later in the week. ('He's stuttering more than ever,' said Dickie Morgan. This was a sure sign that he was under pressure.) Ron didn't care. He had won the game and everyone knew it.

They even knew it back in London. One evening Ron phoned home. Reg told him with glee: 'Nipper's looking everywhere for you, chasing his tail all over London.' Ron and Reg had a good belly laugh at Read's expense. 'He just doesn't know where you are!' said Reg as he laughed himself silly.

Ron thought for a moment. 'Then someone should tell him,' he said casually. Reg decided it would really be sticking two fingers up at Scotland Yard. (When the news of Ron's whereabouts reached Nipper Read, he was furious.)

Ron told Reg of meeting the boxers Tony Zale and Rocky Graziano and he told him all about the Gallo brothers. He talked of the sights and he talked of the welcome he had received from the Colombo family. The news was good – there would be more business and more bonds and he also mentioned the possibility of getting involved in drugs.

'I'm looking forward to getting home,' he told his twin before he hung up the phone.

The trip back was quiet. Cooper sat by himself, not saying a word to Ron or Dickie Morgan. Morgan had bought the presents, as instructed – so there would be enough for everyone when they got back to the UK. Ron sat and thought. Reg had been right all along – Cooper was an unknown entity and therefore a man to fear. Ron made up his mind there and then to get rid of him.

23.

April 1968: The Net

Ron and Reg Kray found themselves in a dominant position towards the end of 1967 and the start of the New Year 1968. Ron had already shot and killed George Cornell and Reg had stabbed McVitie to death. The twins ruled London and after the McCowan case (where all three Kray brothers stood trial at The Old Bailey, on charges of running protection – they were acquitted) they were feeling cocksure. They were free to take over London, the whole country – even the world.

The police had tried on numerous occasions to stop their rise among the criminal fraternity, but without success. One attempt after another had failed – their options were being narrowed and their methods scrutinised by the press. No matter what they did now, the Krays could always shout 'Harassment!' There would always be a newspaper to take up their cause – they were headline material.

The Krays knew that if they could keep control over events and keep their Firm under the cosh, then their future looked secure. Nothing had got out about the Cornell killing – and McVitie had disappeared, there wasn't even a body. No news was good news to the Krays.

In 1967, however, Scotland Yard decided on a change of tactics – they moved things up a gear and put Leonard 'Nipper' Read in charge of the case. The plan was simple – to take the Krays out of circulation once and for all.

Read decided to compile a special team. He wanted fresh faces, specialists from outside where there could be no hint of corruption or coercion. He even wanted somewhere else to work from, away from Scotland Yard and from prying eyes. He chose Tintagel House, a block of government offices on the south bank of the River Thames. It was isolated and protected. Read wanted his plans secure, his information secret, his intentions private. There was to be only the most essential contact with head office at Scotland Yard. Read was on his own.

Read knew the Krays. He had even had a drink with them when invited to attend the celebrations at the Hideaway Club after the McCowan affair, shortly before they changed the name to El Morocco, in honour of Billy Hill. But the newspapers were there too and a photographer had taken a photo of Read having a quiet and all too friendly chat with his adversaries Ron and Reg. He was immediately taken off the case.

Scotland Yard had not had much luck with their investigations of the Krays thus far. First there was the mishap with the Boothby case, where they had to shelve information gathered so painstakingly over several years, when the Yard issued a statement saying that the Krays were not, in fact, under investigation. And then there was this photo of Read, their most gifted detective, drinking openly in public with enemy number one.

But there was no other man capable of handling the case. Read was the best they had, so Scotland Yard gave him complete control. Read now began the long and arduous task of sifting through all the known information about the twins. Charlie Kray didn't concern him at all. Read knew that Charlie was a hanger-on, a part of the structure but no leader of it. The true leaders were Ron and Reg – and he wanted them, no matter what the cost.

Progress was slow for Read and his team. As soon as they started to interview some suspects and witnesses, the news got back to Ronnie and Reggie. The twins knew Read was on their case. But as long as everyone remained silent, there would be nothing the police could do about them. The silence would see them through.

Nipper Read needed a break and it came in the unlikely form of Leslie Payne. Payne knew everything about the Krays. He knew all about their protection rackets, their long-firm frauds and their dealings with the Mafia. Payne had been Ron Kray's business manager and he had at one time complete control over their business arrangements, their accounts and their fortunes. Payne was deeply involved with the Krays – so why would he spill the beans?

The reason was simple. He knew Ron and Reg wanted him dead. He knew too much. They had even paid McVitie to kill him. Payne knew his days with the Krays were well and truly over, now he needed a different kind of protection. And so, in December of 1967, he made a complete 200-page statement to Nipper Read.

Payne was kept at a Marylebone hotel for a period of almost three weeks. Read wanted time to drag everything out of the petrified Leslie Payne, who sweated his way through interrogation after interrogation by Read's team. Eventually they managed to get a full dossier on the Krays – from their rackets to their Mafia dealings. Payne decided that there was only one way to get out of trouble – to tell the whole story to Read and hope that the Krays could be put away for good.

But with all this new information now secured, Read had to prove whether or not it was correct. And could it be used in a court of law? Just knowing that something is right, is not necessarily enough. Read issued orders for his team to investigate. They were told to tell everyone that their statements would not be used unless the Krays were under arrest. He knew that the twins would intimidate the witnesses – so secrecy was paramount. Even Scotland Yard were not told of the move.

Despite all the secrecy about the operations underway at Tintagel House, the twins got to hear that Read was getting close. They knew that Payne had told his sordid tale in the hope of getting amnesty, and they knew that witnesses would be questioned. But Ron and Reg Kray still didn't worry. They had showed that they could beat Scotland Yard time and time again, so why be scared of this little copper with his private army of investigators?

Ron even went out and bought a couple of pythons – one he named Gerrard, after the detective in charge of the McCowan case, and the other he named Nipper. Nothing could scare the twins. One day, though, one of these snakes escaped and the other had to be given back to its previous owner – they were too troublesome for the brothers. Was this a bad omen for the twins?

Ron Kray had always said that Nipper Read was the one to fear. He called him a 'cunning little bastard', but secretly he could see something about the dapper detective that made his heart beat faster, and that caused him nightmares. Read was a supreme organiser. He knew the game and he knew the score. He had proved this many times throughout his career, even organising police for the 1966 football World Cup. But Read's ambitions demanded more – he wanted to join the murder squad and to get responsibility for catching the big boys of English crime.

Capturing the Krays was Read's first major assignment. At only five feet seven inches, Read was small by normal police standards, but what he lacked in height he made up for in energy and enthusiasm. An ex-boxer, originally from the Midlands, Read was a well-spoken, quiet man with a perpetual slight smile on his ruddy face. Read was a bit of a loner, so being in charge of a secret operation suited him. Even his family were not told of his new job at Scotland Yard.

But Read knew that catching the Krays would not be easy. They were old adversaries and old-style crooks, but the Mafia were now well and truly in the picture and these old dogs could learn new tricks.

It was the boss of Scotland Yard's Murder Squad that helped Read set up his new organisation at Tintagel House. John du Rose was a shrewd old-time cop, known as 'One day Johnnie' because of the speed of his work. But even du Rose knew that it would take time and guile to catch the Krays. He encouraged Read to use teams of detectives, similar to the ones du Rose had himself used in catching the Great Train Robbers. Gradually Nipper Read gathered around him a core of experienced detectives, all with one goal in mind – to catch the Krays and to get them convicted.

Nipper Read was in charge at Tintagel House and organised all the leg work, but it was du Rose who made up the game plan. The anonymity of the building, typical of civil service life, was ideal for Read. He and his team could come and go at will – no prying eyes of the media, no chance of the Firm spotting them south of the river, no spies to report on their efforts. Read reported directly to Peter Brodie, Assistant Commissioner, who in turn passed all information on to du Rose.

Brodie and du Rose went to enormous lengths to conceal the true work of the team at Tintagel House. Bulletins were put up at Scotland Yard telling of this new division supposedly dealing with 'corruption', and Nipper Read was ostensibly assigned a murder in Ireland, to keep his name out of the UK press. But things were still difficult for the little man, who knew that the Kray case could be his last at the Murder Squad, so he got du Rose to make him a deal. If he hadn't finished in three months, then he could be transferred to another case, away from the Krays. This was Read's get-out clause.

Organisation at Tintagel House was strict; nothing was left to chance. Everyone was told to be prepared, to get tough, to play by Read's rules. Routines were varied. His team members were told to go home at irregular times, to park their cars in a secure compound and to have shooting practice on a regular basis. They were up against the best. They had to be better than the best.

Nipper Read gradually developed an idea, one that he knew would work. To Read it was all quite simple, if they couldn't catch the Krays, then the Krays would have to get themselves caught. Surely, he pondered, with so many crimes over so many years there must be an awful lot of people out there with knowledge of the Krays and their ways. Someone must surely talk sooner or later. It was his job to make sure it was sooner rather than later. Over only a few short weeks Read had gathered an index of names – one of these would lead him to the Krays.

Scotland Yard supplied the legal assistance needed for his plan to work, and Read had meetings at Scotland Yard to find out exactly what the law required. He had to talk and deal with criminals, so the legality of things must be in order. After protracted discussions they agreed that whatever Read wanted to do was all right with the Yard – just get the Krays!

Read's next big break eventually came after Ron Kray returned from the USA in the spring of 1968. As a way of helping out the US Mafia and to really get them to appreciate the Krays, A.B. Cooper suggested doing the Mafia a favour. And he knew just the right thing. A well-known Las Vegas gambler and club owner, now in London and staying at the London Hilton, had recently had a run-in with the Mob in New York. Killing him would be a feather in their cap – it would save the Mob the expense of killing him themselves.

Ron hired someone to follow the man when he went for his early morning run around Hyde Park. But the assassin never got his chance – and the gambler flew off, away from London and away from the Krays. Ron Kray was furious, but they hadn't told the Mob what they were up to, so Ron simply asked Cooper for another target.

Cooper then came up with the idea of getting rid of a Maltese club owner in London. According to Cooper the man, George Caruana, was an enemy of the Mob so killing him would make the Mafia indebted to the Krays. Ron and Reg thought about it for a moment or two. They agreed.

The twins were still after yet more Mafia business – bonds, or protection of the Mob's clubs in London. They didn't really care what it was, but they wanted it all for themselves. With the Richardsons and the Nash brothers out of the way, they felt that the business was naturally theirs. They had a right to it – and the Mob had to deal with them, no one else.

A killing like this, thought the twins, would show the Mob that they were really getting down to business – and setting up Murder Incorporated, as had been suggested in New York. Their first idea was to bomb Caruana's car. Cooper even suggested a man for the job, a bespectacled youngster by the name of Paul Elvey, and dispatched him to Glasgow to fetch the dynamite. Ron had thought of gelignite, which they'd used in Chicago during the time of Al Capone, but Cooper told him he could get dynamite in Glasgow and it was much safer to use. Ron and Reg had a meeting with Cooper and Elvey in a Bethnal Green pub, where they discussed further killings.

'No problem,' said the young man, slowly sipping his beer.

Elvey made it to Glasgow, but he was arrested when he boarded the flight returning to London and the police found the four sticks of dynamite in his hand luggage.

Under questioning he told the police that his contact man was A.B. Cooper and that he worked for some gangsters down south – the Krays. Nipper Read was overjoyed. He soon had the man in for interrogation himself. The Kray connection was clear and the name of the banker A.B. Cooper was already on Read's list of possible sources of information. Cooper was brought to see Read at Tintagel House.

Cooper surprised Nipper Read by telling him that he had already done a deal with Scotland Yard and had in fact worked for Read's boss du Rose – and also that he was trying to implicate the Krays in an attempted murder plot. Cooper also told Read that he worked for the FBI. Read was furious when his boss at Scotland Yard confirmed the deal struck with Cooper. The good news, though, was that Cooper was now working for Scotland Yard. But somehow Nipper Read was suspicious of the American. He was too quick to answer; too quick to give away the deal with du Rose. Was he friend or foe? Read decided to find out.

Read and Cooper set a trap for the Krays. The deal on the Caruana killing obviously couldn't go ahead. They would have to make up a story to cover their backs. Read persuaded Cooper to fake illness and move into a hospital, pretending to be suffering from an ulcer, all bandaged up with hidden microphones. The plan was to make the Krays talk and record it.

Cooper phoned Ron from his hospital bed. He told him that he was not well – and that he wanted to see him urgently. Ron heard what he said, but he didn't like how he said it. He didn't like it when Cooper stammered. It normally meant that he was lying, so he sent someone else, a member of the Firm. He was told to say nothing, just to hear what Cooper had to say and report back to the twins. The man did his job and Read was left with egg on his face. Read and his deputy, Frank Cater, had been in the adjoining room, waiting for a signal. But the signal never came. The trap, so carefully laid, had failed.

The whole operation was a nightmare for Nipper Read. Now the twins were wise to his games and he would have to be a little more adept in future. Using a man like Cooper was no easy task either. Was he really an FBI agent? What was the deal he had made with du Rose? Would he really have killed Caruana?

The main problem for Read was that Ron Kray appeared to have learned from the Mob in New York. He was now using out-of-towners to do his dirty work, as advised by Frank Ileano. Using the old Mafia trick of putting as many people as possible between the man giving the order and the man doing the killing, was a way of protecting the king-pin, the boss, or the capo. Ron had already done his killing, Read was sure of that.

Soon it was April and Read still didn't have any real information on the death of George Cornell. He didn't know what had happened to McVitie and to Mitchell – and he couldn't establish a connection between the Krays and the publican Freddie Foreman. Rumours abounded, but Read needed hard evidence – proof of the killings. Other members of the Firm had now disappeared. Jack Frost, who sometimes drove for Ron, was no longer around and their old pal 'Mad Teddy' Smith was gone. Were they being killed, one by one? Or were the rats deserting the sinking ship?

24.

May 1968: Gotcha!

Nipper Read had two trump cards – but he wanted more. Payne had already made his statement giving names and addresses of everyone he had known during his time with the Krays, and now it was the turn of the stuttering American banker A.B. Cooper.

When Elvey had been arrested carrying the dynamite, no one knew the full extent of his involvement with Cooper. But on checking the youngster's flat in London the police found a variety of killing machines. They found a suitcase with a hypodermic needle carrying cyanide and they discovered a professional modern crossbow capable of killing at long distances. They could not understand how such an apparently simple-minded person could be so ingenious. The fact was that he wasn't ingenious at all – all the equipment had been supplied by Cooper.

Cooper and Read didn't get on well. From the outset Cooper played Read off against du Rose, the FBI off against the US Treasury department, the Krays off against the US Mafia and everyone else off against whoever else happened to be around. Read was wise to his game. He didn't trust the man an inch.

Read wanted to charge him for three attempted murders – those using the cyanide briefcase, the crossbow and the dynamite. But du Rose came to the American's rescue. He told Read that Cooper had been an informant for over two years and that no charges were to be proferred. Read was stopped dead in his tracks, just when he thought he could get the dirt on the Krays and prove their involvement in murder.

Cooper told Read that his employment with the US Treasury Department had started some time earlier when he had been caught smuggling gold. He was told he could do one of two things: either serve time for smuggling or become an *agent provocateur* and assist the US Treasury team in Paris. Cooper had agreed to help them. He had already laundered bonds for the Krays – bonds supplied by the US Mafia, so he had just the connections that the US Treasury Department needed. They too were interested in the Krays, since their names had come up during Mafia investigations back in the USA.

Gradually the whole story came out. Just how did Cooper supply Ron Kray with a passport to the USA? Answer: He arranged it with the team in Paris, working out of the US Embassy building. How did he convince Ron that he really had connections? Answer: He had actor friends play crooks, telling of past deals and of past crimes. How did he pay for the killing equipment – the cyanide suitcase, the crossbow, the dynamite? Answer: The US Treasury Department paid for it all.

Cooper even had to explain how he had managed to get machine guns and other firearms for the twins. The gun that didn't kill McVitie, he told them – that was one of his. The gun that didn't kill Dixon – that too was one of his. He went on to tell Read almost everything he knew about the Krays, but he said he didn't know where the bodies were buried, he hadn't witnessed any killings and he did all he did under orders from the US government.

'They wanted to establish the connection between the Mob in New York and the Krays in London,' he told Read. 'We had planned on meeting Meyer Lansky, the people from Vegas and some of the top New York families,' he told him, 'but Ron Kray was too hot. No one would come near him!'

Everything, he told the policeman, was done to gain the confidence of the twins and the US Treasury had given him scope for what he did – all went according to plan, and all according to orders. He was doing a dirty job the best way he knew how. Du Rose believed him. Read didn't.

After some eight months of investigations Read had now amassed a huge amount of information on the twins, but still no witness testimonies. They had all left him in the dark. Even his own boss had been playing a double game. Of all the goings on, all the guns and the deals – no information had been passed on to Read and his team at Tintagel House. They had to find it all out the hard way.

Read's only success at this time came during a visit by little Joe Kaufman, the American from New York who knew the US Mafia well and had helped with laundering the stolen bearer bonds. He arrived unexpectedly in London and went to see Cooper at the nursing home. Read taped their entire conversation. Here was another list of names, another crook who could spill the beans on the Krays. Kaufman was most explicit about the deals. He talked openly and freely.

Now, after nine months of investigation, Nipper Read knew a lot about the Krays and their criminal activities. But he still needed proof. Du Rose wanted action; Read wanted more time. In the end it was du Rose who got his way by telling Read to take the Krays in for questioning. At a hastily arranged meeting at Scotland Yard, du Rose told Read to do something, or hand it all over to another detective. Read had no choice if he wanted his career to take off – he had to arrest the Krays.

'We know who to talk to,' Read told his boss. 'We know what happened and we know where it happened, but we still need statements from witnesses.' Superintendent Harry Mooney, present at the meeting, told Read that he was sure he could get the barmaid at The Blind Beggar to talk as long as the twins were safe behind bars. But it was a huge gamble. In the end he had no choice. For Nipper Read, one of Scotland Yard's best detectives, it was showdown time.

Read gathered his team together at Tintagel House on the evening of 8 May 1968. Superintendent Donald Adams arrived early, along with Harry Mooney. Frank Cater was there too – and John du Rose drove over from Scotland Yard. Gradually some 60 police officers gathered at the inauspicious buildings on the south bank with police cars and walkie-talkies. They were prepared for the long haul, but only Read's inner circle knew their real task.

No phone calls were allowed; no contact with anyone, anywhere. Sandwiches were brought in so that no one had to go out for drinks or meals.

Du Rose announced that they were there to arrest the Kray brothers, all three of them. The operation would commence at dawn, on a given signal. 'It must be timed and you must be ready,' he told them. There were in all 26 names on the police's list. They would all have to be arrested simultaneously and the police officers present were told to expect violence.

'There are 24 different addresses to be raided,' said Read. 'The Krays and their gang have been under observation since early morning. At the moment the twins are in a club in the West End. If all goes well, we'll strike at 6 a.m. – they'll be fast asleep, we'll be fast and awake!'

Read distributed photographs to his team of raiders. They all had to be taken into custody, no one must get away. When someone asked Read who would be arresting the twins themselves, he answered in a characteristically modest way.

'Me!'

That evening the twins were entertaining Joe Kaufman, who was still unaware of all the problems he had caused. They were drinking in The Old Horns pub, just off Bethnal Green Road. Kaufman was telling them about Cooper and that failed hospital trick and he brought good news from the USA. 'More bonds are on the way,' he told them. Ron and Reg had a good drink and a good laugh. So the business was starting up again – that meant more money.

But somehow Reg was a little worried. He had noticed a police presence around his offices in the West End. This was not normal. And then there was the worrying lack of information concerning that 'little bastard' from Scotland Yard. They hadn't heard anything of Nipper Read for some time – and no news certainly wasn't good news. Ron laughed it all off – he couldn't care about Read, he was only after a good time with his American pal. Soon they gathered up members of the Firm and headed off to The Astor Club, in the West End.

There was nothing strange about that evening and nothing strange about the other guests at the club. Still, Reg was not in a good frame of mind. When bulbs flashed from a multitude of cameras, Ron took it all in his stride. But Reg took offence and lashed out at one of the photographers. Ron had to calm him down (a rarity in itself), but still Reg was worried. There was something *wrong*, but he just couldn't see it. Ron and Reg, after an evening on the booze, went home to No. 12, Braithwaite House, Bunhill Row. They were high as kites, drunk as lords, pissed as newts.

Simultaneously across the East End, Read's squad swooped. At exactly 6 a.m. they raided the assigned addresses. Nipper Read ordered the door of the Krays' flat to be broken down as they rushed in to find Ron in bed with a young boy. Ron stared at the armed police officers. 'I'd be careful with those,' he told them, looking at the guns. 'They may go off!' He was dragged out of bed and searched. Then the armed policemen searched the flat to look for firearms, knives – anything that could help their case. They found nothing.

Reg too was dragged from his bed and the clutches of a blonde beauty. He was still drunk and had slept for only one hour. At first they didn't even let Reg dress. The janitor appeared complaining about the noise and they knew that it was time to go. After a quick search of the flat the police left with their prize prisoners in tow. Nipper Read took both of the Kray twins to Scotland Yard, where they were officially arrested and cautioned.

That same Wednesday they also arrested Charlie Kray. He was asleep in bed with his wife Dolly, even though he had already planned to leave and set up home with his new flame, Diana Ward. Diana couldn't come down to London, because one of her children was ill. Charlie's marriage was over. Dolly had, in fact, met another man, George Ince, and the affair had upset the twins so much that they had given Charlie a warning: 'You sort it out, or we'll sort it out!'

The police didn't care about Charlie's matrimonial status though when they broke down the door. Charlie had tentatively opened it, still on the safety chain, but the police broke it down. Charlie was almost speechless. 'What's going on?' he demanded as they began to search the house.

Charlie was ushered into one of the downstairs rooms and made to sit down. Another man took the phone off the hook. They weren't dressed as ordinary police. They were obviously not from the 'Met'. This was a special squad and it must be serious. Suddenly Dolly and the kids Nancy and Gary appeared at the door, wondering what the hell was going on. Charlie didn't have long to wait.

One of the policemen spoke: 'You are being arrested on charges of conspiracy to defraud.' Charlie looked at the man, open-mouthed. He continued by saying that anything Charlie said would be taken down and could be used in evidence against him. Charlie was not too worried at this point, he had been through this before and they had always got away with it.

Once dressed Charlie washed and shaved – he even had time for a cup of tea. Dolly chatted with them during this drawn-out process, but eventually the time came for them to leave. One of the policemen came over to Charlie with a pair of handcuffs.

'Are you joking?' asked Charlie.

He wasn't. The officer tried to put the handcuffs on the heavy wrists of Charlie Kray. Charlie had been a good boxer, fit and heavier than the twins. He was no small man and the handcuffs caught his flesh as the policeman tried to get them on him. At last someone told him to stop and he pocketed the cuffs.

Charlie told Dolly not to worry as they dragged him away. He was thrown into the back seat of the police car, officers either side holding onto his arms, and they drove off. The nightmare had begun.

Of the 26 intended arrests the police had managed to capture 24.

On the drive Charlie started to think. Why had they broken down the door if they were only taking him in on suspicion of fraud? And where were they going? Charlie tried to find out as they drove past Bow Street and headed for the West End. It didn't look good. They made straight for West End Police Station in Savile Row.

It was chaos there. Charlie saw some familiar faces as he waited in a secure waiting room, somewhere towards the rear of the building. This was no ordinary arrest. Something was going on and Charlie didn't like it one bit. Suddenly a uniformed policeman appeared and told Charlie he was to be charged with fraud, over stolen bearer bonds. Charlie asked if he could phone his solicitor, but his request was refused. By 8 a.m. Charlie Kray was sitting alone in a cell — with only his thoughts for company.

Read was now a busy man. With the twins behind bars, surely someone would talk? The evidence gathered so far was good, but Read knew that a conviction was by no means a certainty. Read had to show that the witnesses to the crimes had nothing to fear. And that meant keeping the Krays and their Firm behind bars for some considerable time. In the McCowan case Read only managed to put the Krays on remand for two months and that was not long enough for people to start talking. He knew that this time they were in for the long haul alright — six months at least, maybe longer.

Nipper Read was taking no chances with the Krays. First he had them taken over to Bow Street, where they were formally charged — with everything from petty larceny to conspiracy. The police were keeping the books open though, giving themselves time to establish the truth about the Krays and get them for murder.

During interviewing Read took a walk around the room. The Krays were being questioned for identity purposes. When Ron saw Read he turned to talk to him. 'Any chance of bail, Nipper?' he asked.

'I don't think so, Ronnie,' said the little detective.

The Krays and their Firm were transferred to Brixton Gaol. They had recently built a new special-housing unit there, for terrorists and the like. It was just the place for the Krays and their gang. The keys were electronically controlled, the doors were solid and the luxuries of life were nowhere to be seen. Soon, though, the twins managed to find a couple of guards they could bribe for information. Before long they knew exactly what was going on – and who was doing the talking.

The only two men who escaped that morning of 9 May, were Ian Barrie and the Krays' cousin Ronnie Hart. But these two were also soon picked up by the police. Without the Krays their days as top dogs were over – and they knew it. Hart was arrested in a hideaway caravan and Barrie was taken into custody after getting drunk in an East End pub.

Members of the Firm already in custody were starting to talk. John Dickson, Connie Whitehead, Ron Bender and the Lambrianou brothers were all forced to make statements. Some were more willing than others. In the end the only ones not to rat on the Krays were Ian Barrie and Tony Lambrianou. But not talking meant certain imprisonment.

The preliminary hearing was set for July, but the police had a few tricks they wanted to play on the Krays first. At Bow Street they got all three brothers, together with the members of the Firm, into one big room. The guards were taken away and one of the doors was left open. Charlie looked at the open door, dreaming of freedom. But Reg could see the trap. Ron even saw the funny side of things. 'Sorry for wasting your time, Nipper,' he shouted out. 'You must think we're silly!' Read walked in with a wry smile on his face. The twins were wise to these games, they had been playing them all their lives and they weren't going to get caught that way. Even at this stage they thought they could get away with it. The twins had even started to do deals with members of the Firm about who did what. 'We'll take care of your family if you say you did for Cornell,' and 'You take the rap – and we'll see you're all right.' No one took them up on them.

They all settled into the routine life at Brixton Gaol. Charlie and the twins got together every day in the small exercise yard at Brixton to talk about developments. Ron and Reg were convinced that no witness would talk about the killings. Charlie had nothing to fear anyway, he wasn't even there. They cheered themselves up as they took their half-hour stroll around the yard, but Charlie wasn't pleased about being put in the same league as the twins. He hadn't killed anyone, he hadn't witnessed any killing, he hadn't been involved in any way. But he was beginning to worry – to get scared.

What really worried Charlie was the fact that Reg was not willing to take the blame for the McVitie killing. If Reg was not willing to tell the story as it was, then who would believe that Charlie had no involvement in the crime? Ron and Reg were planning their escape by trying to get others to take the blame. So how much blame was Charlie expected to take?

Days dragged by. There were meetings with solicitors, trips to Bow Street and back and visits from the family. Violet and old man Charlie Kray came to visit, so too did Dolly and the kids. Violet brought them meals every day and sometimes she even managed to get them a bottle of wine. Things for the Krays went on very much as usual. They had visits by pals on the outside and their protection money was still being collected. The general feeling in the East End was that the Krays would survive the ordeal – and come out on top, as usual.

Nipper Read and Fred Gerrard also came to Brixton Gaol. They tried to scare the twins, but that tactic soon went out the window. They concentrated instead on members of the Firm and that was when they started to get successful. One of the best talkers was Albert Donaghue, who made a complete statement about the killing of Frank Mitchell, the 'Mad Axeman'. He put it all down to the twins and he even told them the name of the leader of the gang who did the shooting – Freddie Foreman.

At the preliminary hearing at Old Street Magistrates Court, on 6 July 1968, things started to fall apart for the Krays. They had asked that all press restrictions be lifted, to generate as much publicity as possible. 'We want the world to see the diabolical liberties the law's been taking,' said Reg. The twins were scathing about the police and their actions and they were enjoying the limelight once again. The press were having a great time too. They had the front-page story, all about one of the biggest trials in history – and they gleaned every sordid detail with glee.

The man in charge of proceedings was the Metropolitan Chief Magistrate, Frank Milton, and it was his job to ascertain whether or not there were charges to be faced in a superior court. But the circumstances of the hearing were not what he desired. It became a farce, with armed police surrounding the building, the press juggling for position to hear the bloody details of the killings and trying to catch the name of a celebrity or two. Witnesses were under police guard and kept at secret locations around London – even the paperwork was hidden away under lock and key.

Nipper Read attended the hearing, a wry smile on his face. He was sure and convincing – and the twins knew then they were in for trouble. But even they could not have imagined what was to happen next – and how their bandwagon would go one way from then: downhill.

Bill Exley had been a boxer. He was also a thief and a man who had been with the Krays for a long time and he had actually guarded Fort Vallance after the Cornell and Mitchell killings. When he took the stand the whole courtroom went quiet.

The court was told that the witness was frail and suffering from a heart condition, so a chair was placed in the witness box. Exley's appearance confirmed that statement and he looked almost like a living corpse. He told his tale and everyone listened. It was not what they expected. He was telling the truth. He told the court that he had run the long-firm frauds for the twins. He also said he wanted to clear his soul from the burden of the crimes the twins had committed. His frail appearance, his quiet voice, his defeated manner all spelt certain doom for Ron and Reg Kray. But the police weren't finished yet.

Next came the barmaid from The Blind Beggar. Harry Mooney had questioned her at Tintagel House and on promises of protection, she told all – how Ron Kray came in and shot George Cornell, how she was threatened by Freddie Foreman, and all about her fears for her life.

The preliminary hearings over, the twins had some five months to ponder their position – and the police had five months to get the evidence they needed for a conviction. Read wanted all the time he could get. The Krays wanted out.

25.

January 1969: The Trial

The trial opened in number one court at The Old Bailey on 7 January 1969. Ronnie and Reggie Kray were both charged with murder and with being an accessory to murder. Interest in the trial was intense. Seats were even selling on the black market at five pounds a go – something that delighted the twins. Even when it looked bad, the twins still managed to keep their sense of humour, especially Ron who kept on joking and shouting his head off at any opportune moment; always the showman.

By now the twins were certain of their fate. The preliminary hearing had shown that former pals and allies had turned against them. Now, several months later, they were sure that there would be an endless queue waiting to bare all in the witness box. They were resigned to the fact that they would be spending a long time in jail.

Things started slowly. A cage had been erected to house the Krays and their cohorts, but two men were missing. Scotch Jack Dickson and the Krays' cousin Ronnie Hart had turned State's evidence and would be appearing for the prosecution. Nipper had really done his homework – the fate of the Krays was sealed.

Charges were read aloud in court. Ron and Reg were both charged with double murder – of Cornell and McVitie. Charlie was accused of helping to get rid of McVitie's body, together with Freddie Foreman – and the others were implicated in a mish-mash of charges.

Mr Melford Stevenson, the judge for the trial, was solemn throughout, living up to his reputation as a hard but fair man. Like the prosecutor, Mr Kenneth Jones QC, he kept to the facts, the truth – the hard evidence. But at times these men would delve into the realms of the theatrical, to lighten the proceedings and to bring home a point. From day one, the trial was as entertaining as the best of television or theatre. It was the best show in town.

'Gentlemen of the jury,' the prosecutor announced, 'think for a moment of the horrifying effrontery, the terrifying effrontery of this deed. Two men walk into a public house and there, in cold blood, kill another human being.' The room was held in stunned silence.

'I will bring before you the barmaid and she will tell you that she recognises the killer of George Cornell!'

Elements of the cross-examination were a little farcical. John Platt-Mills QC represented Ronnie and Paul Wrightson QC represented Reggie. Try as they could to attack the witnesses, it seemed rather self-evident that they were telling the truth. It was all backed up with statements and witness testimonies. They could not refute the testimonies, they could really only condemn those members of the Firm making the statements. 'So you are saying this to save your own skin?' they would say. But there was no master-plan, no scheme of events for them to hold on to. Day by day the prosecution piled on the statements and the pressure. Day by day a long sentence seemed assured.

Charlie's barrister was Desmond Vowden. He reassured Charlie Kray that there was nothing to worry about. He felt they had a good case against the charges of involvement in the Mitchell killing – and he thought he could prove that Charlie was nowhere to be seen when McVitie was knifed to death. But as the witnesses took to the witness box, Charlie knew that his days were numbered. Ronnie Hart was not telling the truth, neither was Scotch Jack.

The film star Charlton Heston made an appearance in the courtroom one day and other celebrities turned up to see their so-called pals. But Judy Garland couldn't make it, so she sent them a telegram wishing them good luck.

It became clear right from the outset that the majority of the Firm had deserted them. Ronnie Hart was the principal prosecution witness and along with John Dickson, he had thrown in his lot with the police – to get away with it, to stay out of jail free. Altogether some 28 criminals gave their evidence against the twins.

Ron and Reg Kray decided that the only option was to go down fighting, so they tried as best they could to add their own personalities to the proceedings. They both appeared in the dock immaculate as usual. They both refuted the witness testimonies. They both denied murder. They both admitted nothing. Ron even went on to say that he had never been in The Blind Beggar – and that he and Cornell were old friends. But throughout their testimony the court could see their demeanour, their hatred of the law, their lack of respect for the proceedings.

Only once did Reg lose his cool, when the prosecution brought up the death of his wife Frances. 'The police are scum,' he shouted.

Ronnie too only lapsed once, when he shouted at the prosecuting counsel: 'You fat slob!'

But the press were disappointed. There were no juicy names thrown around the courtroom, no secrets revealed about the rich and famous or the celebrities of the time. Ron and Reg Kray were not talking about their influential friends – they never would. 'We never inform,' said Ronnie. 'We believe we're better than the rats who deserted our ship.'

Of all those who testified, only three men refused to talk. Ian Barrie would neither confirm nor deny any involvement, nor would Freddie Foreman. Charlie Kray simply said that he knew nothing of the killings, and that his role was simply as an advisor and nothing else. He didn't know of any murders and he certainly didn't help with getting rid of any bodies.

The Krays were not charged with protection and there were no charges with regard to the US Mafia and the money laundering. The police said nothing about the long-firm frauds. The prosecution concentrated on the killings of two crooks – George Cornell and Jack 'The Hat' McVitie. No one mentioned the psychology of twins and the effect that it had on their relationships. And Reg Kray would not say that it was his brother who had urged him on to that final moment of death.

It was pride that stopped Reg Kray defending himself. It was that 'twin thing' that denied him a fair trial. And it was that same misguided belief in honour that betrayed Charlie.

With Ron and Reg both denying murder, there was no defence for Charlie. The twins did, however, approach Nipper Read on one occasion, nearing the end of the trial, to ask for leniency for their brother. But Read was onto a good thing. He knew that Charlie Kray was no killer, and all three Krays had to go down, and go down for a long time. It was the only way – and the police pulled no punches.

Violet was in court most days, supporting her boys. But she didn't recognise the events recounted by the witnesses. Surely her boys couldn't really do that. Surely they were just her adorable twins – they were *special*. She and old man Charlie had even sold the new family home, The Brooks, in the Suffolk countryside so they could help pay for the costs of the trial.

Other family members appeared in the witness box too. Aunt May received a vicious onslaught from the prosecution, followed by strict words from the judge. Ron and Reg complained about her treatment and so too did Charlie. But it did no good. As far as the trial of the Krays was concerned it had already been decided – the police, the judiciary, the 'slags' of the Firm – they were all in cahoots.

After 61 days, the jury retired to consider their verdict.

26.

March 1969: The Sentence

It had been the longest trial in criminal history – and the most expensive, costing over £150,000. The jury took 6 hours and 54 minutes in all to reach a verdict and they then piled back into the courtroom. Their decision was handed to the judge and Justice Melford Stevenson read it aloud in court at 7 p.m., 8 March 1969.

The twins were found guilty of murder – and Charlie was found guilty of getting rid of the body of Jack 'The Hat' McVitie, even though he was in bed at the time of the actual killing.

'I am not going to waste words on you,' the judge told Ron and Reg. 'In my view society has earned a rest from your activities. I sentence you to life imprisonment, which I recommend should not be less than 30 years!'

Ron and Reg were just 35 years old. By the time they got out of jail, they would be almost pensioners. The thought of 30 years behind bars was something else. They had both been in prison before, but neither could contemplate or appreciate what 30 years actually meant. There was not enough evidence to convict on any of the other charges, so 30 years it was. Charlie was given 10 years for getting rid of Jack 'The Hat' and Freddie Foreman also received 10 years. Ian Barrie got 20 years for his part in the killing of Cornell.

After the previous hullabaloo the sentencing was a rather tame affair. The news reporters ran from the courtroom as the Krays were taken away to start serving their sentences. They had already been on remand for some ten months, but that didn't even scratch the chart as far as the twins were concerned. 'Not less than 30 years,' Justice Melford Stevenson had said. That was a long time and those words were to haunt the Krays during the forthcoming years of their imprisonment.

The twins were put in the cells below. When Ron heard of the sentence they had given Charlie, he was furious.

'The rats gave you ten years?' he asked, too shocked to take it all in.

'Ten years,' repeated Charlie. 'Ten fucking years!'

27.

1969–81: Life

The Kray brothers were all transferred to Brixton Gaol that evening. Their first meeting with the Governor, his assistant and the chief prison officer there was a routine affair. First they had to take off their clothes. They had been wearing their own clothes throughout their days on remand and during the trial itself – Violet had supplied them with clean clothing throughout. But now it was time to put on prison attire. Their own clothes were boxed and shelved.

They then went to their individual cells to dream about prison life and to reflect on their past. For Ron and Reg it was time to adjust, to settle in to a long life of incarceration. They were used to such hardship. But their brother Charlie had never been imprisoned before, except for a short time in Montreal. This was new to him – and it hurt.

Charlie couldn't sleep that night. Since they were all 'Category A' listed, a red lamp burned in their cells all night. By morning he was severely depressed. He was tired, dirty and unshaven. He wasn't enjoying himself at all. 'Champagne' Charlie was devastated.

It was Ron who cheered him up. Rubbing his hands as he strolled from his cell that morning, he greeted everyone with a smile. 'Good morning,' he said. 'What a lovely day.' The Kray brothers all ate a hearty breakfast together before walking out into the sunshine that surrounded the exercise yard. 'I think I'll send off for a holiday brochure,' he told his brothers. 'I'd like to go on a cruise when I get out.' Nothing could put Ron Kray in a flap – he was just like he always was, acting as though there was no tomorrow.

But on 16 May, Reggie and Ronnie were on the move. Reg was sent to Parkhurst on the Isle of Wight and Ron was taken to Durham Prison. Freddie Foreman was sent to Leicester and the others were scattered throughout the country. Charlie found himself alone.

Charlie had to wait in Brixton for his time to start in earnest. Waiting is not the same as serving – there is no time for a routine, for settling in. But soon Charlie was called for – and told he was going to Chelmsford in Essex. Once here he was under constant supervision, constantly under the gaze of the guards and CCTV. This was Charlie's new life – and he hated every minute of it.

For the twins, however, prison life was almost a routine right from the start. Reg met many of his old pals at Parkhurst and soon became the boss of the Gaol. The Great Train Robbers, Tommy Wisby and Roy James, were there and so too was Eddie Richardson. But Reg Kray was the most well-known gangster in the country and soon he had them all jumping to his commands. He was to become the established 'face' of the prison – he would rule the roost inside as he had done outside.

Ron started off well enough, but his tantrums were always a problem – and separating the twins was not an easy option for the authorities. It was also costly, since they were given permission to see each other on a regular six-monthly basis. Twice a year they managed a get-together under the noses of the authorities. It was all cosher – and paid for by the tax payer.

After a year or so at Parkhurst Reg Kray was moved to Leicester. This is normal routine for the authorities (don't let them settle, keep them on the move). But this was only short lived. Soon he would be rejoining his brother Ron, who had now been moved to Parkhurst. When the twins got together again in 1972, they settled in to a daily routine of comparative freedom. They were free to talk to each other, free to make plans together and free to do business together.

Charlie Kray was transferred to Albany Prison in 1972. It was ironic that his brothers were only a few hundred yards down the road at Parkhurst and it made things more straightforward and manageable for the family. Violet could see them all in a day. They were a close knit family, these Krays.

The added advantage of this closeness for the authorities was the fact that Reg could help to control Ron. It was strange how the tables had been turned, since it was always Ron who controlled his twin brother during their days of crime and violence. Ron took his medicine – and the time passed by slowly. But Reg could never totally control Ron. When a new guard refused to give Ron his medicine there and then, he tore into the man. The result of this was another change of scene for

Ron Kray — Broadmoor was to be his new home and his status was to be certified as criminally insane.

Charlie too was soon on the move — in 1973 he moved from Albany to Maidstone. This was good for Charlie who found new freedom here. Soon he was no longer a Category A prisoner — and he was treated with respect by the guards at the prison. The authorities there even gave Charlie a three-day pass in August 1974, so that he could go home to his mum and dad and have a night out and a drink or two.

But Charlie Kray just couldn't get used to being 'free'. His head ached and his thoughts drifted back to the good old days, when the Krays ruled London and when he'd never had it so good. The three days and nights over, he headed back to Maidstone, determined to be a model prisoner — and to get out of jail as quickly as possible. Charlie was eventually freed on 8 January 1975.

He could now see his brothers at will. Reg was still in Parkhurst, apart from a few temporary moves here and there, and Ron was in Broadmoor. But Charlie decided to stay away from prison — he had seen enough of these institutions and was determined never to go back into a jail. So Ron and Reg would have to wait to be reunited with their elder brother.

The only one to see the benefit of Charlie being home was Violet. She could now concentrate on her twins — visiting them twice a week for the entire time they were in prison. And with regular six-monthly visits to Broadmoor, Reg saw more of his twin than he saw of his elder brother Charlie, who now became an unfamiliar sight.

The following years would see the twins growing closer together — and Charlie growing further apart from them, as his world changed and his feeling about being a Kray took on a far less important and significant role. Charlie was not trying to hide, but he was tired of having to talk constantly about his brothers. Although he wrote a book on his release, proclaiming his own innocence, he became less of a Kray and more of a 'Del Boy'. Wheeling and dealing was still the name of the game, but he tried to distance himself from the action — and any heavy business at all. Reg settled into life at Parkhurst and even though he was still a high risk Category A prisoner, he found a certain freedom within the high walls of one of the most secure prisons in the country. He was the 'face', the man in charge — and the person to whom the governor turned when there was trouble. Soon Reg Kray was the boss — the one who called the shots. The authorities didn't tell Reg what to do – they asked him if he would *like* to do it.

To keep Reg happy they turned a blind eye to his homosexual activities, allowing his relationships to develop and remain firm. They were always reluctant to move his 'partner' away from the prison, in case he became angry and caused trouble. In this way Reg Kray truly became the 'Guvnor' of Parkhurst.

Ron too kept up his sexual activities in Broadmoor, becoming their prized inmate. Just like his twin, he took over the asylum. He was again the 'face', the man they all looked up to and respected. This was, after all, Ron Kray – the man who had killed George Cornell. Ron's life soon settled into a routine – one of medication and composure. He rarely mistreated anyone, serving out his time in the manner he had always lived by. His motto had always been, 'If you can't do the time, then don't do the crime.' He had lived by it – and he knew he would die by it.

28.

August 1982: The Last Farewell

Charlie was abruptly woken in the small hours of the morning, as the telephone burst into life. The woman's voice was faint and unknown to him. Who could be calling at this hour, waking Charlie from his drunken sleep – and more importantly why?

Charlie didn't want to hear the words, so he quickly passed the phone over to his girlfriend Diana Ward, lying next to him. The woman on the end of the line spoke in a matter-of-fact tone – without feeling, without pausing. Diana confirmed it all for Charlie. His mother Violet had just died. The date was 5 August 1982 and Charlie's worst nightmare was just about to materialise – he would have to break this news to his brothers Ron and Reg.

It was something that he had thought much about in recent years. All Violet's visits to see Ron and Reg, even the trips to see Charlie when he was in prison, had taken their toll. They all knew they owed her a debt of gratitude and they all knew they had helped to shorten her life. But now that it was over, what would they say and what would they do? So many thoughts flashed through Charlie's sleepy mind. Suddenly he was wide awake.

He got out of bed and went downstairs. He made straight for the drinks cabinet and poured himself a drink – a stiff one. It was a lovely morning with the birds singing and the sun peeking through the curtains – but Charlie wasn't enjoying the drink and he wasn't appreciating the beauty of the hour.

Violet had gone into hospital only a few days before, with suspected pneumonia. Charlie had been to see her and at first she had taken it in her stride. But on the second day Charlie couldn't get much sense out of Violet. He spoke to another woman in the ward and was told that his mum had undergone some tests – and that pneumonia was confirmed.

When a doctor approached Charlie went through it all again. The man was polite and quietly spoken and he explained the routine to the worried son. There had been tests all right and she certainly had pneumonia. But she also had cancer. Charlie was in shock when he heard the words. His mum had always been well. The Lee family all lived long lives – why should this happen to his mum? But Charlie Kray already knew the answer really.

'Can you do something about the cancer?' he asked tearfully. 'She will get well – won't she?' The doctor told him that things were serious, but not impossible. The problem was to get rid of the pneumonia. Before that they couldn't start on any cancer treatment. Charlie was in sombre mood when he got back home.

Another brandy helped to calm his nerves. He knew he would need all his strength to cope with the torment of the funeral and the task of breaking the news to his brothers. It was then that Charlie remembered the date – 5 August was his mum's birthday. She was 73 years old to the day.

The first thing to do was to tell his dad. Diana and Charlie hurriedly dressed and made for Braithwaite House. They talked as they drove. As usual with Charlie, he was the one to take care of the business and he was the one who had to decide which brother to tell first. It wasn't an easy decision, with Reg in Parkhurst and Ron in Broadmoor. But the decision was made for him. Broadmoor was only an hour away – and a visit to see Reg on the Isle of Wight would take at least five long hours. So it was decided: Ron first, Reg second.

Old man Charlie was surprised to see anyone at 7 a.m. 'What's going on?' he asked, bleary eyed.

Charlie told him straight – Violet was dead. His ageing father fell apart before his eyes. Breathless and gaunt, he screamed and ranted. The old man had not been well. His sons had always believed that it would be old man Charlie to go first, so the news of his being alone was devastating. Diana made the tea and the family talked of plans. Young Charlie promised to tell the twins – and he would handle all the funeral arrangements. 'Don't worry, dad,' he told the old man. 'I'll take care of it all!'

When Charlie phoned Broadmoor with his news, he was told that he could come immediately. Charlie wasn't looking forward to seeing Ron. He hadn't seen him for some time and that whole idea of Ron being gay and having gay lovers at Broadmoor was a source of constant pain to him. Charlie was proud of his manhood, and having a brother who was openly gay was something he never could understand or tolerate.

But before the trip to Berkshire, he had to phone Parkhurst and arrange for a visit to see Reggie – and that was a problem. He knew he couldn't make the trip until the following day and the news people would be sniffing around, looking for a scoop. The death of Violet Kray, mother of the Kray twins, would be news indeed.

Fortunately the welfare officer at Parkhurst was well aware of the media situation and he volunteered to talk to Reg in private – and to break the news to him personally, as gently as possible. Charlie agreed, thanking the man for his kindness and thoughtfulness. He would be there the next day, but it was better if Reg didn't hear it on his radio first, which was constantly tuned in to the outside world from his prison cell bedside. Charlie hung up the phone and got ready for the trip to Broadmoor.

They arrived at the hospital at around 11 a.m. Diana and Charlie were kindly and politely shown in to a private room in the hospital wing of the institution – all cosy and neat, with no one to bother them. Ron was then brought in to the room. He had actually long believed that his dad would be passing away – any day he thought. But the shock of the news about his mum from Charlie was most unexpected. Ron Kray broke down in tears as Charlie told him the news of their mother's death.

'Why mum?' asked Ron through his tears. 'I knew dad didn't have long to go, but *mum*!' Again he sobbed as he held his head in his hands,:Charlie broke down too. Talking about it brought back all the grief of the early morning hours – he was reliving that phone call all over again.

Charlie and Diana rose to go – leaving Ron alone in that little room.

'We won't disturb him,' said one of the nurses as Charlie closed the door behind him. Charlie wiped the tears from his face and hugged Diana as they strolled out to the car. Now it was time to check on his dad and to start organising the funeral arrangements.

Back at Braithwaite House, the block of council flats where Violet and old man Charlie lived, Charlie checked on Reg. He hadn't taken it well apparently – not well at all. 'He'll be glad to see you tomorrow,' he was told. Charlie knew it would be the same thing all over again. Whatever he went through with Ronnie, he would have to go through with Reggie. The day came and went, and Charlie could get down to the serious business of the funeral of his mother.

George English & Sos, the Bethnal Green funeral directors, were chosen to handle the arrangements and they did the family proud. The funeral and burial were handled with finesse and dignity. The only thing to spoil the day for the Kray brothers was the mass of police gathered in and around the church, along the entire funeral route and even in and around the cemetery at Chingford Mount. But this was no ordinary funeral – it was the first chance to see the Kray brothers together for over 14 years. Everyone wanted to see the twins, these 'heroes' of the East End, the scourge of the underworld, the celebrities of crime.

Not many in the crowd knew the secret behind the funeral. They didn't know that Reg Kray had recently tried to commit suicide by slashing his wrists. To all intents and purposes the twins were well and looking fine. Some comments were heard about their fine clothes; other suggestions were more ironic, describing them as being 'dressed to kill'.

The 24 August was an important day for the Krays. But it looked like a national day out for the police. They were everywhere – in cars, parked along the streets, in the crowds of onlookers and mourners, in the skies above the route – all the time armed to the teeth.

There were eight cars full of wreaths and many more filled with mourners, friends and family. Diana Dors and her husband Alan Lake were there. So too was the actor Andrew Ray. People had come from far and wide to pay their last respects to Violet Kray – and the media was there to record the events. Just to make things look good on camera and bad for the twins, the authorities had chosen to give the task of 'Kray minders' for the day to their biggest men. It was all done to make the twins look small, but it didn't work. Being hand-cuffed to a giant prison guard was something they could both shrug off with ease. They were, after all, the Kray twins.

The service was held at St John's Church. All was quiet as the twins strolled into the church and were seated for the ceremony. Even here the brothers were not allowed to be seated together, or to talk together privately. Their old pal and ex-gangster boss Billy Hill came to the church, but he couldn't get near to either Ron or Reg. He did though manage a quick chat with Charlie. Once again, they cursed the presence of the police. The twins looked out for Hill, eager for a nod or a wink in their direction – a show of respect. But it was not to be.

Old man Charlie didn't like the police presence either. He felt it was not warranted: unjustified and irreverent. He was not well, but he got through the ceremony all right and even managed to shout at the police once or twice as they guarded the burial plot. Ron and Reg were not allowed to see their mother buried. Once the funeral service was over, the brothers Kray were ushered into their separate transport vehicles and whisked away to Chingford Mount. They spent the whole time at the Police Station, guarded by over 50 police officers. It was all a waste of time and a waste of money. There was no way the Kray twins would do anything to jeopardise the dignity and the sacred nature of the proceedings with a jail break. It was all so unnecessary.

'I don't want all this,' said old man Charlie, as he was led away to the car. Young Charlie agreed – when it was his father's time, he would see to it that the police were kept away. Some eight months later he was dead. The twins decided not to go to the funeral. They didn't see their father buried and they didn't pay any tribute to the man who had helped to bring them into the world.

Charlie was there for the service and the burial, but he was a lonely figure at Chingford Mount Cemetery. Charlie Kray was alone. His brothers were still in jail and still in the headlines – and there seemed no end to this job as chief funeral arranger. It was something that Charlie knew much about of course, since in the old days of the Firm he had often had to clean up after killings, pick up the pieces and hide all the clues. He had performed this task so often that it had earned him that nickname – even the twins used it from time to time: the 'Undertaker'.

29.

December 1985: Another Way of Life

Ron Kray had always done things differently. The doctors could empathise. They could see the disconsolate nature of the man – he needed something that was not readily available at Broadmoor. What he needed was a woman.

Being a homosexual was not going to stop Ron getting married. He had already chosen his bride – Elaine Mildener, mother of two. She had started writing to Reg, but he was too much to handle, so she swapped her attentions to Ron – and *voila*! This mad man of Broadmoor had found himself a soulmate – and an instant family to take the place of his own mum and dad. It meant someone else to call, someone else to visit him, someone else to help him cope with the boredom of Broadmoor.

Ron had his pals, all right – but they all said the same things and had the same rituals. Ron wanted something different. He missed his mum and the femininity that she provided, so he relished getting married and conforming to 'normal' life. Reg was the thinker of the two – too much pressure, too much sincerity, too much planning and scheming. Ron wasn't like this at all. He was easy-going and pleasant to talk with – he didn't have that 'I'd-like-it-done-yesterday' attitude of his twin.

The wedding was a great event in Broadmoor's calendar. Things would never be the same again as journalists gathered in the gloom to flash their bulbs and take their notes and chat with the happy couple. Ron had agreed a tidy sum for the photos and Elaine could start being Mrs Kray with a little style and dignity. But it wasn't easy for her children Andrew and Debbie to understand. In fact they never really appreciated their mother's liaison with the former gangland boss and killer. For them life was never to be the same again.

Ron had always told Elaine that sex was out of the question. His real 'soulmates', he told her, were inside Broadmoor, incarcerated with him.

There were a few close friends nearby and they were all he needed for sexual pleasure – but he wanted something else. It was family, or at least the sense of one, that he longed for. The idea alone made him feel good – it made that medication easier to swallow. Although he was a paranoid schizophrenic, Ron Kray craved normality. He was no longer really alone, no longer really confined to an institution. Now he could hear stories of the kids and listen to the stories of home life, as related by his wife. This, to Ron Kray, was a form of freedom.

But soon the visits became a pressure and a duty to Elaine. She was pleased at first, but the notoriety was something that she hadn't bargained for – and she was soon dreading the visits. And when she talked about the possibility of a divorce, Ron accepted it. It was inevitable, he recalled. 'I could see it wouldn't last, but for a while I was just like any man, married with two kids – and I loved it.'

The year 1985 was a good one for Reg Kray. He had just lost an old 'flame' but he soon found a new friend in the form of the 'cheeky chappie' Pete Gillett. Pete had arrived at Parkhurst after causing trouble in his previous prisons. He was an outward-going youngster with a smile on his face and an amusing word for any difficult or strained situation. Reg Kray and Pete Gillett became bosom pals.

Pete was serving time for armed robbery, where he had driven the getaway car. He knew he had done wrong and he was willing to do his time. But he didn't take to other inmates pestering him, so he stood up for his rights and defended himself at all times. It was this not being able to stand down that had got him sent to Parkhurst. But he settled in and Reg was soon supplying him with a little 'puff' (cannabis) and 'hootch' (strong liquor) made and distributed in Her Majesty's Prisons.

The two got on well. Reg told pals that 'Christmas had come early' and the two built up a strong relationship. Pete was actually beginning to take the place of Ronnie. Ron could see this in the letters Reg sent him every week. He wrote back wishing his brother well in his new friendship. Reg had his gay pals around the prison, but this new friendship was something altogether different. The joke around the prison was that Reg always gave a gold watch to his 'flame', so he could tell the time when he was bending over him. On one occasion an inmate rushed into Pete's cell in the early hours of the morning – he was only wearing underpants and had a full erection. Pete rushed to complain to

Reg. 'I don't need this, Reg,' he said. 'It looked like he had the leaning tower of Pisa in his pants!' Reg called the man in and they had a chat. It never happened again.

But Pete Gillett never got that watch. Instead he became one of the family when Reg made him his 'adopted son'. This was a most strange and fascinating relationship – one that confused the media, who like things cut and dried. Who was this Pete Gillett? And why did Reg make him his 'adopted son'? In the main it was to protect the lad from the goings-on inside jail. Being Reg's 'son' kept him safe from homosexual activity – it meant that Pete could sleep at night.

And as for Pete? Well, he had nothing to lose and everything to gain, or so he thought. Pete Gillett: Reg Kray's 'adopted son' – something that he is still known as today.

30.

1988–94: Double Exposure

The Kray twins were all about image. They would go to extremes to keep one basic premise alive: that they were just a nice couple of lads who got caught up in crime. They had even perfected a role for Charlie: the brother of some really cool guys who were serving time in prison for killing off a couple of nasty crooks. That was the planned image and it worked for many years. But not now!

Through the 1990 film *The Krays* and through their own books, the three Kray brothers tried to perpetuate this idea of innocence. They were engulfed by crime – never did they embrace it. They were forced to kill – it wasn't something they wanted to do. It was their pride that forced them into defending themselves – never did they set out to dominate the underworld. Ron, Reg and Charlie Kray have told these stories through the years and people have listened. But it is far from the truth.

Take the film *The Krays* for instance. From the first instance Roger Daltrey contacted them regarding the project they were interested in only one thing – the money. (Since it was Charlie who was helping to negotiate the deal, it was he who ended up with most of it.) It may be difficult to understand giving money to killers purely because they are killers, but that didn't appear to be difficult back in 1989, when the final deal was struck regarding the film of the life of the Krays. Ron and Reg wanted the fame too – but the money was by far the most important consideration.

Paying Charlie Kray well over £100,000 for being the 'technical adviser' on the film was a good pay-out. After all, he only had to show how Ron killed Cornell and how Reg did for McVitie.

The most surprising fact to emerge regarding the film was that Ron and Reg, who were notorious control freaks, weren't even bothered about reading the script or seeing the stars of the film. When it was shown they were angry about their mother's use of bad language – that was something she would never do. And they complained about the deal that Charlie had done with the film-makers, giving them a flat fee instead of a share in the profits. They could have scrutinised the detail of the film contract, they could have read the script, they could have been in contact with the film-makers while the film was in the production stages. But they didn't and they weren't.

Charlie had, however, done his job well – and the film portrayed the twins as a couple of Eastenders who were forced into crime, reluctant to assume the mantle of Top Dogs of the Underworld and were compelled to kill. Whatever they did, they had to do it. It kept the Kray myth alive and flourishing well into the latter part of the twentieth century and beyond.

The books fulfilled a similar function. Ron and Reg wrote about their lovely and adorable mum, their upbringing as good lads in the deprived areas of the East End, and their enforced imprisonment – first by the army and then by society. It was a sad tale they had to tell and they had to tell it – to keep up appearances. This was the image they wanted for themselves and this is what people were allowed to read.

Others, however, had different ideas. Old members of the Firm wanted to tell a different story – but their tales were buried in the second-hand-book stores and hidden on the back shelves, seldom seeing the light of day. This is exactly what the Krays wanted.

What the twins did and what they wanted people to think they did, were two very different things. When Kate Kray made a pact with Ron that she could sleep with other men, she was told that it was all right as long as she didn't tell the press about it. But she did – and that meant that Ron lost face and lost control in his well-ordered life. Divorce was an inevitable consequence.

Reg was a homosexual throughout his prison life, but he wanted it kept a secret. So he carried on correspondence with the women who wrote to him, he kept up their visits talking about the great sex they would have when he was freed and he got married to give himself the appearance of normality. There was the truth – and then there was the image that he had so carefully selected for himself.

When inmates threatened to spill the beans on Reg and his gay lovers, they were either silenced with money or threatened with violence. Reg didn't care which method he used – as long as it worked and he maintained his image.

It is frightening how manipulative the twins were in their attitude towards the media – and it is amazing that it worked for so long. But now the Krays are dead and there is little to fear in telling the truth and it is only today, in the twenty-first century, that the real story is emerging, pushing and pulling its way to the surface through all the charades and the camouflage erected so painstakingly over the years.

In the days of the Kray 'Empire', it was Ron who dominated. It was Ron who wanted war, it was he who was the first to kill and it was he who wanted more of it. But throughout their imprisonment it was Reg who took control. It was Reg who controlled his prison environment with a fist of iron, it was he who gave the orders to friends and associates on the outside and it was he who put out contracts on people he wanted killed.

Shortly before his death, Ron Kray was attacked in Broadmoor by Peter Sutcliffe, The Yorkshire Ripper. The ferocity of the blows took him completely by surprise and he never really recovered. Unfortunately, he made the mistake of telling Reg all about it. And when Reg found a suitable hitman, who was on his way into Broadmoor, he gave the command: 'Take care of Sutcliffe.' Reg didn't care if it meant dead or alive, he just wanted Sutcliffe to be taught a lesson. Not because he had hurt his twin brother, but because it had damaged his own reputation. He just couldn't let it happen and he couldn't let him get away with it.

To Reg Kray control was the major factor. And he wouldn't let anyone else take care of business. For Reg there would never be a tomorrow – so everything had to happen today.

He was most impatient during the period of the early '90s when his 30 years could soon be over with adequate provision for good behaviour. This was when he began to try to persuade the parole board to give him his freedom. Everything he did from now on was designed to get himself set free.

Ron, however, knew that he would never see freedom again. I asked him back in 1992 what he would do if he was ever released. 'I'd like to sail the world,' he told me. 'I'd pack my bags and I'd go everywhere.'

The twins wove a web of deceit throughout their lives. Ultimately they even deceived themselves – they began to live the dreams, to take part in their own unreal existence of make-believe. They were illusionists of the most persuasive kind, creating their own 'virtual world' – and for a while, they fooled the real world. But even they knew that one day their fabricated lives would be torn apart – and they didn't care, as long as they weren't around to see it.

31.

March 1995: Death of the Don

On 17 March 1995 Ron Kray died quietly in Heatherwood Hospital, Ascot. He had been suffering with heart problems for some time, brought on by his incessant smoking habit, but this was a major heart attack and Ron just didn't have the strength to survive it.

Only a few days before he was joking about the fact that as a 'mad man', certified insane, he wasn't liable to tax – and he kept up his smoking until the end. A hundred cigarettes a day was his usual dosage and no one could stop him. They had warned him of the consequences, but Ron Kray lived for the day. After every heart attack he thought about it for a moment, concluded: 'Well, no one lives for ever!' and just opened a new packet. His motto was 'always live for today, for tomorrow may never come'.

The media were immediately put on alert – one of the Kray twins had died! People asked the same question: 'Was it the mad one who'd died, or was it the other one?' Testimonies of his life's achievements were everywhere – on the television, in the newspapers, on the radio – they all told the same sad story. They all tried to assess his importance in the realm of the gangster and the world of crime.

There were the usual sympathetic words from friends and family and the celebrities had a great time trying to out do each other in the 'kind words' stakes. Reg was in shock and needed tranquillisers, Charlie was horrified that his strong brother should be a casualty of those cigarettes he loved so much, and even Kate had some kind words to say about the man she once called her husband.

The three Kray brothers were no more; the Kray twins were no more, so the obvious question everyone was asking was simply – with one of them dead, why not release the other one? The mad brother, who had apparently caused all the problems, was no longer around – surely Reg should be freed?

Reg himself was quick to join the bandwagon. This moment needed control and the only man for the job was Reg Kray. He had been put on medication even before his brother's death and the authorities at Maidstone Jail had refused to give him permission to run to Ron's bedside. They gave no reason for this, but Reg was furious and medication was the easiest option. Even Charlie couldn't console his brother.

Charlie Kray was also outraged at the refusal from Maidstone Jail. He couldn't figure it out and he complained vehemently to the authorities. It did no good, Ron died alone in hospital. There was no family there to see him depart this earth, there were no friends around him. It was a bleak end to a dazzling career as one of the 'Godfathers of Crime'.

First in Durham prison in 1969, Ron was transferred to Parkhurst in 1972. But Reg couldn't control his brother and after a few years things came to a head. One day, when Ron was due his daily medication, there was a new guard on the wing at Parkhurst. Ron asked for his pills and the man refused. Reg rushed to the office and pleaded with the guard. 'He has to have his pills, or there'll be trouble!' said Reg. It was all too late. Ron went crazy and started to hit out at the guards. One by one they went down, one by one they raised the alarm. Eventually they carted Ron away in a strait-jacket.

Broadmoor, in Berkshire, was to be his home for the next 20 years. It had taken them over seven years to determine Ron's condition, although Long Grove Asylum had diagnosed paranoid schizophrenia all those years ago, back in 1958. But the treatment at Broadmoor worked and he was reasonably well throughout his stay at the institute. He settled in to a daily routine and didn't appear to mind the seclusion. He had nothing to worry about – and he had promised the authorities there that he would never escape, so they trusted him and did their best to assist him if they could. There was also a plentiful supply of gay lovers to keep him busy.

Ron was a good patient at Broadmoor. With the correct medication his condition was kept under control and he did what he could to stop the boredom. At times he wrote books, although the last money he received from a publisher had to be returned – he couldn't think of anything to say. But in the main Ron helped his friends. 'What can I do with the money?' he once asked me. 'When my friends leave here, they need my help. It's only money, after all!'

Ron was right, he had everything he could possibly need in Broadmoor, so why hang on to the money? So he gave it all away. When he died he was broke.

I have fond memories of Ron Kray. When I first went to see him in 1992 I was a little apprehensive about meeting him. I had been told all the stories – 'His eyes will look right through you. Watch out for his fierce handshake. Keep your cool.'

Some months later I told him about a report in the press concerning Broadmoor. The talk was that the loonies had taken over the asylum. 'Where have they done that?' asked Ron.

'Here, Ron,' I told him.

Ron stared at me and laughed. 'Why hasn't anyone told me?' he said.

Ron tended his garden at Broadmoor and caused no one any harm. The news of the latest political scandals didn't bother him, the fact that they weren't about to release him didn't bother him – nothing appeared to bother him.

His death was front page news on 18 March, with his last words blazoned across many a tabloid: 'Oh God, Mother, help me!'

Charlie was almost in tears as he told them, 'Ron would be buried in the family plot in Chingford.' But he had to confess – Reg would be handling all the details of the funeral this time.

Reg was kept busy. One of his gravest concerns was the fact that he had let a pal borrow his black suit, so he had to get it back in a hurry. And there was the funeral proper to plan. It had to be big, something the entire East End would be proud of. Ron's last wish was that he would be transported in a hearse pulled by six black horses, plumes and all. Reg wouldn't let his twin brother down.

Unknown to Reg and Charlie was the fact that Ron's brain had been removed at the autopsy. As the heavies guarded the coffin, no one knew that the brain was being studied by scientists.

The authorities at Maidstone didn't want the same shambles that had happened at the death of Ron Kray, so they decided to let Reg out for the day so that he could attend the funeral. John Altman (Nick Cotton in *Eastenders*) and page-three girl Debee Ashby were at the prison to console Reg and they too argued the case for him being allowed to attend the funeral. The stars were beginning to join in in their droves, getting all the publicity they needed. It was all arranged for Wednesday 29 March. It would be a day they would never forget.

From English & Sons funeral parlour to the church in Bethnal Green, some 60,000 people lined the streets. The procession was stunning, headed by the hearse carrying the flower-covered coffin, pulled by six black horses with their plumes swaying in the wind. The sides of the hearse were glass covered so the public could all get their last view of the box that carried Ron Kray to his grave.

The guests included those killers 'Mad Frankie' Fraser and Freddie Foreman (who had only recently admitted to the killing of the 'Mad Axeman' Frank Mitchell). Naturally enough, there were tributes from the likes of Barbara Windsor, Roger Daltrey – and the US Mob. It was a time to show respect and Reggie and Charlie Kray were there to see that all due regard and respect was shown to their brother, now that he was so sorely departed.

Reg was the first of the brothers to speak to the press. 'Ron had a great humour, a vicious temper, was kind and generous,' he told them. 'Above all he was a man.'

The 30-vehicle cortège moved slowly towards the church, where Father Bedford was ready to conduct the ceremony. The coffin was carried into the church by, amongst others, Charlie, that old rival Johnny Nash and the Kray's hired killer, Freddie Foreman – all to the tune of Frank Sinatra's 'My Way'. Poems were first on the service list and then the hymns, including 'Morning Has Broken' and 'Fight the Good Fight'. Whitney Houston sang them out of the church with 'I Will Always Love You'.

Once outside, Father Bedford felt he should explain his reasons for conducting the ceremony. 'It was my duty to commend Ron's soul to God,' he told them. 'I don't make judgements. God does, and thankfully he is far better than me.'

The pallbearers carried out the coffin and everyone piled into their Rolls Royces, Daimlers and the like. It was now time to transport Ron to his final resting place at Chingford Mount Cemetery and there was a police escort to see that he got there on time. In fact there were so many police around that day, that they outnumbered the hoods by some three to one.

Reg and Charlie waved to the crowd – they had to please their public and maintain that image. The following day the tabloids captioned a photo of Reg Kray, 'The Grinning Gangster'.

At Chingford Mount the coffin was placed alongside the grave. It was a similar grave to the ones the Krays used to bury their victims in all those years ago. The oak coffin was a beautiful sight, complete with gold-plated handles – and Reg even threw a red rose on top of the coffin as it was laid in the ground next to their mum, their dad, and Reggie's first wife Frances.

Some of their old pals had a get-together at a local pub afterwards, but for Reg it was time to get back to Maidstone Jail. His last sight as Ron was laid to rest was of his wreath, saying simply: 'To the other half of me.'

Reg returned to Maidstone, still handcuffed. This was all part of the deal that Reg was forced to enter into for his freedom for that one day. For the rest of the party, including Charlie and the pallbearers, the time was ripe for a little reminiscing. They recalled the good old days, they talked of the scams and of the deals – and of old pals who never survived their gangster days. The funeral was over, but it would never be forgotten.

At the end a painting was laid by the grave as an everlasting tribute to Ron Kray. It was a painting of the twins and it reminded everyone of their glory days as bosses of organised crime. But the painting, so painstakingly laid by the graveside, was stolen during the night. And who says that there is honour among thieves?

Also stolen that night was a floral boxing glove, given by the prisoners of Maidstone Jail. Ron had nothing when he died – and he took nothing of value with him to the grave – except the knowledge of the real harm they did, the facts about where those bodies are really buried and the real truth of the Krays and their killings. Ron Kray was dead and buried, but the myth would survive.

32.

June 1997: The Dope

Re-produced by kind permission of Mainstream Publishing from *The Kray Files* by Colin Fry

'Gotcha!' said the police officer as he arrested Charlie Kray. For Charlie it was all a case of déja vu, or as he put it, a case of mistaken identity. But it was he who had mistaken the identity of the man with whom he had just made a two kilogram cocaine deal, with the promise of supplying five kilograms every two weeks for the foreseeable future. For the man, known as Jack, was really an undercover officer from the Metropolitan Police, masquerading as a northern businessman who wanted a new supplier of dope – his previous supplier, he said, had been killed.

The date was 31 July 1996, just another pleasant Wednesday – and a new Kray prosecution was imminent. Charlie Kray had been settling down for the evening with his girlfriend Judy Stanley to watch television at her home near Croydon, south London. He was well aware of the fact that the drugs deal was going down, since he had played a major part in setting it up, but he had covered his tracks well, or so he thought, by not being there when the drugs changed hands. This was an old trick and it had helped Charlie Kray out of many a hole. He was often there or thereabouts, but was never caught with his pants down. This time, however, he had supplied his own evidence for his own downfall. For unknown to him at the time, his incriminating conversations with Jack and his friends had been recorded on tape. He was soon to be his own irrefutable witness, his own worst nightmare.

Charlie Kray was led away by jubilant police officers to Ilford Police Station, next door to the regional criminal operations unit, where he was questioned about the £80 million deal. Plain-clothes detectives, involved in the arrest, quizzed him about his part in the drugs syndicate and the subsequent supply of cocaine. He maintained his innocence throughout, even though he was informed of the capture of his two partners in crime, Ronald Field and Robert Gould.

The case against Charlie looked convincing, but it all rested on police evidence; evidence that had to stand up in a court of law. And Charlie had usually been able to wriggle out of trouble. The only real exception here was back in 1969 when he was found guilty of helping to get rid of the body of Jack 'The Hat' McVitie and was subsequently sentenced to ten years in prison. On that occasion, however, his luck was not with him, since he had not actually taken any part in the killing, where other members of the Firm disposed of the body at sea. So what did he have to fear this time around?

Judy Stanley stopped to talk to the press as she left Ilford Police Station that night after a vain attempt to see her lover. 'Charlie has done nothing wrong,' she said tearfully. 'We are utterly amazed.' As a parting gesture she asked them, 'Can you imagine a 70-year-old man who has a hatred of drugs being involved in the distribution of them?' No one answered. Later, back at her Sanderstead semi-detached house she spoke again to the press. 'Someone has thrown his name into the hat because of what he is,' she said. 'He is no stranger to all this, but he's 70 now and doesn't need the hassle.'

The police issued a statement saying that it was 'one of the largest and most significant drugs raids this year'. Indeed, the Metropolitan Police had been very busy that evening, arresting 31 people in south-east London

Charlie Kray had much to think about as he sat in his cell that night. What kind of case did the police really have against him? Would the others talk and implicate him in the deal? How long would he spend behind bars if found guilty? When would he be permitted to see his lawyer, Ralph Haems, a close Kray family friend?

It reminded him of the days when he was behind bars in Canada. That time he was thrown out of the country, because of lack of evidence. His Mafia pals had played their cards right, unlike their English cousins who had had a traitor in their midst and a man who almost led them to life in the 'Tombs', Montreal's own top-flight prison. But the Mob weren't around this time, so who could he rely on? Charlie Kray began to think, to wonder why it had happened this way – to speculate on the outcome and to reflect on the events that had led to this most terrifying ordeal. The only question that concerned him was the reason why.

'Done, mate.' That was all it took to secure the multi-million pound drugs deal. Charlie Kray was feeling fine. It was the deal of a lifetime, but he had to be careful. 'I put people together,' Charlie told Jack. 'But I won't go there when they do these things because I have too many eyes on me.' How right he was.

Jack too had to be careful. He needed the right kind of proof of Charlie's complicity in the deal, so a hidden tape recorder was always at hand. It wouldn't do to tip anyone off accidentally, since this was hardcore drugs trade – intruders were dealt with speedily and for ever. There was no room for errors of any kind.

The idea of the sting came in May, when a phone tap revealed the name of Charlie Kray. The Metropolitan Police were aware of drugs deals being set up in and around London, and they had arranged for numerous phone taps to try to gain useful information concerning future drugs trade. They felt sure that the known drugs barons would be involved somewhere along the line, but the name of Kray must have been a real bonus. High profile, high status – a good career move in the making.

However a recent cocaine bust involving Dave Courtney, a friend of Reg Kray's and the man in charge of security at Ron Kray's funeral, may also have played a part in calculations. He had been arrested at Heathrow Airport with £1 million of cocaine. Further back in time there was the cocaine bust involving Pete Gillett, Reg Kray's adopted son – and then there was the bust involving Joe Pyle, ex-Kray Firm member. There was no end to cocaine connections in the Kray family.

An introduction was made through a go-between, establishing Jack (not his real name) as a northern businessman, with connections in the underworld and in need of a supplier. Cocaine was his chosen vital ingredient and Jack did all he could to impress Charlie Kray with his good humour, his money and lots of champagne. They didn't call Charlie Kray 'Champagne Charlie' for no reason.

It worked well and soon Jack was invited to attend a party, a benefit for Charlie's son Gary who had recently died of cancer. Jack and another plain-clothes man called Brian (again, not his real name), met with Charlie Kray and the discussion inevitably came around to drugs. Ronald Field, a 49-year-old builder, and Robert Gould, a 39-year-old electrician, were introduced to Jack and Brian as a good supply source of cocaine.

Later, Charlie would be thankful that his son, Gary, was not alive to witness the depths of depravation that had enticed his father into dealing in drugs, something that his brothers, even in their heyday, had never resorted to. But drugs were not then the scourge of society that they are now. If Reg and Ron Kray were starting on a life of crime today, then it would be difficult indeed not to be involved in one way or another in drugs.

Soon afterwards, Jack invited Charlie and his accomplice Ronald Field to visit with him in Newcastle. This was to seal the connection and to show good faith. Once again, throwing money around as though there was no tomorrow had apparently worked, and Jack became just another do-gooder in the long line of Kray benefactors. The two Londoners stayed at The Linden Hall Hotel at the expense of Jack and his friend Brian — although in reality every tax payer in the UK was footing the bill. But Jack had set things up very well. The scheming had paid off. Charlie and Ronald Field fell for the bait — they took it hook, line and sinker. Jack, on behalf of the Metropolitan Police and the country, and in order to trap Charlie Kray once and for good, agreed to pay £31,500 per kilogram, for an initial drop of two kilograms, the money to be paid in cash at a time and a place to be determined later by mutual agreement. The arrangements included future supplies of five kilograms, every two weeks for at least the following two years – a deal that would net Charlie and his pals a cool £8 million. And it was all recorded for posterity on a hidden tape recorder, to be used later in the trial of *Regina* v *Charles Kray*.

The deal was done and all the men shook hands on a prosperous business venture. And that is what it was to Charlie Kray, just another deal. It was another chance to make a fortune and to give Judy Stanley the good life he thought she deserved. This was, to him, a last chance – a chance to gain some kind of prestige and to live the rest of his petty life in some kind of grandeur.

But Charlie Kray wasn't through playing his mind games. He was well aware of the fact that he was now playing very near the line, the barrier between good and evil — some would say that he had already crossed over to the other side. If Charlie could find a way of getting the money (and that was what this was really all about) without really going through with the deal, then he would jump at the chance. After all, it had often worked on previous occasions of petty crimes. This time, however, the deal could not be termed petty. How could anyone call £80 million anything but a major scam?

There were numerous delays to the deal going through, as Charlie tried to evade the question of drugs and to get onto the question of the money. He even managed to borrow a small amount (about £500) from Jack, saying that he had recently lost £1 million on a deal that had gone wrong. Now that doesn't appear to be far-fetched considering Charlie's proven track record, but anyway it did the trick for the time being. 'Something is better than nothing,' has always been Charlie's motto. Again, the State footed the bill.

Eventually Jack and Brian managed to fix a meeting with Field and Gould at The Swallow Hotel, in Waltham Abbey. The date was 31 May 1996. The drugs would be delivered and the money would change hands – £63,000 in cool cash. Charlie Kray would not be present at the exchange.

As planned the cocaine was handed over in a brown paper bag, to the undercover policemen Jack and Brian in the early part of the evening at the chosen venue. The deal done, Field and Gould left the scene with their ready cash, also in brown paper bags. Jack and Brian inspected their delivery of the cocaine and phoned in to headquarters that the sting had gone off well and that Operation Crackdown was a success.

When Ronald Field and Robert Gould stopped to refuel their car at the Lakeside Service Station, on the M25 London orbital motorway at Thurrock, police swooped to capture both men and cash. Further drugs were also seized. Jack was right, Operation Crackdown had been a complete success. At the same moment officers were on their way to visit Charlie Kray – his champagne days would soon be over, possibly for good.

On Friday, 2August 1996, Charlie Kray appeared in Redbridge Court, East London, charged with plotting to supply and supplying drugs. The 30-minute hearing was a simple affair. Charlie smiled to Judy – Judy smiled back. Charlie even managed to blow her a kiss as he stood quite motionless in his smart navy-blue suit, waiting for a decision. He and the other accused were given a further 28 days in remand, although this was later changed to six days since the magistrates had made just a little mistake regarding their powers in such a case. But the major details remained the same: conspiring to and arranging to supply approximately £80 million of cocaine.

Judy took it well and vowed to continue her fight to save her

Charlie, a man who, according to her, hated the mere mention of drugs.

The following days, weeks and months saw a routine of visits to court for all three accused. They were in deep trouble and the police were not about to release any of them just so they could conveniently leave the country or intimidate witnesses or anything else for that matter. So they would remain in jail until a date could be fixed for a trial.

They had a long wait. On Monday, 2 December 1996 Charlie Kray stood in court at Woolwich, South London, and was duly remanded in custody for plotting an £80 million cocaine importation and supply deal. His pals Ronald Field and Robert Gould were in court with him, accused of the same crime and therefore all three men would await the same fate.

Judy was there again, but there were no kisses this time. The only good thing to come out of this period for Charlie Kray was that he didn't have to feed himself, or to supply a roof over his own head. And his debtors couldn't get hold of him. The problems hadn't gone away, since he still owed money – they had been shelved for a while and time, as they say, is a great healer. But it hadn't worked before, so why should it work this time? Sooner or later, Charlie Kray would have to face up to his problems, his debts, his deals and his nightmares.

Charlie Kray was soon standing in Woolwich Crown Court, accused of offering to supply cocaine, supposedly to the value of £39 million. Why the figure had been reduced from £80 million is not quite clear – it may have been market forces at work. But still it was enough to put him away for a very long time indeed. It was now Wednesday, 14 May 1997 and Charlie Kray had already spent almost a year in custody.

John Kelsey-Fry, for the prosecution, opened with a few general remarks addressed to the jury. First of all he told them that 'Kray is an unusual name and you may have guessed that the defendant, now over 70 years old, is the brother of the Kray Twins, Reggie and the late Ronnie Kray'. He continued to tell them: 'You will appreciate that no man is his brother's keeper, and whatever his brothers may or may not have done 30 years ago cannot adversely reflect on this defendant.' In the same vein he added, 'The brothers' past actions can in no way help you determine his guilt or innocence of these charges.' Well, that was plain enough and it must surely have helped to set the record straight. The seven women and five men of the jury were, I am quite certain, put at ease by these remarks. However, to put their minds completely at rest, they were told that they were being put under police surveillance throughout the expected six weeks of the trial, just as a security measure. That remark must surely have helped their concentration.

The Kray name now established, it was time to continue. 'As the evidence unfolds it will become clear that Charlie Kray presents himself as an affable, slightly down-at-heel character much liked for his amusing tales of the old days and the twins,' said the learned prosecutor. But he added, just for good measure, 'the Crown alleges that behind that affable and charitable image there was another side to Charlie Kray. He was a man prepared to be involved in the drugs trade.' John Kelsey-Fry had made his point and everyone in the courtroom knew it.

The prosecutor told the court that Charlie Kray took care never to be present when the drugs were handed over – this was routine practice. He also reminded the jury of the Kray name and all the associations and implications that go with it. 'But he was the kingpin, the link in the chain without whom the deal could not be done.' Details of the cocaine itself were also outlined in the courtroom – it was 92 per cent pure, and lethal. A five kilogram, delivery every other week would have had serious consequences. And then Kelsey-Fry delivered a telling blow by informing the jury that the other defendants in the case had admitted their involvement; Field from Raynes Park and Gould from Wimbledon had pleaded guilty prior to the trial. Charlie Kray was the last man standing.

Charlie had not helped his case by refusing to answer questions that night at Ilford Police Station, when he was first taken into custody. Mr Kelsey-Fry pressed home his advantage by repeating this fact several times and added that they would be hearing tape recordings of Mr Kray setting up the deals. Also on the recordings, according to a somewhat jovial John Kelsey-Fry, they would be hearing Charlie Kray talking about his old friends Rocky Marciano and Frank Sinatra. But the main point, he confirmed, was to listen out for those matters involving the proposed cocaine deal. These first tape recordings were taken at Charlie Kray's 70th birthday party in Birmingham. It was here, according to the prosecution, that the first talk of supplying drugs took place. The jury would hear Mr Kray himself admitting to be able to supply cocaine. These were damaging remarks indeed – and the trial had only just begun.

The first witness in the case was our old friend Jack the undercover policeman and to protect his identity he was hidden behind a screen. Jack told his story of the sting, and of the eventual handing over of the cocaine. He missed nothing out about Operation Crackdown and even talked about his back-up story of being a northern businessman with criminal connections. 'I told Mr Kray that my dealer had been topped,' he told the jury. He continued to relate a tale of intrigue and guile. 'Kray said he had people who were sat on a ton [of cocaine] and he could put my name on it,' he told them. '"That is a lot of puff," I told him.' Charlie Kray was then reported to have said: 'I know it is not the place, we will talk in the morning.' But no mention was made of who it was who set up the initial meeting with Charlie Kray and how his name had come up in the phone-tapping part of the investigation.

Still, the prosecution had a good case against Charlie Kray and the jury heard a lot of incriminating evidence against him during that first week of the trial. It was just something that he had to get through, before he could have his own particular day in court. But a betting man wouldn't have given him very good odds during this first part of the trial.

The whole idea and presentation of the interrogation of Jack had all been a little bizarre. It had been staged to impress the jury and it had been very convincing, although more at home in an American TV trial. The press had been there in force – no one wanted to miss an historical Kray trial and it was well reported throughout the media. But it didn't look as though the force was with Charlie Kray this time around. It was soon to be even more peculiar and theatrical – acrimonious even. For it was now the turn of Jonathan Goldberg QC, for the defence.

On Thursday, 22 May 1997, Jonathan Goldberg QC was ready and eager to cross-examine Jack, the prosecution's main witness. Was this to be a revival of good fortunes for Charlie Kray? Or was it just a last-ditch gamble, with all the cards stacked against him? At first it looked as though all he had were jokers in his hand.

'Did you tell a barmaid at a hotel in Essex that you and Brian, a colleague, were into security guarding wealthy Arabs and jewels?' he asked a surprised Jack. Was this Mr Goldberg's trump card? Jack replied that he couldn't remember.

It was now time to add a little spice into the trial of Charlie Kray. The defence QC continued to attack Jack on that point. Referring to an evening that Jack and Brian had spent with The Spice Girls at the Essex hotel where the drugs deal was supposed to be shortly concluded, he asked if Jack had said to the barmaid 'Why don't we kidnap Victoria Adams, better known as "Posh Spice", then release her and put ourselves forward as bodyguards?' Victoria is now Mrs David Beckham. His intention was to imply that Jack and his colleague Brian had compromised themselves and the investigation by drinking and partying with the girls at the hotel. Four hours of such behaviour, remarked Mr Goldberg QC, was surely tantamount to misconduct.

Jack denied that he had said anything of the kind to the barmaid. Jonathan Goldberg continued to talk about the 'Spice Girl' incident; something that appeared to have happened by chance after the girls had appeared on *Top of the Pops*.

Questioned about making phone calls that evening, Jack admitted phoning Michelle Hamdouchi, a hostess he had met at Charlie Kray's 70th birthday party, to ask her over to the hotel. The undercover policeman was asked if he had said, 'Come and have some drinks with Posh Spice.'

Jack replied that it had all been a prank, but that she had surprisingly arrived at the hotel. It was apparently a surprise to both Jack and to his colleague.

But Jonathan Goldberg wasn't finished with his questioning yet. 'Isn't it true that Miss Hamdouchi and your colleague Brian went for a "quickie" in the bedroom?' he asked. The idea was that both Jack and Brian wanted their own bit of spice entering their lives, at the taxpayers' expense too.

'I don't think so, sir,' said Jack solemnly.

The aforementioned sleeping together had not apparently been reported to superior officers in subsequent reports and Mr Goldberg suggested that the whole thing had been one huge cover-up to disguise their own misdemeanours as a genuine 'sting' operation, in which they were 'setting up' his client. 'You got caught trying to protect him [referring to Brian] and both of you have ended up telling a tissue of lies.'

It had all been a case of 'Give me what I want, what I really, really want,' suggested Jonathan Goldberg QC. Brian had managed to get what he wanted, but it certainly looked as though the whole thing could have back-fired on them and blown their cover. It was a sorry and sordid episode, if a bit of a joke, and Jack had difficulty in answering the many questions put to him that day. There had been a couple of cops whoopin' it up in the Swallow Hotel Saloon but for the moment they appeared to have got away with it. For Jack and Brian that Thursday couldn't end quickly enough.

If these previous days had been a comedy of errors, then what awaited the jury on Monday, 2 June 1997 was a character assassination. The man doing the assassin's work was none other than Jonathan Goldberg QC. And the man being crucified was his client Charlie Kray

First Mr Goldberg had a few words to say about the treatment of his client. Outside Woolwich Crown Court armed police were on patrol. People going into the court were searched and their luggage was searched. His client had been kept at Belmarsh Prison, 'Category Triple A' security (like IRA prisoners). 'The hype surrounding his case is the biggest obstacle I face in defending him,' he concluded.

Now the assassination could begin. 'Charlie Kray is no more than a skint old man trying to charm cash out of his victims.' Now that was pretty bad, but worse was to come. 'He is a pathetic old has-been, cashing in on the family name and cadging drinks whenever he can'.

Charlie Kray stood motionless in the dock, head down, while his life was torn to shreds. What a sight he made. He wore a smart suit, a clean shirt and polished shoes. But behind the façade stood the real Charlie Kray with his fake watch, schooled smile and false reputation. In tears he told of how he couldn't even bury his own son, who had died of cancer at the age of 44 the year before. His brother Reg, he told the jury, had paid all of Gary's funeral expenses. He spoke quietly and in a subdued way about living with his girlfriend Judy Stanley, a headmaster's daughter, at her semi in Sanderstead, and of how he shared the home with her three sons. It was a sad experience for everyone there.

Mr Goldberg didn't let up, however. He said that police had lured a foolish old man into a carefully laid trap. 'This old fool thought he could string them along and con them.'

A pitiful Charlie Kray, his reputation in tatters, had to continue to have his life pulled apart. It must have been a terrifying ordeal for a man who had lived his life with pride. For no matter what he had done or had tried to do, Charlie Kray was indeed a man who had tried to live up to a certain code. It may not have been a recognised moral code, but it was in the main the style of a man with dignity. It may appear strange to an outsider but Charlie Kray was not all bad. However, he did have difficulty in telling right from wrong, and this time he had gone just a little too far across that line between good and evil.

The jury were now witnessing a curious double act. First Jonathan Goldberg would say something quite detrimental about his client. Then it would be Charlie Kray's turn to do himself damage and to imply a simplicity in his actions. The reason for these actions, as stated by both men, was simply to get money out of a punter. Charlie Kray didn't care who the punter was – just how much money he could con out of him.

Charlie Kray now told that jury that he had even had to borrow £50 that night when he first went out to meet Jack and his pal. He said that he had always been broke, with no bank account, no credit cards, nothing. Now that is something of a little white lie, however, since I just happen to have a copy of a cheque from Charlie Kray in my possession. Certainly, he didn't have the account for very long, but it did exist and it is not difficult to prove. However, the police were not interested in such sordid minor details. They had a fish to catch, and bank account or no bank account, they wanted their man.

Jonathan Goldberg continued the act. 'Charlie Kray is nothing, but he looks everything,' he told the court. He was quoting Lady Bracknell, from *The Importance of Being Earnest* where Oscar Wilde is describing Algernon. 'He might seem suave, like a million dollars, but he is just an old trouper doing his best.' It might have been his best, but it wasn't working.

Something new was needed, and the defendant himself had, once more, to step into the breach. 'It was just a load of bull,' he told them. 'I swear on the grave of my son that it's just a load of rubbish.' He was clearly trying to establish the fact, alluded to earlier, that he was trying to con money out of Jack and his pals – not trying to supply drugs.

Mr Goldberg took up the argument once again by telling the jury how Charlie Kray had 'frittered away the money from the Kray film'. Perhaps he forgot to tell them the amount involved – maybe £99,000 would have made a different kind of impression on them. He may also have forgotten to tell them of the problems Charlie Kray had with his brothers over his handling of the deal. Instead of over £1 million, they only received around £297,000 between them. (This included Charlie's payment as technical adviser.) Charlie, as usual, needed the money fast and took a huge discount to get cash. Ron and Reg Kray were furious with him at the time and didn't speak to him for almost a year. But that was of little interest to Mr Goldberg.

'Charlie Kray has been a victim of his surname throughout his life,' said the defence council. This may have been right, but it was also his 'cash cow' and he had milked it for all he could get. 'He is sociable, loveable, anti-crime, a wonderful father, anti-drugs and anti-violence,' he continued. And for good measure he added: 'He is a man with a heart of gold, naïve and gullible.'

Well, I may very well agree with some of that, but really, to call Charlie Kray anti-crime is like calling Tony Blair anti-politics. Charlie Kray was always on the fringes of criminal activity, and how any man can say such garbage about the man who laundered stolen bearer-bonds from the US Mafia, is really quite beyond me.

But Jonathan Goldberg did hit the right note when he began to argue the case against the police, saying that the whole case looked like 'an elaborate and devious sting'. To clarify matters he added, 'No doubt it has been quite a feather in the cap of many officers to nick the last of the Kray brothers.' The police, he said, had acted like 'agents provocateurs'. There may have been some truth in this, but Charlie Kray didn't have to do the business to arrange for the supply of cocaine.

It was revealed in court that Charlie Kray had been involved in various businesses. He had managed a failed pop band, gone bankrupt with a clothing company, existed as a celebrity doing talk shows and interviews and so on. Again the talk came around to famous film stars such as Judy Garland and Frank Sinatra, but it reminded Charlie of the time Ron shouted at Judge Melford Stevenson at the trial back in 1969, 'I could be dining with Judy Garland instead of being here.' It wasn't the kind of thing a QC should be reminding the jury of in such circumstances.

The only other conviction that Charlie had against his name, apart from disposing of the McVitie body, was a £5 fine for theft in 1950.

To change tack a little, Mr Goldberg asked Charlie about his brothers. Ron had been ill, he said, but he could be kind-hearted. Reg, he said, went crazy after Frances died, but they always treated normal people with respect. He didn't, however, explain what he meant by 'ordinary people' – he probably meant anyone who didn't get in their way.

The day was drawing to an end and it was time to make a point or two. To explain the way Charlie looked at people and money, Mr Goldberg said, 'Charlie Kray would offer to sell Scud missiles if he thought he could get some cash out of the deal. But only as a con.' This was indeed a dangerous ploy, for it showed a devious side to Charlie's character. 'Anything for money' was not really the kind of thing to say to a jury, and certainly not one trying a Kray. To balance things up the QC added that the police officers in the case had swilled champagne and had actively encouraged Charlie to deal with them. But seeing that kind of money was too enticing, he had just explained that in open court. It was an apparent fact that Charlie Kray was a crime waiting to happen!

To Jonathan Goldberg QC, Charlie Kray was 'a pathetic old has-been, a thoroughly washed-up figure whom the hype by the police and prosecution has made to appear something he is not'. The day was over for Charlie, no time for elaborate excuses. No time for any cosy chat over a pint down the pub – only time to remember. It had been a gruelling day for everyone and now Charlie Kray had only his thoughts for company.

If anyone had imagined that this trial would continue with a whimper, then they were very much mistaken. Wednesday 4 June started with a bang!

'My brother found out before I did that they had removed Ronnie's brain after he was dead for experiments. Everyone was ringing up about it and was very upset about it and wondering why.' Charlie Kray was near to tears as he continued his grim tale. 'Finally they returned the brain in a casket and it was re-buried,' he told the court. (Exactly how anyone had recognised the brain of the deceased murderer was not exactly made clear. It probably had a label on it saying 'Ron Kray's brain'.) The family had complained to the Home Office about it, but no one had had the decency to explain the need for removing the brain, or the need for keeping it such a secret. So the complaint had not yet been resolved.

'They didn't admit it at the time,' said Charlie. 'We thought we were burying the full body.'

In actual fact brain tissues were removed by Home Office pathologists and pickled in a jar. No one said whether it was strawberry or raspberry, and I am sure Ron Kray wasn't bothered – but the tissues did find their way to Oxford for testing. A statement was issued at the time, but hidden away for only academics to find. A spokeswoman for Wexham Park said, 'Tissue is sent away to specialist centres if we don't have the right facilities.' She added: 'They can find out if there was any damage to the brain or any illness. It is not standard but it happens in about one in three cases.'

Radcliffe Infirmary in Oxford had been in possession of the tissues for almost a year. Tests were carried out in order to establish whether Ron Kray had suffered any brain damage or illness prior to his death. However officials denied that tests were linked to research into criminality. But still the brain tissue had been removed without consent when the post-mortem examination had taken place at Wexham Park, near Slough.

It was confirmed by Radcliffe that researchers had not found any abnormalities in Ron Kray's brain cells. Ron would have been pleased to know that.

For the moment Jonathan Goldberg QC was content to repeat his summing up. He said once more that the police had lured his client because of his name and that he was a 'foolish old man' who had been trapped by devious methods. Mr Goldberg had used all his aces. The only cards left were character witnesses, who were due to appear the following week. But could convicted villains like 'Mad Frankie' Fraser and actors, such as William Murray from ITV's *The Bill*, really get Charlie Kray out of trouble? Only time would tell.

'Charles is a lovely, lovely man who would not know how to steal a penny,' said 'Mad Frankie' Fraser, replying to a question put to him by Jonathan Goldberg QC. 'He wouldn't say boo to a goose,' he continued as he poured praise on the man in the dock. The trial had moved on to Monday, 9 June 1997 and the former Richardson gang member (some would say 'executioner') was presented as a character witness in the case. It may appear puzzling that a villain such as Frankie Fraser was in court at all, especially when he was not standing in the dock. For during his 73 years he had been inside for 41 of them, and had openly admitted to killing two people. This was the kind of man who was now acting as a character witness on behalf of Charlie Kray.

'To this day the Krays are quite rightly idolised,' he said, when questioned about his relationship with the Krays. As a Richardson enforcer he had spoken with Charlie and his brothers many times, mainly to sort out minor problems that had arisen between the gangs, he told the court. He even went on to talk about the time when Ron Kray shot and killed George Cornell and when questioned further he said 'Theory has it that he [Cornell] had called Ronnie a big fat poof.'

Asked by John Kelsey-Fry for the prosecution as to whether he thought Charlie Kray could deal in drugs, 'Mad' Frankie replied, 'He could not do it, not for a single day. You are probably more into drugs than him.' This was gradually developing into the 'Mad Frankie' Fraser show, and it was not helping Charlie Kray one bit. But then 'Mad' Frankie has always had a way of helping himself. As a final gesture to the jury he told them 'This is the first time I have come out of court free'. He was free all right, but his so-called pal Charlie Kray was beginning to pray for a miracle, because that was what he needed now.

Next in line as a character witness was William Murray, the actor who plays Det. Sgt. Beech in *The Bill*. Charlie Kray was a gentleman, he told them all – he had even been helped by the Krays early on in his career.

Then came a procession of well-wishers such as Eileen Sheridan-Price, the first ever Miss UK; Robin McGibbon who had written a book with Charlie Kray some years earlier; Michelle Hamdouchi, who had been sleeping around with Jack's colleague Brian and had been mentioned earlier in the trial.

It was all very interesting, but not interesting enough. The tape recordings previously played 'live' in court, where Charlie openly talked about supplying drugs, had done their trick for the prosecution. From then on it had been downhill all the way.

Charlie Kray had now spent a lot of time in the dock behind the glass screen. His only companions had been two prison officers standing by his side and his only movement was for a glance or two upwards, to see who was testifying. The five-week trial was over and the jury of four men and seven women (one man had been excused during the trial) had to bring in their verdict. Guilty or not guilty?

On Friday 20 June, the jury brought in their verdict. They had deliberated for three whole days. The verdict was delivered soberly and simply. Charlie Kray had been found guilty on all counts. He was guilty of offering to supply undercover police officers with a consignment of cocaine every fortnight for two years. He was guilty of supplying two kilograms of cocaine worth £63,000 the previous July, 1996. They could have added that he was also guilty of being a man named Kray.

Judy Stanley wept as she sat in Woolwich Crown Court, her hands covering her face. Other women in the packed public gallery started to cry, while the men just shook their heads in amazement.

But all this time Charlie Kray sat in the dock without the slightest emotion. He knew it was all over bar the shouting, and when it came it was something of a relief. Judge Carroll had already, earlier in the day, told him that he could expect a custodial sentence. He rose from the dock to shake hands with his barrister, Jonathan Goldberg QC. As he shook his hand he also found time to blow Judy a kiss, but he didn't smile on this occasion, although he did manage to receive one back. He knew he faced a possible life sentence.

Outside the court Judy Stanley was too upset to speak to the press, so friends said a few words on her behalf. Diana Buffini told them that there was evidence that the jury were not allowed to see. And Maureen Cox, a former *Sun* page-three girl said: 'Our biggest fear is that he will not come out alive.' Later Judy did speak to the media, but only to say, 'I am in a state of shock.' Their only hope now was a light sentence and everyone stressed Charlie's age, over 70 years old, and the problems of incarceration at that time of life. For Charlie Kray any sentence could be for life.

Judge Michael Carroll began proceedings on Monday, 23 June 1997, by launching a withering attack on Charlie Kray, whom he called a veteran villain. 'You show yourself to be ready, willing and able to lend yourself to any criminal enterprise,' he told him. 'But when caught you cried foul,' he continued. 'I'm pleased to see that this jury saw through that hollow cry.' He sentenced Charlie Kray to 12 years imprisonment, part of which was to be as a 'Triple A' prisoner. 'Throughout this case you have professed your abhorrence of drugs, but the jury's verdict has shown your oft-repeated protestations to be hypocrisy.'

Charlie showed no emotion as the sentence was passed. The game was up. 'Those who deal in class-A drugs can expect justice from the courts, but little mercy,' said Judge Carroll bitterly. Judy Stanley waved goodbye to her ageing lover as she left the court.

It was left to Mr Goldberg QC, a man who had torn his own client to pieces, to say that he thought Charlie Kray would have trouble in prison and be a target for thugs. 'Every young hoodlum will want to take a pot-shot at Charlie Kray. Public interest does not require a sentence that means he dies in prison,' he said. Perhaps Jonathan Goldberg had already said enough. Giving young offenders ideas of that nature is not a good thing to do. Charlie Kray had been a survivor all his life, but this was the beginning of the end.

The irony of the case is that his accomplices, Ronald Field and Robert Gould, received nine years and five years respectively. And these were the men who actually did the business.

Reg Kray immediately complained about the verdict and the sentence. He thought the whole case had been arranged and that it was a set-up to lengthen his own prison term of 30 years. Then he quietly set about trying to find the man who had fingered his brother.

All the stories of stars such as Jackie Collins, Muhammad Ali, Sonny Liston, Judy Garland and Frank Sinatra, hadn't helped. The stories of Posh Spice and the 'quickie' incident hadn't helped. The demeaning summing-up by his own defence council hadn't helped. Nothing had helped.

As trials go it was an expensive and protracted series of outlandish events, more at home on the cinema screen than in a crown court. It was a tale of iniquitous dealings and personalities, with a debilitating series of assaults on the personal character and credibility of the accused, Charlie Kray. The country had incurred all the costs and would continue to do so for the next three years.

'We will appeal,' said Judy Stanley, finding her voice at last. 'Twelve years is a long time, but Charlie will be fine.' She left to start proceedings for the appeal and to drown her sorrows. She began to cry again. Judy Stanley was right, Charlie Kray was an old man who didn't deserve 12 years imprisonment, but she was wrong about him being able to survive.

Further down the road, however, stood a happy and contented man. Detective Superintendent Gavin Robertson, the man who led the enquiry known as Operation Crackdown, was overjoyed. He wasn't amazed at the verdict or at the sentence. 'No sad old fool has the capacity to produce that amount of cocaine,' he said solemnly.

When I was writing my book *The Kray Files* back in 1997, I asked Scotland Yard for information regarding this case against Charlie Kray. No one wanted to speak to me. Instead, I tried a different approach and asked for permission to see Scotland Yard's own files on all three Kray brothers held at Kew, with main reference to the events prior to their arrest in 1968. Initially I was told on the phone that there should be no problem, since it was presently covered by the 30-year rule which was about to run out.

I wrote to Scotland Yard's Department of Public Affairs, as instructed, and waited for a reply. What I got was a shock. It came in the form of a phone call – saying simply that 'Someone has imposed the 75-year rule. No one can see the files for 75 years!' Well, that was that. All this talk of freedom of information was a complete waste of time.

But why should Scotland Yard put these files away for such a long period of time – surely they aren't protecting the Krays, so just who are they protecting? This question remains unanswered.

At their trial back in 1969 the Krays received long sentences, not for the killings alone, but for all of their crimes, most of which could not be proven. Was Charlie Kray getting 12 years for being a Kray and for being involved in crimes that Scotland Yard couldn't prove? The secrecy around Charlie's trial in 1997 and that of all three Kray brothers back in 1969, is a worrying sign. Are criminals now getting sentences because of what is proven in a court of law, or because of what the police think they have done? Surely a freedom of information act worthy of the name would help to solve this riddle.

Throughout the following three years Charlie was in and out of court, appealing against his sentence. It hadn't helped during the trial and it didn't help afterwards. His appeals over, there was nowhere to go and nothing to do. Charlie Kray was a finished man. He became the second of the Krays to die in custody.

After his death the prison authorities found an address book in his cell. It included some of the key names of his fellow accused and a possible 'Mr Big' from the north. Police are still investigating the case.

33.

July 1997: Married to the Mob

Roberta Jones is an honours graduate in English Literature and not the kind of woman you would normally think of as romantically connected to the Krays. But on 14 July 1997, she married Reg Kray.

The new Mrs Kray was then an unknown entity. She had been born and raised in Stockport, where her father had taught at the Birkdale School for Hearing Impaired Children. He and his wife doted on their daughter, who did well academically and they were delighted when she decided to go to university. But her father died of cancer when she was still in her teens and she never really got over it.

In one of her first interviews with the press she told a journalist 'When I lost my father, I lost my protector – the member of my family who looks after problems and sorts thing out.' By the time she met Reg Kray she had lived in London for almost 20 years and she had apparently not been able to find a replacement for her father during this time. Now she had found Reg Kray, gangster supreme – and things had changed.

Her mother, Gladys, did her best to protect her daughter, much as her father had done. But the world of the prison, seen as a virtual reality experience by anyone on the outside, supplied Roberta with a kind of security. She could visit Reg and talk about all the things they would do when he was free – and then she could go home and have a good bath. They were worlds apart, separated by culture, education and up-bringing.

But there was a spark in Roberta's eyes every time she met her gangster pal – and that was enough. It told her that here was someone different, someone who could look after her and take care of her problems – someone she could trust.

The cynics among us will naturally say that it was all a scam, at least on the part of Reg Kray. He wanted to show that he was an ordinary guy, with ordinary dreams and 'ordinary' sexual needs. The fact that getting married could possibly help with his parole, I am sure never entered his head.

Pete Gillett, his adopted son from Parkhurst, was no longer in favour. In fact it had been said that Reg had put a contract out on his life. So there was now a need in his life – something missing. Roberta Jones fulfilled that need very nicely.

'Reg Kray is my life,' she told the press. 'Everything I do, everything I am, is about Reg.' She was getting used to the attention and she was beginning to enjoy herself. She had not only found a father figure, she had found wealth and fame.

Roberta became involved with the Krays when she agreed to stand in for a friend, who had made arrangements to visit Reg in Maidstone Prison. Just why meeting the aged 'Godfather of the Underworld' was one of her top priorities has never been questioned. They started talking about Ron, but soon the conversation got around to personal details of a sexual nature, something that Reg was good at. He couldn't actually do anything about it, being a prisoner in a man's world, but he could talk about it and dream about it – and Reg enjoyed his intimate chats.

Roberta soon moved down to Maidstone to be near her virtual lover. She attended his every need – well, almost every need. There were just some things that were not possible to take care of in the visiting room. But she kept the rented two-bedroomed terrace house in tidy order – waiting for her man to come home.

Reg was 63 years old – the exact age of her father when he died. 'Reg believes he has found a soul mate in Roberta, despite their 25-year age gap,' said a well-wisher. (The words were not well chosen, since soul mate sounded a little too much like cell mate.) 'The cold showers help keep his potency,' he added somewhat unnecessarily. But Reg needed the showers, to keep his spirits up – as well as his masculinity. Being a gay in a man's world had made things bearable for Reg, who had always longed for real sex with a real woman. He had made his mind up – Roberta would be the one.

'Regarding our love life,' she told the media folk, 'I have just switched myself off.' If that was truly the case, then Roberta Jones was truly a remarkable woman. There must be many men – and women – all over the country busily trying to find that switch! 'We can touch and hold hands but we both look forward to the day we can lie beside each other,' she added. But none of the press asked about 'lying on top', which was what they were all really interested in – that would be too sordid, too shocking.

Reg proposed on the phone from Maidstone Jail. Roberta asked him to get down on one knee and ask again. This he did – and Roberta told him she would think about it. But she had found her surrogate father – she had found a man of substance, who could combine all her dreams into one. Reg Kray was wealthy, famous and stuck in jail – he was the perfect choice.

The Double R was back in business when Reg and Roberta were married in Maidstone Prison. The authorities were pleased with the move – it really looked as though Reg Kray was thinking about the future. He needed a stable environment if ever he was to be released from incarceration. And he needed a woman to take care of him. So they allowed the marriage to go ahead – and Reg laid on his usual glam slam of a show.

'The bride was late,' said the press the following day. But Reggie Kray had all the time in the world – he wasn't going anywhere. Roberta wore a white wedding dress and only a few close personal friends were invited. The only outsiders to see the actual wedding were the security people who caught it all on camera – now wouldn't that be worth the seeing?

Reg had laid on a laser show for the ceremony. He had also arranged for huge bunches of flowers to decorate the chapel and naturally enough, friends sent flowers from all over the country. Even brother Charlie sent flowers, although he couldn't attend in person, seeing as he was banged up in prison for cocaine dealing at the time. Bradley Allardyce, a prison 'pal' of Reggie's, was the best man and the Brentford FC manager Dave Webb turned up for the ceremony too. After only 20 minutes Roberta Jones uttered those immortal words 'I do', and it was all over – she was now Mrs Reg Kray.

They all left the chapel to the tune of 'Amazing Grace'. It could just as well have been 'My Way'. The wedding was over and Reg actually managed to kiss the bride. But that was all he did. Soon Reg was shown back to his cell. But he had proved his manhood to his prison pals, even though some of them knew the real Reg Kray, and not the one he had been so careful to project over the years. Reg may have been a homosexual, but now he was married.

Roberta made her way out through the metal detectors and all the security that went with a Kray wedding. Some of the festivities had even been laid on by the prison.

Outside the jail, the lawyer Mark Goldstein, a man who has started sending me carefully worded letters of late, stood outside to address the press. 'Mr Kray and Miss Jones wish to thank their family and friends for their love and support and look forward to the time when Reggie is released and they can spend the rest of their lives together.' Just why he called them 'Mr Kray and Miss Jones', is anyone's guess and using 'Reggie' instead of 'Reg' or 'Reginald', made the words seem familiar. It was all designed to create a feeling of well-being, of warmth and admiration.

But the cameraman, 'clipped' by Roberta's Jeep on her way back home, didn't have many kind words to say about the new Mrs Kray. She didn't look back. She didn't ask if he was all right. She didn't, apparently, care.

'I live in the present,' said Roberta, when she was questioned by reporters about the wedding. But there was not much of a present left for Roberta Kray. She knew she had to forgive the past, she should not even consider the future – and she had to forget the present.

Now Mrs Roberta Kray has a new man to support her, in the form of their lawyer Mark Goldstein. As stated earlier, he has written to me recently trying to get me to be quiet by stating that anything I have on the Krays is the copyright of Reg Kray's estate. He has even told me that I must ask for permission from Roberta before publishing any material, letters and such. This, I feel is a little like overkill – are they afraid of the truth, do they fear the future, are they worried about what I may dig up, literally, from the past?

The real truth behind the wedding may never be known, but both benefited from the experience. Roberta now has the Kray wealth, the Kray name – and the Kray cohorts behind her. When she speaks, people listen because she carries the name of Kray and after all, there aren't many of them around any more. We haven't heard the last of the new Mrs Reg Kray. Watch this space.

34.

April 2000: Death of a Clown

Charlie Kray was a crook. He was the brother of the Kray twins and he was always on the look out for a nice little earner. But did that mean he had to die a pauper, a prisoner – and a condemned drug dealer? He died broke, homeless and a lonely man. On 4 April he succumbed to the effects of a sudden heart attack and quietly passed away at St Mary's Hospital. He was, at the time, serving a 12-year stretch at nearby Parkhurst Prison, on the Isle of Wight, for his part in a £39 million cocaine smuggling plot.

The elder Kray brother was again in the headlines – but again for all the wrong reasons. I am sure he would have enjoyed all the media hype, even from his death bed.

Charlie had first noticed problems the previous year, when he had chest pains. The doctors called it a stroke – in reality though, he was on his way out. All the courtroom appearances, all the troubles and tribulations of being in prison – it was all too much for 'Champagne' Charlie Kray. He had poor circulation, causing problems with his legs and feet – and Frankland Prison (where he was before he was transferred to Parkhurst) was no place for a 73-year-old man, literally on his last legs.

He now openly admitted to close friends that he had made a mistake – possibly the biggest mistake of his life. He had nothing left to fear and spoke openly for the first time about the cocaine deal. He had wanted the money, nothing else – and since he was a Kray, he knew a man who could get him what he wanted. Getting cocaine was no problem.

Being a Kray had many drawbacks, but it had some plusses too. One of these plusses was having connections. Everyone would confide in Charlie, he knew where the bodies were buried, but he would never talk. He had a code, the old code of the old criminal. It was what he called respect, a moral identity, honesty among thieves, something that bound people together – it was a tradition that he took to the grave.

It was a sting operation that had put him in prison – and the sting still hurt. He felt outrage and bewilderment at the process of the law and of the appeal procedure, his thoughts naturally going back to the days of his first period in prison. At that time he was serving a stretch for getting rid of the body of Jack 'The Hat', something he swore he never did. He was at home in bed, fast asleep – he only heard about the killing the next morning well after the event and after the body was dumped at sea. But it felt the same. He kept asking the same question, over and over. 'Why me – why me?'

He had promised himself then that he would never be sent to prison again, but he hadn't reckoned with the law's vendetta and their case against the Krays. The police wanted all three Kray brothers behind bars – and they achieved their goal.

Charlie had never been a true member of the Firm, he had never been on the board of any Kray company – and he had never killed anyone. But he was a Kray – and to the police that was good enough.

His latest conviction and sentencing meant a new spell behind bars. This stretch, first in Frankland and then in Parkhurst, was tough for Charlie Kray. He was 70 years of age and a pensioner. He became a pitiful, frail, ghostly image of his former self when he lost much of his hair after the first stroke and there were the continuous problem with his blood circulation. So when Charlie started complaining of stabbing chest pains, the medical centre at Parkhurst rushed into action. They immediately sent him to St Mary's for observation. Their suspicions were well founded – Charlie Kray had suffered a major heart attack.

On Saturday 18 March, the news reached Reg Kray in Wayland Prison, Norfolk. The message said simply: 'Charlie is dying – get here quick!' He immediately contacted the authorities at the prison and arrangements were hurriedly put together for him to visit Charlie on the Isle of Wight. He had acted quickly. Charlie had barely been in St Mary's for 24 hours, but Reg knew in his heart that he would probably be seeing Charlie for the last time, so speed was an important factor. In fact, Reg Kray hadn't seen his brother Charlie for some five years – not since the funeral of Ronnie, back in 1995.

Reg knew Parkhurst like the back of his hand. The idea of going back to a place where he had spent some 17 years of imprisonment was not ideal for Reg – in fact he hated the mere thought of it. He understood the system; he knew the rules inside and out – and he didn't like it. But Charlie was close to death and he had to move quickly – there was much to do and much to say.

The following day, Sunday 19 March, Reg Kray made an early start. At 6.45 a.m. the dogs searched the transport vehicle, just in case of drugs, before Reg was unceremoniously placed on board. Together with three trusted wardens he left Wayland Prison in Norfolk, travelling in a white van through the huge gates and out into the outside world of the pleasant green fields of East Anglia.

First stop was Winchester Prison, where they were due to take lunch. The meal was the usual thing – something good for the wardens, something else for the prisoners. Normally Reg would have been looking forward to a change of diet, but not on this occasion. In fact he couldn't eat much at all – he kept on thinking of his brother Charlie.

The ferry crossing to the Isle of Wight was the normal routine and soon the white van was approaching the dark walls of Parkhurst. Still hand-cuffed, Reg was shown Charlie's cell and told that he could stay there until they were ready at St Mary's. He had been hand-cuffed all day and it was beginning to look as though he would be hand-cuffed all night.

But finally they got their act together at Parkhurst and Reg was taken the short trip to the hospital, still under guard and still hand-cuffed. Reg was lucky – Charlie was awake, at least enough to have a chat and shake hands with his brother. Reg could hardly recognise him. He stared at Charlie, mouth gaping and tears running down his cheeks. Never had Reg shown such emotion, never had he been so sorry for any one else. They talked about everything and nothing – and about his poor condition and sorry state. Charlie was under no illusions as his legs slowly turned black and his breathing deteriorated. Reg knew it was all true – his brother Charlie was about to die.

St Mary's issued the usual reports to the eager press. Charlie was 'comfortable and cheerful' (which later became 'extremely unwell'). And the statement issued by Parkhurst put it all in context. They said simply 'Reg Kray can stay in his brother Charlie's cell as long as he likes!'

The press were there when Reg emerged from the hospital, still hand-cuffed, but looking all right given the nature of the visit. He was smartly dressed in blue jeans and a casual jacket, with the jacket hiding the hand-cuffs, but he was not a happy man. Sources at the prison told reporters that the reunion had been emotional. 'Both men are old,' they said. 'And they know they haven't got long left.' Reg was shown back to Charlie's cell – and the wait began.

Charlie Kray was still fighting, but the end was in sight. It was the toughest fight of his life, but he didn't have the strength anymore. He had never wanted to throw in the towel, but this time it was different. There was no going back, nothing he or others could do.

Reg knew he wasn't going to like being back at Parkhurst, but this was something completely unexpected and undesired – waiting in Charlie's cell, surrounded by all of Charlie's possessions, brought back memories of the old days. It was what Charlie had cherished; what the twins had cherished. Time dragged by as he sat quietly in the cell waiting for Charlie to die. It was the worst time of his life.

Soon he had been there for more than a week. Just how long could Charlie hang on? Every day saw a deterioration in his condition – now he could hardly talk or even open his eyes. On the evening of 4 April, the news he had been dreading was confirmed by the prison authorities – his elder brother Charlie had died peacefully in his sleep at 8.50 p.m.

Earlier that same day Reg had talked with Charlie in the hospital. They spoke of the problems that existed between them – of the books Charlie had written, of the film *The Krays*, the deal for which Charlie had rushed through for his own benefit and not for the benefit of the family as a whole – and of the cocaine deal that had brought about his untimely conviction. Charlie knew he was taking his last gasps of air and he was glad he had made peace with his brother. The smile on his face told Reg that they were back together. As Reg talked to him, Violet came alive. Aunt Rose was there too – and Gary, Charlie's son who had died a few years earlier. Charlie could see them all and in a way, he was looking forward to the reunion after death. Everything was forgiven.

But now Charlie was fading fast and his breathing was intermittent. His legs were as black as coal and his body was quite still. The only movement came from the slight beating of his heart. The hospital rushed out a statement. 'He has had heart problems and respiratory problems,' they told the press. 'His condition is giving cause for concern.'

Reg wanted to continue the chat but the doctors asked him to leave. Once back in Charlie's cell, he thought of all the things he would like to have said. But there was never again any opportunity to put the record straight. He never saw his brother alive again.

Reg was rushed to Charlie's bedside, but there was nothing he could do, there was nothing he could say, there was nothing he could even think of doing. His mind was in freefall. He thought of everything and nothing as he sat and stared at his brother's ashen face and his bruised body. In the end there was nothing he could do to help his brother.

Five years earlier he hadn't been able to help Ron, who died at the hands of his favourite cigarettes. And now he found himself in a similar position with Charlie. All he could do was arrange and pay for the funeral. If only he had helped Charlie when he was begging for salvation, for instance when Gary died. He had paid for that funeral and he was about to do the same all over again. This had not been the reunion he was looking for.

Gary's death had been a momentous event in Charlie's life – and it was all downhill from then on. Not being able to afford to bury his son was one of the main reasons for his getting involved in cocaine smuggling. He was broke, unemployable and had only a few close friends around him. There was nothing left to try, no hope for the future. Charlie needed a reason to live, but Reg couldn't give him one.

The crying game was not normally Reg Kray's style, but that night he cried himself to sleep. Once again, he had to arrange a brother's funeral and it brought back many unpleasant memories. He thought of his mum's funeral, when they all laid her to rest. He thought of Ron's funeral, with the plumed horses and the crowds of spectators. What should he do for brother Charlie?

He considered all the options and listened to anyone who cared to voice an opinion. But in the end he did it his way. This was Reg Kray's brother who had died and so he deserved the best that other people's money could buy. He understood those who asked him to keep it low-key, but in the end his own pride had to be satisfied. It would be big – even bigger than Ron's.

Always willing to please the press, he granted interview after interview. 'I visited him twice a day, once in the morning and then a long session in the afternoon,' he said pitifully. 'He looked terrible. He was just lying there on his back sucking in air from an oxygen mask. He was breathing really heavily and he was out of it.' It was a heartbreaking moment for Reg as he said, 'His chest was going up and down and he couldn't hear me.'

He piled on the praise for his brother. 'I've been through so much and even though it has been hard coping with the loss I have remained strong in mind. But it has been so sad to lose Charlie – prison was not the place for him, he was too old to endure it.'

Wednesday 19 April saw the funeral of Charlie Kray. It was held at St Matthew's Church in Bethnal Green, home territory for the Krays. It was a spectacular event – more a pageant than a funeral procession, but it honoured Charlie the only way possible. Reg couldn't express his love for his brother in real life, so he would tell the world after his death. All the usual crowd were there, villains and celebrities alike. It was a who's who of the criminal world, both past and present – even their old enemy Charlie Richardson came along to pay his last respects.

The police decided that they too would be there that day – not to pay homage to Charlie Kray but instead to play a different kind of game. It was called 'spot the crook'. All the helicopters overhead and the police cars and bobbies on the beat made the ceremony look like something out of a Hollywood film. Charlie would have loved to see it. And the guns on view would have made Charlie feel at home, since he had always likened the East End to the Wild West of America.

English's Funeral Parlour had done Charlie proud. He had been laid out like a king in an open coffin. Well wishers were coming and going – all paying their respects. Some brought wreaths, some best wishes for the afterlife. As bodyguards guarded the body, flowers were laid all around him. In fact it reminded me of a brush with Buster Edwards, the great Train Robber, who had a flower stall at Waterloo Station. Once, when I had come up to town to see Charlie, we'd met at Waterloo. Suddenly Charlie dragged me over to the other side of the road and away from the flower stall I was standing at. When I asked why all the rush, he replied, 'It's that Buster, he's always trying to get me into trouble.' That just about summed up Charlie's life.

The flowers and the wreaths all paid tribute to Charlie. There was one shaped like a boxing ring, fashioned from red roses and carnations, from brother Reg. And there was another one saying 'Grandad'. And yet another from 'C' Wing at Parkhurst. Then there were the lilies from Barbara Windsor. It all brought back memories of Charlie and Babs in the old days – what a carry on.

The crowd was buzzing. Everyone was waiting for the other star of the event to show. Reg was due any time now and it was getting to be a warm day. Those shirt collars felt tight and the mascara was beginning to run as the clock moved ever so slowly towards 11 a.m.

Charlie's coffin was brought out onto the street covered in wreaths and flowers. The heavies moved in and placed the coffin in the back of the first of the two hearses – the second one was there to carry the flowers. Everyone was ready, but Reg hadn't yet appeared, so there was still time to check out the wording on the side of the hearse – it spelled out 'Gentleman' in lovely flowers. People were beginning to stretch their necks trying to witness the whole choreographed sequence of events, so where was Reg Kray?

At last he made his scheduled appearance. Everyone gasped as they saw the blue Mercedes pull up outside the funeral parlour. Friends reached out their hands as Reg sat quietly in the back, hand-cuffed once again – but this time to a pretty woman police officer. Slowly the procession was under way along Bethnal Green Road. People threw flowers in the path of the cars as the cortège passed by, stretch limo after stretch limo – 18 in all. A white-robed minister and a mourner, complete with black top hat, walked into Vallance Road. The Krays were back home.

Reg could hardly recognise the road where the family had lived for so many years. But it brought back memories of the old days all over again. He remembered his mum and his dad, and all the good times they had together. But it didn't last long. Soon they were on their way to the church.

Reg waved to the crowds as they made their way there. He looked surprisingly well, if a little thin and pale. But his pinstripe suit seemed to fit all right and his hair was well groomed as usual. He looked well, but he looked old.

St Matthew's Church was where the ceremony was to take place and it had been adorned with flowers and other decorations, on the request of Reg and Roberta. They wanted things to go well and their organisational skills had been put to good effect. The vehicles stopped at the church and the crowds gathered in, for a close look at the old Godfather of crime. It was all staged for the media and for the enjoyment of Reg Kray – it was what he had wanted, and what he wanted he usually got.

There was ample protection at the church with the local Hell's Angels out in force, all spruced up for the occasion and all standing to attention. It was strange to think of all these leather-clad bikers – some joker even mentioned they were 'Charlie's Angels'. But Charlie's Angels protected people from crime, they didn't go out of their way to honour gangsters. As Reg walked through the rows of mourners and onlookers, he shook many a hand and acknowledged many a welcome. The hugs and the kisses were real enough – it was showtime, and the main event was this appearance of Reg Kray.

'Up Close and Personal', by Celine Dion, rang out loud and true from the church loudspeakers as Charlie's coffin was paraded into the church by six pallbearers. It was one of Charlie's all-time favourite songs and it matched perfectly all the glittering array of jewelled merchandise on display.

But there were many highlights of the day, including the sighting of Charlie's old pal Billy Murray, from *The Bill*, and his old drinking partner the actor George Sewell. But these were the stars of yesterday – Charlie was the star of today.

Father Ken Rimini, who had known Charlie for many years, took over proceedings as the congregation broke into song. The hymns had been chosen well – and they meant much to Reg, as he sat and listened to the voices around him. He couldn't sing the words himself, but he listened to every one. 'Morning Has Broken' echoed around the church, then 'Fight The Good Fight' and 'Abide With Me'. The tears flowed as Reg held his head in his hands.

'Many things have been said about Charlie,' said Ken Rimini, 'some true and some very untrue and hurtful. I can't judge him. He now stands before a greater authority than this life.' He then went on to talk about Charlie's son Gary, who had died of cancer aged just 44 years. He talked of how it had affected Charlie and his outlook on life – and what it did to his belief in God. 'It broke his heart,' he told them pitifully.

The guest-list was again well chosen, with friend after friend remembering Charlie as a kind man, a true friend and a great man to be with. Jamie Foreman, son of the old gang member Freddie Foreman, told them 'Charlie's smile will be ingrained on my heart'.

Reg put his head on his young wife's shoulders as the guests spoke of Charlie. All the pain, all the sorrow – it all came flowing back. For a moment, he only thought of his brother Charlie, everything else blacked out in his mind.

The finale itself was a recording made by Reg. It was of a poem he he told everyone that he had written for Charlie and he had it played through the speakers, filling the open space above them with nostalgia. His voice was weak, his tone sympathetic as he spoke the words.

I am not there, I did not die,

I am a thousand winds that blow,

I am diamond glints on snow.

Another of Charlie's favourite singers sang them from the church. It was Shirley Bassey, a friend from the old days, who sang 'As Long As He Needs Me'. Reg kissed the coffin as it was lifted by the chosen few and he wiped the tears from his eyes. He straightened himself up, tidied his clothes, and prepared to meet the crowd.

They cheered as he entered into daylight. 'Mad Frankie' Fraser shouted out 'Three Cheers for Reggie' as they all joined in the tribute. It had been well worth the 50-minute wait and well worth the price of admission – after all it was a free show – although some may have called it a freak show. But the service was over, the crowd had had their fun, and the cars pulled up to take the coffin away to its final resting place.

It reminded Reg of Ron's funeral procession, where crowds lined the eight-mile stretch all the way to Chingford. It was orderly and neat, all ship-shape and Bristol fashion, just like a military exercise. The journey was soon over and it was time to lay Charlie to rest.

Reg wandered among the graves, until he came to the family plot where his first wife, Frances, was buried. Suicide is not easy to get over and some say that Reg never truly came to terms with his wife's death at the tender age of 23. He stopped by the headstone and stroked it gently, before turning to the journalists and the cameramen – it may have been Charlie's funeral, but it was also a photo opportunity.

As Charlie was laid in the ground, Reg stood flanked by the policewoman on the one side, and Roberta on the other. Even with no hands free he managed to throw a red rose onto the coffin as it disappeared underground and he looked around him for a quick glimpse of freedom. But it was soon all over – all he had left of his day of freedom was the return journey to Wayland Prison.

Some remained longer at the graveside. One of these mourners was Charlie's common law wife, Diane Buffini. 'Charlie would have loved the sunshine,' she told reporters, as once again the crowd started to cheer. 'Free Reg Kray!' they sang. 'Take the hand-cuffs off!' they shouted. Reg would have agreed with them, but he was long gone.

'Reg wants me to thank you all for coming,' said Big Paul, as the press stood and listened patiently. 'He wishes you all well and he hopes to be among you soon!' More cheers followed the blue Mercedes as it sped away from the cemetery and the old-time gangster boss disappeared in the dust. Reg had gone from view but not from their memory.

Twin brother Ron was dead and buried, so too was elder brother Charlie – so when would it be the turn of Reg Kray, the last surviving member of the Kray gang, once the most feared organisation in the annals of British crime?

No one outside the prison system knew that Reg had already developed a stomach condition that was causing them some concern. Already at this time he had cancer.

35.

August–October 2000: Freed – to Die!

By the summer of the year 2000, Reg Kray was fading away. He had become a bag of skin and bones – and his condition was causing the prison service some real headaches. Being a Kray, he was always in the news and soon speculation began to take hold among media people throughout the country – was the last of the Krays a dying man?

Previously a boxer of some renown, Reg Kray had been a fitness fanatic all his life, both in and out of jail. He was fit to the extreme, muscles firm and flexed, a man of almost superhuman capabilities. But everyone could see how this once dynamic individual had changed – the metamorphosis was almost complete, he was now a frail old man with only time to kill.

Reg Kray had already confirmed his place in our history. He had become a legend in his own lifetime – a part of the system and a celebrity by right. He was now some 65 years old – a pensioner and of no danger to anyone.

But the rigid prison diet had taken its toll on the gangster supreme and his hearing was beginning to fail. Like it or not, Reg Kray was not the man he used to be – and it was clear to all who knew him that he would be lost in the outside criminal world, a place where he and his brothers used to reign with a vicious brutality that had shocked the nation.

The Krays had killed their way to glory. They had done whatever they wanted to do to maintain their dominance of the criminal fraternity – and they showed no remorse. The Krays had their sticky fingers in any illicit scheme going, where they could cream off the dosh and skim on the goods. From protection, to long-firms, to laundering stolen bearer-bonds for the US Mafia, they were the villains who could handle the villains. No one could ever tame the Krays.

But the record shows that the twins were only convicted of one killing each – Reg for McVitie and Ron for Cornell. So why did they get 30 years each, a sentence of outsized proportions by modern standards – and why did Scotland Yard impose the 75-year rule on their files?

Ron Kray often used to say 'If you can't do the time, then don't do the crime!' and in the end, it was his brother Reg who was actually doing the time – all 30 years of it. Towards the end, even the man who captured the Krays, Leonard 'Nipper' Read, said that the time was right to free Reg Kray.

The former public enemy number one was no longer a threat to society, so why was he still being kept in jail? He had never tried to escape and he had no intentions of starting now, when he couldn't even have managed to climb the gentle wire fence of Wayland Prison. All he had to live for was his wife Roberta – and his dream of freedom.

What was happening around him didn't help. Freddie Foreman, the man who the Krays had hired to kill the 'Mad Axeman' Frank Mitchell, was in the news. He had admitted to the shooting of Mitchell (along with other killings) and to getting rid of the bodies at sea – and all on prime-time television. The police were after him, but there was just a case of double jeopardy to sort out first. Foreman had been tried at The Old Bailey, together with the Kray brothers, back in the '60s and they had all been acquitted, but it was really looking as though the case would go to court all over again.

The story of Freddie Foreman and his revelations about the Kray empire of old was not what Reg wanted to hear. The public had read his book and now they had seen the television programme. Everyone in the country now knew that Ron, Reg and Charlie had all been involved and that they had ordered Foreman to kill Mitchell.

Reg hadn't wanted it to go to trial again. Foreman's past made front-page news. They brought up the killing of Mitchell and they told of how Foreman had been involved in the Securities Express job in London in 1983, along with a gang including the ex-husband of Barbara Windsor, a certain Ronnie Knight. The takings were some £7 million – something for everyone to remember. But the story didn't last and Reg was off the hook. Ultimately Scotland Yard had to give up.

The first serious signs of trouble appeared in July, when Reg was rushed to the medical wing of Wayland Prison. He had doubled up in agony in his cell complaining of intense stomach pain. At the medical centre he was immediately given antibiotics to keep infection at bay –

and also something for the pain, which was still severe. It appeared as though his liver was inflamed and the signs were not good at all for the ageing mobster.

A prison source said, 'There is no doubt about it – he's caused some serious damage with his drinking.' No one said where he was getting it from. On reflection however, I had my suspicions.

The name of Kray was a regular feature in many a newspaper throughout the early summer of 2000, but it was all with reference to the Kensits, pals such as Dave Courtney and Lenny McLean and celebrities like Martin Kemp and Craig Fairbrass. They all mentioned Reg, but none of it would affect his chances of parole. Reg had to play a waiting game – but how long did he have to wait?

'I feel like I'm dying!' screamed Reg as he was taken to the medical unit at Norwich Prison, just a few days later. The 20-mile trip was covered by ambulance in record time. Reg Kray was the prison's prize offender. It didn't look good, not good at all. Reg was in agony as he grabbed at his stomach and rolled from side to side.

'Reggie was found in pain, clutching his stomach. He is very ill – and he's lost the will to live. No one knows what will happen,' said a prison spokesman. The weight loss was the first sign – and soon he was on liquid food and painkillers. This was not the fitness freak of the past 30 years.

The pain got worse and on 3 August Reg Kray was rushed to the Norwich and Norfolk Hospital to undergo surgery for a suspected tumour. Several operations followed, the first only a few days into his hospitalisation. After some four hours the doctors said that the operation had gone well and that they had removed a malignant tumour from his small intestine. Roberta told the press: 'The obstruction is a secondary growth and we are awaiting further scans to determine the source.' She also confirmed that Reg Kray's lawyer was asking for his immediate release, on compassionate grounds.

Reg Kray was now in and out of the operating theatre like a yo-yo and the news was bad. On 19 August a hospital spokesman announced: 'Reg has terminal cancer and there is nothing anyone can do for him. Doctors have still not found the source of the cancer so there is more out there. It is terminal.' A parole hearing had to be postponed due to his illness – something that had never happened before. The lawyers were now very busy indeed.

Celebrities such as Barbara Windsor, Mike Reid, Billy Murray and

Johnny Briggs were urging for his release as photos of Reg in hospital were made public for the first time. They showed Reg Kray in a hospital bed wearing an oxygen mask – he was, like his brother Charlie when he died, gasping for breath. The photos were scary. They showed an old man in a pitiful state, with tubes all over his body. He may have been alive, but he looked half-dead. There was no life left in his eyes and his famous stare was non-existent. He was frail and gaunt, more like a victim of the holocaust than a prisoner of the land, fed three times a day at the expense of the taxpayer. 'There is no greater punishment this Government can inflict upon him now other than denying him his last, small taste of freedom,' said Roberta. 'We've written to Jack Straw on numerous occasions but never once had a reply from him, not directly,' she told the press.

Reg's solicitor, Trevor Linn, now applied to the Home Secretary, saying that there was a suitable case for release on compassionate grounds. The wait was on – what would happen? Roberta settled in to a daily routine at the bedside, waiting for news and praying for haste. There was a good side to the story, however. 'I'm virtually living at the hospital and stay in a room overnight,' she told reporters. 'It's been hellish, but the one good thing is we've been able to spend time together since he's been here.'

Johnny Briggs, of *Coronation Street* fame said: 'Reggie has been in prison a long time and has paid his debt to society. It's time to let him go home.' Barbara Windsor added: 'I have always said it is time to let Reggie out. In the light of this latest sad news about his cancer it's only right to let him come home with Roberta.' Even tough-guy actor Billy Murray showed compassion. 'Reggie has more than done his time,' he told the press. 'It would be only humane to let him go home. Reggie needs to be with his family.'

Glen Murphy, from TV's *London's Burning*, said simply: 'Reggie should be allowed home. He can't harm anyone now. He should be freed to spend this time with his family.' Most of the country agreed with him.

On Saturday, 26 August 2000, Reg Kray was officially freed from prison by Home Secretary Jack Straw. The reason for his release – compassionate grounds. At last he was a free man, but it turned out that this 'free man' couldn't even get out of bed.

The news announced: 'In the early part of August Reg had been rushed to the Norfolk and Norwich Hospital from Wayland Prison, complaining of severe stomach pains. The trouble that had started back in the summer of '96 has once again reared its ugly head – he has stomach cancer.'

A spokesman for the prison service put it bluntly, 'The operation to remove the tumour went well, but the cancer had spread. Most of his internal organs are now infected, especially damaged are the bladder and bowel regions. It is clear to everyone concerned that Reg Kray doesn't have long to live.'

The hand-cuffs were removed and the guards withdrawn from the bedside. Roberta was overjoyed, but Reg was still very ill – he had to overcome the biggest fight of his life. He was now very much alone. Getting used to being free was not an easy matter for a man who had spent over 30 years behind bars and it was strange with no uniformed people in the room. He may have been free, but he was not free to go home, the hospital wouldn't let him.

'It's about time they released him,' said Mike Reid. 'I'm over the moon for him and his family.' Billy Murray was on hand again, to endorse the message. 'It's wonderful news, but it should have happened sooner. It's a shame it's so late because he is very ill, but hopefully he will get to spend some quality time now with Roberta.'

Others were soon to add their congratulations. 'It's brilliant news. Now he can spend some time with his loving wife,' said Barbara Windsor. 'I sent flowers to the hospital a couple of weeks ago,' she told the media. And in a parting gesture she said tearfully, 'Reg is an old man now – he is dying.'

Anne Osborn, the acting chief executive of the Norfolk and Norwich Hospital, said later that same day, 26 August, that she could confirm that Reg Kray was currently too ill to leave hospital. He was freed from the shackles he had worn for over three decades, but he was still not free to go.

He had been ill for a long time, but he just didn't show it. He knew his time was up – it was only his powerful physique and his considerable mental strength that had kept him going. It was not a question of what he wanted to do now that he was free, but rather what would he be able to do and how much time did he have to do it in?

'We are satisfied that there is no risk of him committing further offences,' said the Home Office – as if an old man who couldn't even get out of bed would cause them any trouble.

'I'm hoping Reggie will confound the experts,' said his lawyer,

Trevor Linn. 'He's as tough as old boots.' As they talked Reg had his first real haircut for over 30 years and it didn't cost him a penny – the hairdresser did it for the privilege. He was now a celebrity and provided a feather in the cap of the hairdresser – he could live on that tale for many years to come.

Reg was now even more willing to talk to the press. He may have been very ill, but he was keen on doing the business and that meant keeping the media sweet. 'I've been cooped up for 32 years,' he told a news conference. 'I want to be able to sit out and smell the fresh air – then I'll really feel free.' He let them take his photo again, as long as they didn't let anyone know where he would be living when he got out of hospital. The semi-detached house had been front-page news earlier in the week, but the press had been kind enough not to say exactly where it was located. So this was his way of paying them back.

He was talking about dying happy, savouring every minute of freedom, enjoying his new life. He was much better now. The chat and that new sense of freedom was working well, encouraging him to plan for the times ahead.

When asked about his dreams, he replied: 'I'd like to sit down by a swimming pool and have a nice gin and tonic.' He was feeling better; doing things. For a moment he forgot all about his troubles and spoke like the Reg of old. He told them of the things he and Roberta would be doing later in the year if they got the chance.

The news conference over, the nursing staff resumed his medication. He was still receiving treatment for the pain and they were all busy discussing the next course of action. Checking the records, the doctors noticed that the problems had started back in 1996, when Reg first showed signs of stomach disorder. In fact this news made Mark Goldstein, Reggie's civil lawyer, write to the prison service. He was actually considering a claim for neglect on their part.

Over the following days Reg felt better and the staff saw an improvement. In fact Roberta was able to take a stroll in the gardens, pushing Reg around the flower beds in his wheelchair. It was a lovely time for Mr and Mrs Kray, but soon Roberta had to leave – she had a meeting with the Governor of Wayland Prison. The purpose of this meeting was all very straightforward – Roberta had to collect a piece of paper from the prison, saying that Reg Kray was a free man.

'I heard about my release on the radio,' he told the press (another chat, another nice little earner). 'I never wanted to be a criminal,' he said coyly. 'But that's where the circumstances took us.' There was also something about not being used to getting his letters unopened, but most of the journalists missed that one.

He was resigned to his fate – he would be dying, and probably sooner than later. He knew the game was lost but he still wanted that last true taste of freedom. So a room was hurriedly arranged for Mr and Mrs Reg Kray at a nearby hotel, The Town House, in Thorpe St Andrew. It was just a few miles from the hospital and close enough for emergencies – but the surroundings were peaceful and Reg would be away from that feeling of being institutionalised. Reg had chosen the place himself – his last resting place.

Suddenly a Rolls Royce was brought to the hospital and Reg Kray climbed on board. It wasn't quite the taste of freedom that he had in mind – but it would do. Roberta had sent the heavy brigade ahead to book the room and everything was ready for them – they had even taken over the honeymoon suite from a newly married couple. The poor youngsters were furious, but the minders involved were big. It was a reminder of the old days, when everyone lived in fear of the Krays.

Reg was now very ill. He couldn't leave his room, not even for a drink at the bar. And he couldn't make the launch of a new book, apparently shedding light on his years of incarceration. He was so ill that he couldn't even get out of bed to wine and dine with his gangster pals. He was fading, and fast.

On 1 October 2000, Reg Kray died of the inoperable bladder cancer that had attacked his body during those final years of incarceration. Reg had a quiet night but by noon he was dead. Roberta was there for his final gasp, so too were his old pals Freddie Foreman and Jerry Powell. But the game was over – the last of the Kray brothers was dead.

His lawyer Mark Goldstein told the press that there would be a big funeral. 'He was an icon of the twentieth century,' he told them. But there were many who were glad that the twentieth century was over – and that the last of the fearsome trio was dead and soon to be buried.

'He was equally, if not more, aggressive than Ronnie,' said Nipper Read. 'He was known to be an aggressive character – the sort of guy, if you said two wrong words to him, he would immediately attack you.'

Norman Brennan, of the Victims of Crime Trust, made similar statements with regard to Reg Kray. 'Reggie Kray was no hero or celebrity and should be remembered as neither,' he told the press. 'He was a career criminal and a convicted murderer and anyone who believes differently will have forgotten that he held part of east London to ransom. To believe otherwise is to be detached from reality,' he added.

Reg had once said, 'I believe that Ron and I were predestined to become known – either by fame or infamy.' But the Krays were never celebrated. Their notoriety would see to that. But they helped to create their own image, so much so that there are still celebrity pals who extol their virtues. One such pal is Barbara Windsor.

'He was charming and polite,' she often said about Reg Kray. 'Over the years I just kept in touch with him. We would often have a chat. He usually wanted me to do something for charity for him.' Barbara Windsor supported the 'Free Reg Kray Campaign', as did many others, and she was glad that Reg had been released. But, like many old pals, she thought that it was too late and grossly unfair. 'I never stood there with banners, but I think if somebody gets 30 years for murder it should be across the board.'

Dave Courtney, a close friend of the Krays, put it differently. 'Reggie is a prime example of how you should teach your children not to behave,' he said solemnly. But for Roberta, he only had glowing words. 'The best thing that ever happened to him,' he said. 'She's an absolute diamond. Most people think someone who marries a prisoner must have something wrong, but there's nothing wrong with her.' He was telling it straight, as he saw it. There were many people around the country pondering that same possibility.

Reg Kray was buried on Wednesday 11 October, at Chingford Mount Cemetery, in the same plot that holds his twin brother Ron and the rest of his close family. He was carefully placed on top of the coffin holding the body of his twin brother, so even now in death, the Kray twins are back together again. The plot also houses their mum and dad, and brother Charlie. Reg Kray's first wife Frances is there too.

Arrangements for the funeral had been made well in advance, but Roberta wanted a change to Reggie's plans. She didn't like the idea of killers such as Freddie Foreman carrying the coffin, so she got some of her new friends to help out. Mark Goldstein had promised assistance, so too had Tony Mortimer who used to be with the pop group East 17. And there was the young boxer Alex Myhill and Reggie's old prison pal Bradley Allardyce too.

Freddie Foreman was angry at being left out, marginalised by the new Kray widow. I can see his point of view – after all, he had shown throughout his sordid life that he was good at getting rid of bodies so one more wouldn't have made much of a difference.

But Roberta carried out most of the wishes made by her late husband. She had arranged for the Spitfire flypast, as requested, but this was dependent on the weather around the airfield at Duxford, Cambridgeshire. It was expected to fly over the grave at Chingford – a final salute to an army deserter who never fought for his country; a man who considered it stupid to fight for anyone else other than himself and his twin brother; a man who went out of his way to lie, cheat and to kill.

Reggie's coffin was carried out of St Matthew's Church in Bethnal Green, to the strains of Frank Sinatra singing 'My Way'. A ripple of applause spread around the onlookers as the coffin was carried to a waiting hearse. It was all very ceremonious and refined, elegant but altogether rather obligatory. It was what the crowd wanted – and they got it.

The proceedings started, as they had done with Ronnie and with Charlie, from the Bethnal Green Road – and the W. English & Son funeral parlour. Crowds followed the hearse, drawn by six black stallions adorned with feathered head-plumes and wearing patent leather and silver harnesses. It was all pomp and circumstance – and sentimentality was in overdrive.

The carriage was adorned with four large and elaborate wreaths. One said 'Reg Beloved', another said simply 'Free at last'. Another wreath lay on the roof, in the shape of the word 'Respect' and at the rear of the hearse the crowd could see 'Reg'. Not that the crowd could see very much; with a procession including 16 black funeral limousines and two flower hearses, the ordinary public were put at a distinct disadvantage. But that was not the reason for the parade.

The procession had been planned for the image that it would represent. As in life – as in death. And Reg Kray wanted to go out in style. The show was being put on for the media and all the wreaths and the flowers were designed to promote that image, of a man who had left his mark on the twentieth century. The messages were clear. There was a wreath shaped as a boxing glove, another like a football. The one from Barbara Windsor was prominent. It said simply 'With Love'.

Perhaps the most significant tribute came from Reggie's old henchman Freddie Foreman. The chrysanthemums, carnations and roses were formed in a circular arrangement. Maybe it represented that 'what goes around comes around' or possibly it showed the cycle of life and death. The mourners couldn't ask Freddie Foreman or his son Jamie, close companion of Patsy Kensit. They weren't allowed to be there, discarded as unwanted merchandise by Roberta, who had taken over all the funeral arrangements at the last moment.

Of all Kray funerals, this was probably the least important in terms of imagery. At Ron's funeral, Charlie and Reg had been present. At Charlie's funeral Reg was there to please the crowd and to placate the press. But now there were none of the notorious brothers, no Kray gangster leader who could become the centre of focus.

Billy Murray of TV's *The Bill* was there. So too was old pal 'Mad Frankie' Fraser and the man who portrayed George Cornell in the film *The Krays*, Steven Berkoff.

But the majority were hangers-on, heavies with an eye for the theatrical who wanted to show off their tattoos behind their leather jackets and dark glasses. The gold chunky rings had been taken out of their boxes and displayed prominently around their bruised knuckles. Shaven heads were in abundance and no one smiled as the hand shaking routine was performed to perfection.

The badge-wearing minders, with the letters RKF (Reg Kray Funeral), mixed with the traffic police, in their yellow jackets as usual, as the procession made the nine-mile journey to Chingford Mount. The procession slowly progressed along Roman Road and through Victoria Park, where the twins had fought each other all those years previously. Leyton High Street was packed with thousands of people and it was the same throughout Walthamstow and Chingford.

At the cemetery the bodyguards kept control of the crowd. One nine-year-old boy was told to 'show a bit of respect' when his mobile phone sparked into life. He was almost in tears as he sought protection from the heavy mob.

The Spitfire never materialised. The weather conditions were not right at Duxford, so the flypast never happened. Perhaps it was all for the best.

An era had come to an end. The memory of the Krays, of their violence and their crimes, was now consigned to the history books. How will they be remembered? Will we still use the name Kray as the epitome of the criminal, a name that says it all, a name that screams fear and angst? Or will their name just fade away with the passing of the years and the changing of the seasons?

We cannot change the past, but maybe we can still learn from it. The imposition of the 75-year rule, however, has made that most difficult indeed. How can we learn when we are not allowed to know all the true facts of the case against the Krays? And just who do Scotland Yard think they are protecting now that Ron, Reg and Charlie Kray are all six feet under?

The Krays are all dead – but they will never be forgotten.

Epilogue

Even before their deaths the Krays had become folk heroes of a kind, exploited but glamorised by the media – especially the tabloids. Their myth, started many years ago by well-wishers and news people alike, was that they only hurt their own kind – but in recent years this has been disproved time and time again. Now, with the passing of the last Kray, no one seems to care about this mistake.

The celebrities are all still there, some coming out of the woodwork for the first time about their experiences. The twins have become 'Ronnie' and 'Reggie', and not the old familiar Ron and Reg. This has had the effect of making them friendly and affectionate characters, the loveable rogues so favoured by the movie makers – not the deadly villains they actually were in real life. Ronnie Biggs came in for this treatment – so too did Frankie Fraser. The legends have now become more interesting than the people themselves.

The Krays have continued the legacy of other myths like Robin Hood and Dick Turpin and the public appetite appears to be insatiable as news still emerges of the Krays – sometimes even from the grave. In recent months a letter appeared in *The People* – a letter proclaiming that Reg Kray was bisexual. It wasn't the fact that it was being said out loud that was interesting, but rather the fact that it was written by none other than Reg Kray himself. It was a final confession to having homosexual leanings.

The letter came about due to blackmail attempts by fellow inmates, who had seen the hard man of British crime in action and knew all about his extra-curricular activities. He was terrified of being branded a 'queer' or a 'poof', something that had happened to his brother Ron. But Ron didn't care about the name-calling, unlike Reg. Reg had carefully crafted an image of himself over the years: he was hard but fair; he was a man's man and no 'poof'; he was a philosopher and a writer and no killer of innocent men, women and children. Nothing must change that perception – not while he was alive.

As it happened, he managed to buy them off. No one talked. But Reg had handed a letter over to a journalist who kept it on the promise that it would be published if ever anyone brought up the subject of Reg and his 'lovers'. No one ever did when he was alive, but on his death the journalist, Ian Edmondson, had the scoop of a lifetime. Ian had been reporting on the Krays for many years – he knew them better than most and being a twin himself certainly helped. It was this 'twin thing' that had started my interest in the Krays, all those years ago, so I fully understood his fascination. And I, like Ian, had been threatened by the Krays – so I knew that no one can say that he didn't earn and deserve his exclusive.

It appeared that Reg had pestered fellow inmates for favours of a sexual nature. He had bought them expensive gifts to win them around, and he had even had himself checked for AIDS as a precautionary measure. He told the world that he was really bisexual, mainly due to all those years of incarceration. He hated blackmailers, he said, and he talked about not living a lie. But that is exactly what he had done for all those years – remember, it took a long, long time for him to admit that he actually killed McVitie.

The legend of the Krays has much to do with sexuality. It has excited men and women alike, but for different reasons. Whatever those reasons are, the movie folk are into them in a big way. 'Don't question it,' they say – 'exploit it!' And so we have a profusion of home-made British films, all about loveable and not so loveable rogues, people with a sense of humour backed up with knuckle-dusters and machineguns.

Comparisons with Dillinger and Bonnie and Clyde are commonplace. Ron Kray has been likened to the American Mafia boss, John Gotti – called the 'Dapper Don'. Naturally enough, this is mainly due to the attitude of the Mafia capo who went out of his way to seek publicity. It was this search for fame that finally brought him down – just as it did with the Krays. Over the years other Mafia bosses became friends and allies of the Krays. Tony 'Ducks' Corallo, representing the Lucchese family of New York, visited London and hired the Krays for his business dealings in the UK. So too did Joe Pagano, respected hit-man for the Gambinos. I have been informed that Pagano even managed to visit Reg in jail, using a false identity – just to wish his old pal well.

This Mafis involvement brought the Krays into the higher echelons of organised crime – and it brought them publicity.

Our fascination with American culture has now turned into idolism. We are inundated with American this and American that. Our lives are run through the world of media, twisted and turned by the makers of the programmes – the 'good' becoming better and the 'bad' becoming even worse. Everything today is of outsize proportions.

It was America who first invented the 'hero-crook'. It was a retrospective move trying to make sense of a shallow and corrupt past. The avenging cowboy with the gun became a symbol of their age, even though they never really existed. So will the Krays survive as folk heroes – or will we some day learn the lessons and remember the facts as they really were?

We can't blame the Krays for our society, but we should try to understand their effect on our lives and put their achievements into some kind of perspective. They achieved the fame they were after. They even received a gift from Apollo 11 astronaut Buzz Aldrin in the mail. It was shirt, with a note attached saying simply 'To Reg, best wishes Buzz Aldrin'. 'Notoriety' rather than 'fame', however, is possibly a better word to use when talking about the Krays.

The Kray brothers were different. No one previously had terrorised the nation as they had done. No one had killed as many as they apparently killed; no one had flaunted their achievements as they did. As far as gangsters go they were the biggest – and the best.

But individually they were not alike at all. Ron did what he did because he wanted to do it, on the spur of the moment, on a whim. Reg planned every single day of his life by the clock, a routine that would enable him to survive the rigours of prison life – and fight all the way. And Charlie continually followed the smell of success, trying to grab a bob or two on the way.

The whole truth of the Krays will never be known. There are too many secrets hidden away. But things are changing and gradually voices of old pals and old adversaries are being heard, faintly, in the distance, calling out the names of the dead.

I have spoken with many contemporaries of the Krays and their evidence is imposing. There was the guy who ran the pig farm feeding arms and legs to the animals; there was the helper at the funeral parlour who packed bodies two by two into coffins carried by the heavy brigade, and there was the man with the incinerator who shovelled in corpses.

The village of Nazeing hides bodies buried in the garden centres, and Steeple Bay holds the secret to the end of both Jack Frost and 'Mad Teddy' Smith. Reg went on record, on his death bed, to admit to the killing of one more, although he was reluctant to go further. Nipper Read suggests that it was 'Mad Teddy' Smith, but others told of how 'Mad Teddy' escaped to South Africa. Reg never told how many his twin brother had slain.

Yet more people were reportedly killed by the Krays, including the tobacco baron Ernie 'Mr Fix it' Isaacs and Billy Stayton of the Richardson Gang. Many others had contracts on their heads, including Peter Sutcliffe, The Yorkshire Ripper, for having attacked Ron in Broadmoor, and Pete Gillett, Reg Kray's adopted son, who knew too much about their organisation and their killings. Reg had even put out a contract on the policemen involved in Charlie's recent drug case. Reg never stopped his violent ways, although he tried to tell everyone he had time and time again. Some believed him. Others didn't.

The following story about Peter Sutcliffe is proof that he hadn't stopped. Sutcliffe had been visited by Diane Simpson, who was trying to gain the confidence of The Yorkshire Ripper to help the police. Someone from the press was at Broadmoor to see Ron and noticed this blonde woman talking with Sutcliffe. Naturally, the reporter found out who out she was and wrote an article about her visits for his newspaper. Sutcliffe thought it had been Ron who had told the journalist the story – and decided he had to be punished. Sutcliffe's attack on Ron Kray was unprovoked and unwarranted and it left Ron a weak man. Reg didn't like it – he didn't like it at all. So he put a contract out on Sutcliffe and got a pal to do the job. Sutcliffe was stabbed in the eye and required immediate hospitalisation.

Pete Gillett managed to sort out his troubles with Reg by promising not to tell the truth about him and his twin brother while they were still alive. He kept his promise.

The Krays couldn't stop at killing just one man. One murder wasn't enough. Ron discussed 'Murder Incorporated' with the Mafia in New York – he had a desire to kill and felt that it gave him strength and power. Even asking others to do his dirty work was a show of strength and Ron never flinched from taking that most final of decisions – to kill or not to kill.

Villainy was indeed deep rooted when it came to the Krays. Reg Kray especially was most devious in his attempts to pry money from the punters. His last book (*A way of Life*) has been well publicised by the publishers Macmillan. 'This is Reggie's story,' they told us. 'It is a story of courage and remorse, revelation and friendship,' they said.

But it didn't take courage to stab poor McVitie to death and to order the execution of countless men, all done in the name of honour and respect. And how can you talk of remorse, when it took some 20 years for Reg Kray to admit to the McVitie killing – and he has said that he would have done it all again. 'It was him or me,' he said in his books. There was no remorse, no sense of pity for McVitie's family, no mention of doing anything wrong. Revelation is something else that I find contentious, since there are no real revelations here – certainly not about the old days of the Firm. This is what people really want to know about, not the antics of a gay prisoner and his young lovers behind bars. When he died, Reg Kray had very few friends around him. Perhaps these are the people who really know where the bodies are buried?

What Reg kept a strict secret was the fact that he hadn't even written the book himself. This was carried out initially by his adopted son, Pete Gillett, while Reg was in Lewes Prison in the early '90s. Pete visited him regularly and Reg told his stories. Then Pete would go home and write it all up. Reg asked Pete to keep the original as his pension, telling him that it was only to be released on his death. But Reg couldn't wait – and anyway by this time he was a married man, his allegiance had changed. He had the stories copied and did the deal with Macmillan.

Even Reg Kray's agent, Robert Smith, was not informed about the copyright to the book. Reg told him that it was he, and only he, who had written it – and everyone accepted it as a fact. No one doubted the word of Reg Kray – crook, killer, con man and king of the underworld. He had, in fact, done this kind of thing before – doing a deal with one publisher and then trying to do the same deal with another. Reg didn't mind where the money came from, as long as he had enough of it. The Krays were something else, they were the top gangsters of this country and the name is known in almost every house in the country. Even after death they are still in the news.

The twins, Ron and Reg Kray, were sentenced to a minimum of 30 years each because Scotland Yard knew the body count – they just couldn't prove it. This was *the final countdown* – the one they never managed to complete.

Charlie was there when the order went out to kill Frank Mitchell, and he got rid of many a body for his brothers. The 'undertaker' didn't like his work, but he was good at it. The saddest occasion was when he had to dispose of a young kid. He wasn't a member of a gang, he wasn't anyone in particular and did Ron no harm at all — he was just a penniless lad from the streets. He had been taken in by Ron Kray and used for his pleasure — then summarily executed. Ron pulled a gun and shot him dead — just for the pleasure of it. They were all guilty, no doubt of that.

However, Charlie was a victim too, of the aggression and pure lust for killing that his brothers exuded throughout their lives. He was forever picking up the pieces and, of course, trying to gain something in the process. Charlie would have preferred it another way, but he never got the chance.

Where his brothers were concerned, Charlie was always in the right place and at the right time — one step behind, cleaning up as he followed in their footsteps. He suffered the slings and the arrows, and he never quite got used to it!